GERIATRICS, GERONTOLOGY AND ELDERLY ISSUES

# MEDICAID

## ACCESS, PROGRAM INTEGRITY AND IMPROVEMENTS NEEDED

# Geriatrics, Gerontology and Elderly Issues

Additional books and e-books in this series can be found on Nova's website under the Series tab.

# Congressional Policies, Practices and Procedures

Additional books and e-books in this series can be found on Nova's website under the Series tab.

GERIATRICS, GERONTOLOGY AND ELDERLY ISSUES

# MEDICAID

## ACCESS, PROGRAM INTEGRITY AND IMPROVEMENTS NEEDED

ALICE HOLT
EDITOR

New York

**Library of Congress Cataloging-in-Publication Data**

ISBN: 978-1-53614-829-9

*Published by Nova Science Publishers, Inc. † New York*

# CONTENTS

# PREFACE

The Centers for Medicare & Medicaid Services (CMS)—a federal agency within the Department of Health and Human Services (HHS)—and states jointly administer and fund the Medicaid program. States have flexibility within broad federal requirements to design and implement their Medicaid programs. States must submit a state Medicaid plan to CMS for review and approval. A state's approved Medicaid plan outlines the services provided and the groups of individuals covered. While states must cover certain mandatory populations and benefits, they have the option of covering other categories of individuals and benefits.

Chapter 1 - Under PPACA, states could choose to expand Medicaid coverage to certain uninsured, low-income adults. As of December 2017, 31 states and the District of Columbia chose to expand Medicaid to cover these adults, and 19 states did not. GAO was asked to provide information about the demographic characteristics of and access to health care services for low-income adults—those with household incomes less than or equal to 138 percent of the federal poverty level—in expansion and non-expansion states. This chapter describes 2016 national survey estimates of (1) the number and demographic characteristics for low-income adults who were uninsured in expansion and non-expansion states, (2) unmet medical needs for low-income adults in expansion and non-expansion states and by insurance status, (3) barriers to health care for low-income adults in expansion and non-expansion states and by insurance status, and (4) having a usual place of care and receiving selected health care services for low-income adults in expansion and non-expansion states and by insurance status. GAO obtained 2016 NHIS estimates from the National Center for Health Statistics (NCHS), the federal agency within the Department of Health and Human Services that maintains these survey data. NHIS is a household interview survey designed to be a nationally representative sample of the civilian, non-institutionalized population residing in the United States. Estimates were calculated for demographic characteristics for uninsured, low-income adults. In addition, estimates were calculated for unmet medical needs, barriers to health care, and having a usual place of care and receiving selected health services for low-income adults in expansion and non-expansion states and by insurance status. The estimates were based on responses to selected survey questions. GAO selected these survey questions from the Family and Adult Access to Health Care and Utilization and another section of the 2016 NHIS. GAO took steps to assess the reliability of the 2016 NHIS estimates, including interviewing NCHS officials and examining the data for logical errors. GAO determined that the data were sufficiently reliable for the purposes of its analyses. The Department of Health and Human Services provided technical comments on a draft of this chapter, which GAO incorporated as appropriate.

Chapter 2 - Medicaid, a joint federal-state health care program overseen by CMS, is a significant component of federal and state budgets, with total estimated expenditures of $596 billion in fiscal year 2017. Medicaid allows significant flexibility for states to design and implement program innovations based on their unique needs. The resulting diversity of the program and its size, make the program particularly challenging to oversee at the federal level and also vulnerable to improper payments. In fiscal year 2017, estimated improper payments were $36.7 billion in Medicaid, up from $29.1 billion in fiscal year 2015. Further, the Medicaid program accounted for about 26 percent of the fiscal year 2017 government-wide improper payment estimate. This testimony focuses on the (1) major risks to the integrity of the Medicaid program, and (2) actions needed to manage these risks. This testimony draws on GAO's reports issued between November 2012 and May 2018 on the Medicaid program.

Chapter 3 - Medicaid, a joint federal-state health care program overseen by CMS, is a significant component of federal and state budgets, with total estimated expenditures of $596 billion in fiscal year 2017. Medicaid allows significant flexibility for states to design and implement program innovations based on their unique needs. The resulting diversity of the program and its size make the program particularly challenging to oversee at the federal level. For example, in fiscal year 2017 estimated improper payments were $36.7 billion. Further, the Medicaid program accounted for about 26 percent of the fiscal year 2017 government-wide improper payment estimate. This testimony focuses on the (1) major risks to the integrity of the Medicaid program, and examples of actions CMS has taken to address these risks; and (2) other actions needed to strengthen oversight of the program. This testimony draws on GAO's reports issued between November 2012 and July 2018 on the Medicaid program, and information on a program integrity strategy CMS announced in June 2018.

Chapter 4 - Medicaid has grown by over 50 percent over the last decade, with about $370 billion in federal spending in fiscal year 2017. CMS is responsible for assuring that expenditures— reported quarterly by states— are consistent with Medicaid requirements and matched with the correct amount of federal funds. CMS's review of reported expenditures has become increasingly complex due to variation in states' Medicaid programs and an increasing number of different matching rates. GAO was asked to examine CMS's oversight of state-reported Medicaid expenditures. In this chapter, GAO examined how CMS assures that (1) expenditures are supported and consistent with requirements; and (2) the correct federal matching rates were applied to expenditures subject to a higher match. GAO also examined the financial impact of resolved errors. GAO reviewed documentation for the most recently completed quarterly reviews by 3 of CMS's 10 regional offices for six states that varied by Medicaid program expenditures and design. GAO also reviewed policies, procedures, and data on resolved errors; and interviewed CMS and state officials. GAO assessed CMS's oversight processes against federal standards for internal control.

Chapter 5 - Federal spending on services paid for under Medicaid managed care was $171 billion in 2017, almost half of the total federal Medicaid expenditures for that year. Federal and state program integrity efforts have largely focused on Medicaid fee-for-service delivery where the state pays providers directly, rather than managed care, where it pays MCOs. As a result, less is known about the types of payment risks under managed care. GAO was asked to examine payment risks in Medicaid managed care. In this chapter, GAO (1) identified payment risks; (2) identified any challenges to state oversight and strategies to address them; and (3) assessed CMS efforts to help states address payment risks and oversight challenges. To do this work, GAO reviewed findings on managed care payment risks and oversight challenges from federal and state audits and other sources. GAO also interviewed 49 state program integrity stakeholders in 10 states selected based on size, the percent of population in managed care, and geography. Stakeholders included the state Medicaid managed care office, state Medicaid program integrity unit, state auditor, Medicaid Fraud Control Unit, and an MCO.

In: Medicaid
Editor: Alice Holt
ISBN: 978-1-53614-829-9


*Chapter 1*

# MEDICAID: ACCESS TO HEALTH CARE FOR LOW-INCOME ADULTS IN STATES WITH AND WITHOUT EXPANDED ELIGIBILITY*

*United States Government Accountability Office*

## ABBREVIATIONS

| | |
|---|---|
| CMS | Centers for Medicare & Medicaid Services |
| FPL | federal poverty level |
| HHS | Department of Health and Human Services |
| NCHS | National Center for Health Statistics |
| NHIS | National Health Interview Survey |
| PPACA | Patient Protection and Affordable Care Act |

* This is an edited, reformatted and augmented version of United States Government Accountability Office Report to the Ranking Member, Committee on Finance, U.S. Senate; Accessible Version, Publication No. GAO-18-607, dated September 2018.

## WHY GAO DID THIS STUDY

Under PPACA, states could choose to expand Medicaid coverage to certain uninsured, low-income adults. As of December 2017, 31 states and the District of Columbia chose to expand Medicaid to cover these adults, and 19 states did not.

GAO was asked to provide information about the demographic characteristics of and access to health care services for low-income adults—those with household incomes less than or equal to 138 percent of the federal poverty level—in expansion and non-expansion states. This chapter describes 2016 national survey estimates of (1) the number and demographic characteristics for low-income adults who were uninsured in expansion and non-expansion states, (2) unmet medical needs for low-income adults in expansion and non-expansion states and by insurance status, (3) barriers to health care for low-income adults in expansion and non-expansion states and by insurance status, and (4) having a usual place of care and receiving selected health care services for low-income adults in expansion and non-expansion states and by insurance status.

GAO obtained 2016 NHIS estimates from the National Center for Health Statistics (NCHS), the federal agency within the Department of Health and Human Services that maintains these survey data.

NHIS is a household interview survey designed to be a nationally representative sample of the civilian, non-institutionalized population residing in the United States. Estimates were calculated for demographic characteristics for uninsured, low-income adults. In addition, estimates were calculated for unmet medical needs, barriers to health care, and having a usual place of care and receiving selected health services for low-income adults in expansion and non-expansion states and by insurance status. The estimates were based on responses to selected survey questions. GAO selected these survey questions from the Family and Adult Access to Health Care and Utilization and another section of the 2016 NHIS.

GAO took steps to assess the reliability of the 2016 NHIS estimates, including interviewing NCHS officials and examining the data for logical errors. GAO determined that the data were sufficiently reliable for the purposes of its analyses.

The Department of Health and Human Services provided technical comments on a draft of this chapter, which GAO incorporated as appropriate.

## WHAT GAO FOUND

According to the 2016 National Health Interview Survey (NHIS), an estimated 5.6 million uninsured, low-income adults—those ages 19 through 64—had incomes at or below the income threshold for expanded Medicaid eligibility as allowed under the Patient Protection and Affordable Care Act (PPACA). Estimates from this nationally representative survey showed that about 1.9 million of the 5.6 million uninsured, low-income adults lived in states that chose to expand Medicaid under PPACA, while the remaining 3.7 million lived in non-expansion states—those that did not choose to expand Medicaid. In 2016, over half of uninsured, low-income adults were male, over half were employed, and over half had incomes less than 100 percent of the federal poverty level in both expansion and non-expansion states.

The 2016 NHIS estimates showed that low-income adults in expansion states were less likely to report having any unmet medical needs compared with those in non-expansion states, and low-income adults who were insured were less likely to report having unmet medical needs compared with those who were uninsured. Among the low-income adults who were uninsured, those in expansion states were less likely to report having any unmet medical needs compared with those in non-expansion states.

The 2016 NHIS estimates also showed that low-income adults in expansion states were less likely to report financial barriers to needed medical care and other types of health care, such as specialty care, compared with those in non-expansion states, and low-income adults who were insured were less likely to report financial barriers to needed medical care compared with those who were uninsured.

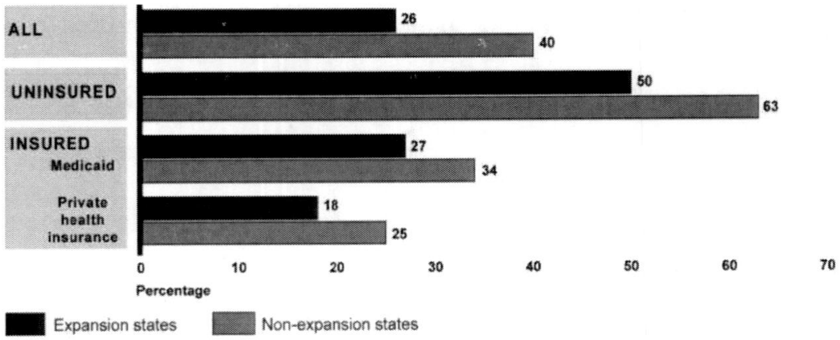


Source: GAO summary of the 2016 National Health Interview Survey estimates produced by the National Center for Health Statistics. | GAO-18-607.

Notes: The difference between all low-income adults in expansion and non-expansion states was statistically significant at $p < 0.05$ (a common indictor that denotes statistical significance). The difference between low-income adults who were uninsured in expansion and non-expansion states was statistically significant at $p < 0.05$.

Differences between low-income adults who were uninsured in expansion or non-expansion states and low-income adults who were insured—Medicaid or private health insurance—in expansion or non-expansion states were statistically significant at $p < 0.05$.

Low-Income Adults Who Reported Having Any Unmet Medical Need in Expansion and Non-Expansion States and by Insurance Status, 2016.

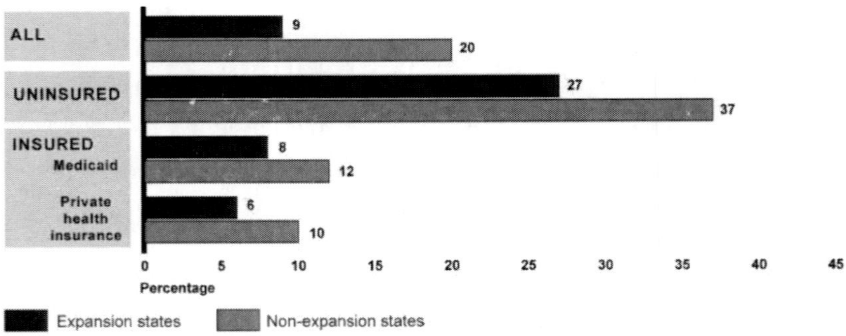


Source: GAO summary of the 2016 National Health Interview Survey estimates produced by the National Center for Health Statistics. | GAO-18-607.

Notes: The difference between all low-income adults in expansion and non-expansion states was statistically significant at $p < 0.05$. The difference between low-income adults who were uninsured in expansion and non-expansion states was statistically significant at $p < 0.05$.

Differences between low-income adults who were uninsured in expansion or non-expansion states and low-income adults who were insured—Medicaid or private health insurance—in expansion or non-expansion states were statistically significant at $p < 0.05$.

Low-Income Adults Who Reported Financial Barriers to Needed Medical Care in Expansion and Non-Expansion States and by Insurance Status, 2016.

Among low-income adults who were uninsured, those in expansion states were less likely to report financial barriers to needed medical care compared with those in non-expansion states.

Finally, the 2016 NHIS estimates showed that low-income adults in expansion states were more likely to report having a usual place of care to go when sick or needing advice about their health and receiving selected health care services compared with those in non-expansion states. The estimates also showed that low-income adults who were insured were generally more likely to report having a usual place of care and receiving selected health care services compared with those who were uninsured. Among the uninsured, relatively similar percentages of low-income adults in expansion and non-expansion states reported having a usual place of care. Similarly, estimates showed that relatively similar percentages of low-income adults who were uninsured in expansion and non-expansion states reported receiving selected health care services, such as receiving a flu vaccine or a blood pressure check.

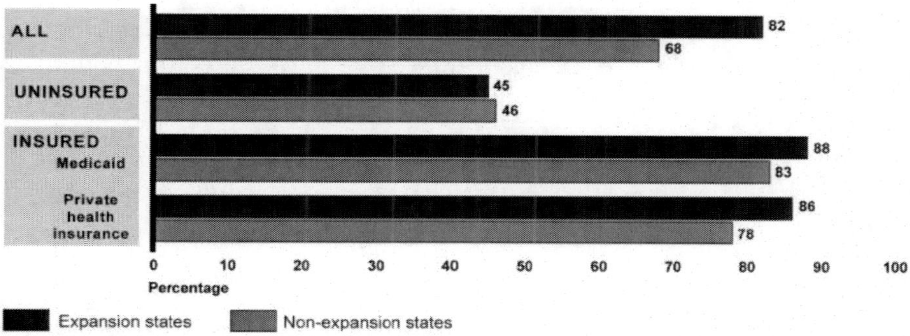


Source: GAO summary of the 2016 National Health Interview Survey estimates produced by the National Center for Health Statistics. | GAO-18-607.

Notes: The difference between all low-income adults in expansion and non-expansion states was statistically significant at $p < 0.05$.

Differences between low-income adults who were uninsured in expansion or non-expansion states and low-income adults who were insured—Medicaid or private health insurance—in expansion or non-expansion states were statistically significant at $p < 0.05$.

Low-income Adults Who Reported Having a Usual Place of Care in Expansion and Non-Expansion States and by Insurance Status, 2016.

September 13, 2018
The Honorable Ron Wyden
Ranking Member
Committee on Finance
United States Senate

Dear Mr. Wyden,

Historically, eligibility for Medicaid—a federal-state health care financing program—has been limited to certain categories of low-income individuals, including children, parents, pregnant women, and individuals who have disabilities or who are aged 65 and older. Beginning in 2014, the Patient Protection and Affordable Care Act (PPACA) gave states the option of expanding Medicaid eligibility beyond these categories to include certain adults with incomes that do not exceed 138 percent of the federal poverty level (FPL).[1] As of December 2017, there were 31 "expansion states"—those states and the District of Columbia that chose to expand Medicaid eligibility—and 19 "non-expansion states"—those that had not expanded Medicaid eligibility to this additional adult population.

Several years have passed since PPACA gave states the option of expanding Medicaid eligibility. You asked us to provide the most recently available information on the demographic characteristics of uninsured, low-income adults, and the extent to which low-income adults are accessing health care services in two groups of states: expansion states and non-expansion states.[2] This chapter describes what 2016 national survey estimates showed regarding:

---

[1] Under PPACA, enacted on March 23, 2010, states may opt to expand their Medicaid programs to cover non-elderly, non-pregnant adults who are not eligible for Medicare, and whose income does not exceed 133 percent of the FPL beginning January 1, 2014. Pub. L. No. 111-148, 124 Stat. 119 (2010), as amended by the Health Care and Education Reconciliation Act of 2010, Pub. L. No. 111-152, 124 Stat. 1029 (2010). PPACA also provides for a 5 percent disregard when calculating income for determining Medicaid eligibility, which effectively increases income eligibility from 133 percent of FPL to 138 percent of FPL. The FPL is based on household income and family size, using the U.S. Census Bureau's poverty thresholds. In 2016, 138 percent of FPL for an individual was $17,231 and for a family of four was $33,897. PPACA also permitted an early expansion option, whereby states could expand eligibility for this population, or a subset of this population, starting on April 1, 2010.

[2] In this report, we use the term "low-income adults" to refer to individuals, ages 19 to 64, with household incomes that do not exceed 138 percent of FPL.

1) the number and demographic characteristics for low-income adults who were uninsured in expansion and non-expansion states,
2) unmet medical needs for low-income adults in expansion and non-expansion states and by insurance status,
3) barriers to health care for low-income adults in expansion and non-expansion states and by insurance status, and
4) having a usual place of care and receiving selected health care services for low-income adults in expansion and non-expansion states and by insurance status.

To address our research objectives, we used data from the 2016 National Health Interview Survey (NHIS), from the Centers for Disease Control and Prevention, National Center for Health Statistics (NCHS).[3] These data were the most recent data available when we conducted our analyses.

To describe the number and demographic characteristics for low-income adults—individuals ages 19 to 64, with incomes that did not exceed 138 percent FPL—who were uninsured in expansion and non-expansion states, we requested that NCHS calculate estimates based on responses to survey questions on demographic characteristics.[4] Responses to survey questions were calculated as an estimated percentage of the total population for three groups of low-income adults: those in expansion states, in non-expansion states, and for all states.[5] We also requested that NCHS test for statistically

---

[3] The NHIS is a cross-sectional, household interview survey designed to be a nationally representative sample that covers the civilian, noninstitutionalized population residing in the United States. Several segments of the population are not included in the NHIS. Examples of persons excluded from the survey are patients in long-term care facilities, persons on active duty with the Armed Forces (though their dependents are included), persons incarcerated in the prison system, and U.S. nationals living in foreign countries.

[4] We asked NCHS researchers to produce estimates from the NHIS data because state identifiers, which are not in the public use file, were required to conduct these analyses. For the purposes of these NHIS analyses, we excluded low-income adults who were noncitizens, were covered by Medicare, only received health care services through military health care or through the Indian Health Service, or had Supplemental Social Security Income. We also excluded adult females from the Sample Adult file who reported being pregnant.

[5] We classified the 30 states and the District of Columbia that expanded their Medicaid program prior to July 1, 2016, as expansion states. The states classified as expansion states were Alaska, Arizona, Arkansas, California, Colorado, Connecticut, Delaware, Hawaii, Illinois, Indiana, Iowa, Kentucky, Maryland, Massachusetts, Michigan, Minnesota, Montana, Nevada, New Hampshire, New Jersey, New Mexico, New York, North Dakota, Ohio, Oregon, Pennsylvania, Rhode Island, Vermont, Washington, and West Virginia. The remaining 20

significant differences between expansion states and non-expansion states. Using these estimates, we summarized the uninsured, low-income adult population by expansion states, non-expansion states, and all states combined for demographic characteristics including race and ethnicity, gender, and employment status.

To describe unmet medical needs, barriers to health care, and having a usual place of care and receiving selected health care services for low-income adults in expansion and non-expansion states and by insurance status, we requested that NCHS also calculate estimates using the 2016 NHIS. Estimates were based on responses to selected survey questions and composite measures—NCHS-developed measures based on responses to NHIS questions on related topics.[6] We selected survey questions and their

---

states were classified as non-expansion states, including Louisiana, which expanded Medicaid on July 1, 2016. The other non-expansion states were Alabama, Florida, Georgia, Idaho, Kansas, Maine, Mississippi, Missouri, Nebraska, North Carolina, Oklahoma, South Carolina, South Dakota, Tennessee, Texas, Utah, Virginia, Wisconsin, and Wyoming. For 3 states, we included NHIS respondents for part of calendar year 2016. Two of the 3 states—Alaska and Montana—we excluded respondents who were surveyed during the first 6 months after the state expanded Medicaid to allow for the effect of expansion to take place. For Alaska, which expanded Medicaid on September 1, 2015, we excluded responses from those surveyed from January through February 2016. For Montana, which expanded Medicaid on January 1, 2016, we excluded responses from those surveyed from January through June 2016. Because Louisiana was classified as a non-expansion state, we included NHIS respondents interviewed from January through June 2016, when Louisiana was a non-expansion state. See R.A. Cohen and E.P. Zammitti, *Coverage, Access, and Utilization by Medicaid Expansion Status: Estimates from the National Health Interview Survey, United States, 2016,* (Hyattsville, Md.: National Center for Health Statistics, December 2017), accessed December 12, 2017, https://www.cdc.gov/nchs/health_policy/coverage_and_access.htm; and R.A. Cohen and E.P. Zammitti, *Access and Utilization by Medicaid Expansion Status for Low-Income Adults Aged 19-64: Estimates from the National Health Interview Survey, United States, 2016*, (Hyattsville, Md.: National Center for Health Statistics, January 2018), accessed January 17, 2018, https://www.cdc.gov/nchs/health_policy/coverage_and_access.htm.

[6] The analysis included two composite measures: (1) any unmet medical needs, which was based on six underlying survey questions that asked respondents about whether during the past 12 months they needed medical care but did not get it because they could not afford it; delayed seeking medical care because of worry about the cost; or did not get prescription medicines, mental health care or counseling, eyeglasses or dental care; and (2) any non-financial barriers to health care, which is based on five underlying survey questions that asked respondents whether they delayed care in the past 12 months for any of the following reasons; could not get through on the telephone; could not get an appointment soon enough; waited too long to see the doctor after arriving at the doctor's office; the clinic/doctor's office was not open when respondent could get there; and did not have transportation. Estimates of the composite measure on non-financial barriers to health care and the underlying survey question are in appendix V.

related composite measures from the Access to Health Care and Utilization and Health Behaviors sections of the 2016 NHIS.[7] These survey questions and composite measures allowed us to summarize access to health care for low-income adults in terms of unmet medical needs, barriers to health care, and having a usual place of care and receiving selected health care services. Responses to survey questions and composite measures were calculated as an estimated percentage of the total population for eight groups of low-income adults: (1) those in expansion states, (2) those in non-expansion states, (3) those who had Medicaid in expansion states, (4) those who had Medicaid in non-expansion states, (5) those who had private health insurance in expansion states, (6) those who had private health insurance in non-expansion states, (7) those who were uninsured in expansion states, and (8) those who were uninsured in non-expansion states.[8] We also requested that NCHS test for statistically significant differences between the groups of low-income adults, specifically:

- all low-income adults in expansion states compared with all low-income adults in non-expansion states;
- uninsured, low-income adults in expansion states compared with each of the four groups of insured, low-income adults—low-income adults who had Medicaid in expansion states, low-income adults who had Medicaid in non-expansion states, low-income adults who

---

[7] NHIS data are organized into several data files. Files used to develop estimates for our study include the Person and Sample Adult files.

[8] Health insurance classification was based on a hierarchy of mutually exclusive categories in the following order: private health insurance, Medicaid, other coverage, and uninsured. Low-income adults with more than one coverage type were assigned the first appropriate category in the hierarchy, and those with other coverage were excluded from these analyses. Low-income adults were classified as having private health insurance if they reported that they were covered by any comprehensive private health insurance plan, including health maintenance and preferred provider organization plans. Private health insurance excludes plans that pay for only one type of service, such as accidents or dental care. Low-income adults were classified as having Medicaid if they reported that they were covered by Medicaid or by state-sponsored health plans with no premiums or if it is not known if a premium is charged. Low-income adults were classified as uninsured if they did not have any private health insurance or were not enrolled in Medicare, Medicaid, the Children's Health Insurance Program, a state-sponsored or other government-sponsored health plan, or a military plan. An adult was also defined as uninsured if they had only a private plan that paid for one type of service, such as accidents or dental care.

had private health insurance in expansion states, and low-income adults who had private health insurance in non-expansion states;

- uninsured, low-income adults in non-expansion states compared with each of the four groups of insured, low-income adults; and
- uninsured, low-income adults in expansion states compared with uninsured, low-income adults in non-expansion states.[9]

We took steps to assess the reliability of the 2016 NHIS estimates, including interviewing NCHS officials and checking frequency distributions for missing estimates, outliers, and obvious errors. Based on this work, we determined that the estimates were sufficiently reliable for the purposes of our reporting objectives. Appendix I provides additional information on our scope and methodology.

We conducted this performance audit from May 2017 through September 2018 in accordance with generally accepted government auditing standards. Those standards require that we plan and perform the audit to obtain sufficient, appropriate evidence to provide a reasonable basis for our findings and conclusions based on our audit objectives. We believe that the evidence obtained provides a reasonable basis for our findings and conclusions based on our audit objectives.

## Background

In fiscal year 2016, Medicaid covered an estimated 72.2 million low-income and medically needy individuals in the United States, and Medicaid

[9] We also requested that NCHS test for statistically significant differences between low-income adults who had Medicaid in expansion states and those who had Medicaid in non-expansion states, and between low-income adults who had private health insurance in expansion states and those who had private health insurance in non-expansion states. We did not request that NCHS test for significant differences between low-income adults who had Medicaid in expansion or non-expansion states and low-income adults who had private health insurance in expansion or non-expansion states. Estimates of all survey questions and composite measures we reviewed and results of all tests for statistically significant differences are in appendixes IV through VI.

estimated expenditures totaled over $575.9 billion.[10] The federal government matches most state expenditures for Medicaid services on the basis of a statutory formula.[11] States receive higher federal matching rates for certain services or populations, including an enhanced matching rate for Medicaid expenditures for individuals who became eligible for Medicaid under PPACA.[12] Of the $575.9 billion in estimated expenditures for 2016, the federal share totaled over $363.4 billion and the states' share totaled $212.5 billion.[13]

The Centers for Medicare & Medicaid Services (CMS)—a federal agency within the Department of Health and Human Services (HHS)—and states jointly administer and fund the Medicaid program. States have flexibility within broad federal requirements to design and implement their Medicaid programs. States must submit a state Medicaid plan to CMS for review and approval.

A state's approved Medicaid plan outlines the services provided and the groups of individuals covered. While states must cover certain mandatory populations and benefits, they have the option of covering other categories of individuals and benefits.[14]

PPACA permitted states to expand coverage to a new population—non-elderly, non-pregnant adults who are not eligible for Medicare and whose income does not exceed 138 percent of the FPL. This expansion population comprised 20 percent of total Medicaid enrollment in 2017. (See Figure 1).

---

[10] In fiscal year 2016, the estimated Medicaid total enrollment included enrollees in all states, the District of Columbia, and five United States territories. See Department of Health & Human Services, Office of the Actuary, Centers for Medicare & Medicaid Services, *2016 Actuarial Report on the Financial Outlook for Medicaid.*

[11] Under this formula, known as the Federal Medical Assistance Percentage, the federal government pays a share of Medicaid expenditures based on each state's per capita income relative to the national average. Federal law specifies that the Federal Medical Assistance Percentage will be no lower than 50 percent and no higher than 83 percent.

[12] States that chose to expand their Medicaid programs under PPACA receive a federal match of 100 percent beginning in 2014 for expenditures for newly eligible low-income adults, gradually diminishing to 90 percent by 2020. Certain states that expanded Medicaid coverage for low-income adults prior to the enactment of PPACA in 2010 may also receive an enhanced federal match for Medicaid expenditures for this expansion population.

[13] See Office of the Actuary, *2016 Actuarial Report*.

[14] Mandatory benefits include inpatient and outpatient hospital services, and laboratory and x-ray services, among others. Optional benefits include prescription drugs, physical therapy, and dental services, among others.

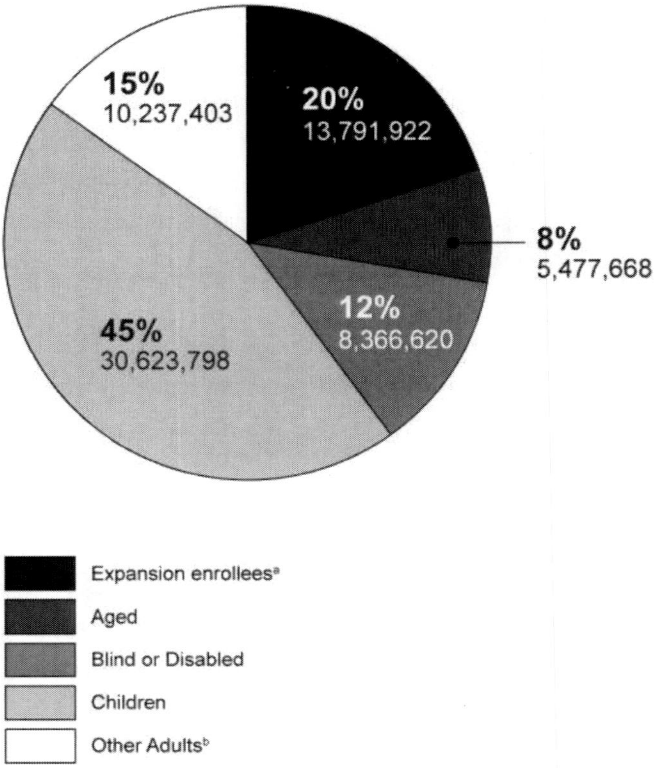


Source: GAO summary of Centers for Medicare & Medicaid Services' data. | GAO-18-607.

Note: Medicaid enrollment numbers are from CMS-64 enrollment data and may differ from other data sources. Average monthly enrollment was tabulated from the CMS-64 enrollment report for fiscal year 2017, which was accessed on April 4, 2018.

[a]Expansion enrollees refers to individuals ages 19 to 64, without children, who are not disabled or pregnant, and have household incomes that did not exceed 138 percent of the federal poverty level. In 2017, 138 percent of the federal poverty level was $22,411 for a two-person household in the contiguous United States.

[b]Other adults refers to adults who are not aged and not disabled.

Figure 1. National Medicaid Enrollment by Eligible Population, December 2017.

As of December 2017, 31 states and the District of Columbia had expanded Medicaid eligibility to the new coverage population allowed under PPACA and 19 states had not.[15] Figure 2, an interactive map, illustrates

[15] Louisiana expanded Medicaid eligibility on July 1, 2016. For the purposes of these NHIS analyses, Louisiana was classified as a non-expansion state and we included low-income

states' Medicaid expansion status. See appendix II for additional information on Figure 2.

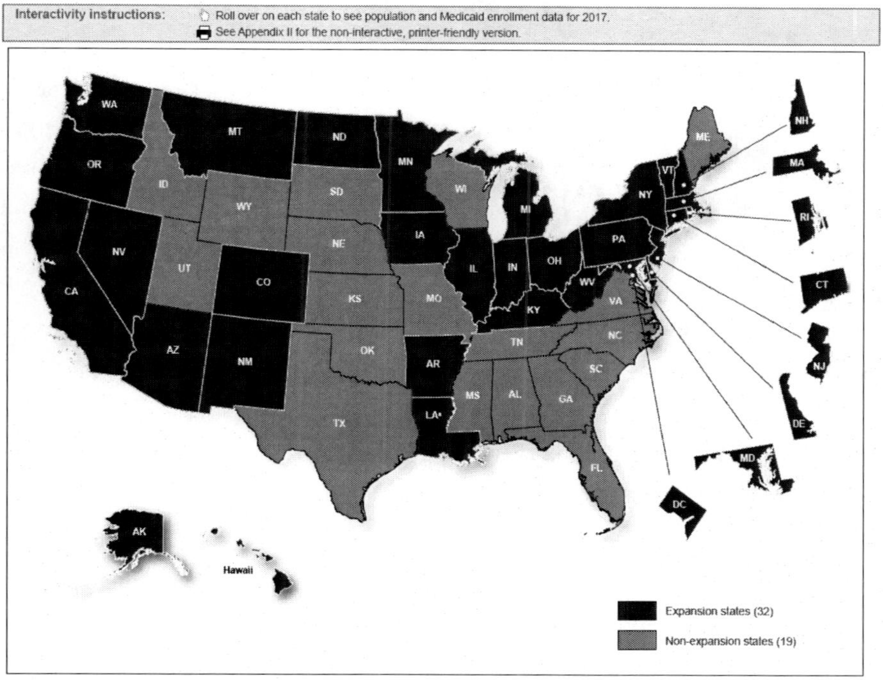


Sources: GAO summary of U.S. Census Bureau, Centers for Medicare & Medicaid Services, and Kaiser Family Foundation data (data); Map Resources (map). | GAO-18-607.

Notes: Census population estimates are as of July 1, 2017. Medicaid enrollment numbers come from CMS-64 enrollment data and may differ from other data sources. Average monthly enrollment was tabulated from the CMS-64 enrollment report for calendar year 2017 that was accessed on April 4, 2018.

[a]Louisiana expanded Medicaid eligibility on July 1, 2016. For the purpose of the NHIS analysis, Louisiana was classified as a non-expansion state and we only included low-income adults interviewed from January through June 2016 when Louisiana was a non-expansion state.

Figure 2. Status of Medicaid Eligibility Expansion by State, as of 2017.

---

adults interviewed from January through June 2016 when Louisiana was a non-expansion state.

## SURVEY ESTIMATES SHOWED 5.6 MILLION UNINSURED, LOW-INCOME ADULTS HAD QUALIFYING INCOMES FOR EXPANDED MEDICAID COVERAGE

According to the NHIS estimates, 5.6 million low-income adults were uninsured in 2016. Of these 5.6 million, an estimated 1.9 million uninsured, low-income adults resided in expansion states, compared with an estimated 3.7 million in non-expansion states. Estimates of uninsured, low-income adults comprised less than 1 percent of the total population for all expansion states and 3 percent of the total population for all non-expansion states.[16]

NHIS estimates also showed that over half of uninsured, low-income adults were male, over half were employed, and over half had incomes less than 100 percent FPL. For some demographic characteristics, there were some statistically significant differences between uninsured, low-income adults in expansion states compared with these adults in non-expansion states. For example, expansion states had significantly larger percentages of uninsured, low-income males than non-expansion states. (See Table 1).

See Table 6 in appendix III for additional demographic characteristics of uninsured, low-income adults. Estimates from the 2016 NHIS showed some statistically significant differences in the health status of uninsured, low-income adults in expansion and non-expansion states. In particular, expansion states had a larger percentage of these adults who reported that their health was "good" and a smaller percentage who reported their health as "fair or poor" than those in non-expansion states. However, the percentages of uninsured, low-income adults with responses of "excellent or very good" in both expansion and non-expansion states were large—47 percent or larger, and the differences between the two groups of states were not statistically significant. (See Figure 3). See Table 7 in appendix III for additional information about the health status for uninsured, low-income adults.

---

[16] The 2016 total population for expansion and non-expansion states were derived from the U.S. Census Bureau, Annual Estimates of the Resident Population: April 1, 2010, to July 1, 2017. See https://factfinder.census.gov/faces/tableservices/jsf/pages/productview.xhtml?pid=PEP_20 17_PEPANNRES&src=pt, accessed on June 11, 2018.

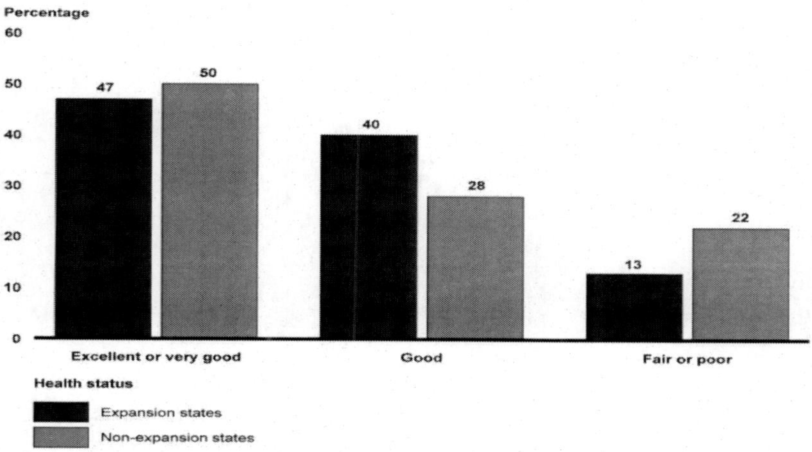


Source: GAO summary of the 2016 NHIS estimates produced by the National Center for Health Statistics. | GAO-18-607.

Notes: Estimates reflect those included in the Family and Sample Adult Core components of the National Health Interview Survey (NHIS). Estimates are based on household interviews of a sample of the civilian, noninstitutionalized U.S. population.

For the purposes of these NHIS analyses, low-income adults are individuals ages 19 to 64, with family incomes that did not exceed 138 percent of the federal poverty level. These analyses excluded low-income adults who were noncitizens, were covered by Medicare, only received health care services through military health care or through the Indian Health Service, or had Supplemental Social Security Income. We also excluded adult females from the Sample Adult file who reported being pregnant. An individual was defined as uninsured if they did not have any private health insurance, Medicare, Medicaid, Children's Health Insurance Program, state-sponsored or other government-sponsored health plan, or military plan. An individual was also defined as uninsured if they had only a private plan that paid for one type of service, such as accidents or dental care.

For the purposes of these NHIS analyses, the 30 states and the District of Columbia that expanded their Medicaid programs prior to July 1, 2016, were classified as expansion states. The remaining 20 states were classified as non-expansion states.

For Good and for Fair or Poor, the difference between expansion and non-expansion states was statistically significant at $p < 0.05$.

Figure 3. Health Status of Uninsured, Low-Income Adults in Expansion and Non-Expansion States, 2016.

## Table 1. Demographic Characteristics of Uninsured, Low-Income Adults in Expansion and Non-Expansion States, 2016

| n/a<br>Demographic characteristics | Expansion states | Non-expansion states | All states |
|---|---|---|---|
| | Percent (standard error) N = 1,915,000 | Percent (standard error) N = 3,721,000 | Percent (standard error) N = 5,639,000 |
| Poverty status[a]: Less than 100% FPL | 59 (3.28)[b] | 69 (2.05)[b] | 65 (1.81) |
| Poverty status[a]: 100% to less than or equal to 138% FPL | 42 (3.28)[b] | 32 (2.05)[b] | 35 (1.81) |
| Sex: Male | 63 (2.33)[b] | 51 (1.49)[b] | 55 (1.31) |
| Sex: Female | 37(2.33)[b] | 49 (1.49)[b] | 45 (1.31) |
| Race and ethnicity: Hispanic | 22 (2.64) | 20 (3.26) | 20 (2.30) |
| Race and ethnicity: Non-Hispanic, white only | 53 (3.40) | 45 (2.70) | 48 (2.14) |
| Race and ethnicity: Non-Hispanic, black only | 17 (2.47)[b] | 30 (2.32)[b] | 26 (1.73) |
| Race and ethnicity: Non-Hispanic, Asian only | NA | 1 (0.57) | 2 (0.60) |
| Race and ethnicity: Non-Hispanic, other | 3 (1.02) | 4 (0.98) | 4 (0.73) |
| Employment status: Employed | 64 (2.43) | 56 (1.60) | 58 (1.37) |
| Employment status: Unemployed | 14 (1.85) | 17 (1.35) | 16 (1.10) |
| Employment status: Not in workforce | 22 (2.17)[b] | 28 (1.60)[b] | 26 (1.30) |

Legend: NA = Not available because of estimates did not meet the NCHS standards for accuracy and precision.

Source: GAO summary of the 2016 NHIS estimates produced by NCHS. | GAO-18-607.

Notes: Estimates reflect questions included in the Family Core component of the National Health Interview Survey (NHIS). Estimates are based on household interviews of a sample of the civilian, noninstitutionalized U.S. population. Estimates were not available when they did not meet the National Center for Health Statistics' (NCHS) standards for accuracy and precision. The percentages may not sum to 100 percent due to rounding. For the purposes of these NHIS analyses, low-income adults are individuals ages 19 to 64, with family incomes that did not exceed 138 percent of the federal poverty level (FPL). These analyses excluded low-income adults who were noncitizens, were covered by Medicare, only received health care services through military health care or through the Indian Health Service, or had Supplemental Social Security Income. We also excluded adult females from the Sample Adult file who reported being pregnant. An individual was defined as uninsured if they did not have any private health insurance, Medicare, Medicaid, Children's Health Insurance Program, state-sponsored or other government-sponsored health plan, or military plan. An individual was also defined as uninsured if they had only a private plan that paid for one type of service, such as accidents or dental care. For the purposes of the NHIS analyses, the 30 states and the District of Columbia that expanded their Medicaid programs prior to July 1, 2016, were classified as expansion states. The remaining 20 states were classified as non-expansion states.

[a]The FPL is based on family income and family size, using the U.S. Census Bureau's poverty thresholds. The 2016 NHIS imputed income files were used to help create the poverty variable, and this variable is based on reported and imputed family information. See https://www.cdc.gov/nchs/nhis/nhis_2016_data_release.htm.

[b]Difference between expansion and non-expansion states was statistically significant at $p < 0.05$.

# SURVEY ESTIMATES SHOWED LOW-INCOME ADULTS IN EXPANSION STATES AND THOSE WHO WERE INSURED WERE LESS LIKELY TO REPORT ANY UNMET MEDICAL NEEDS

The 2016 NHIS estimates showed that smaller percentages of low-income adults in expansion states reported having any unmet medical needs compared with those in non-expansion states; and smaller percentages of those who were insured reported having any unmet medical needs compared with those who were uninsured, regardless of where they lived, for example:

## Low-Income Adults in Expansion and Non-Expansion States

Twenty-six percent of low-income adults in expansion states reported having any unmet medical needs, compared with 40 percent of those in non-expansion states.[17]

## Low-Income Adults Who Were Insured and Uninsured

Thirty-four percent or less of the low-income adults who had Medicaid or private health insurance in expansion or non-expansion states reported having any unmet medical needs, compared with 50 percent or more of those who were uninsured in expansion or non-expansion states.[18] Further, among the uninsured, 50 percent of low-income adults living in expansion states reported any unmet medical needs, compared with 63 percent of those in non-expansion states.[19] (See Figure 4). See Tables 8 and 9 in appendix IV for estimates of the composite measure we reviewed on any unmet medical needs.

---

[17] This difference was statistically significant at $p < 0.05$.
[18] These differences were statistically significant at $p < 0.05$.
[19] This difference was statistically significant at $p < 0.05$.

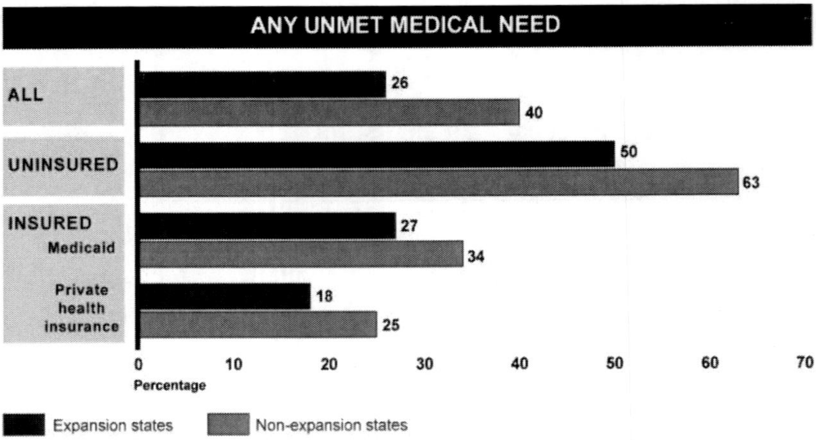


Source: GAO summary of the 2016 NHIS estimates produced by the National Center for Health Statistics. | GAO-18-607.

Notes: Estimates are for a composite measure, which was based on responses to questions from the Access to Health Care and Utilization sections of the Family and Sample Adult Core components of the 2016 National Health Interview Survey (NHIS). For the purposes of these NHIS analyses, low-income adults are individuals ages 19 to 64, with family incomes that did not exceed 138 percent of the federal poverty level. These analyses excluded low-income adults who were noncitizens, were covered by Medicare, only received health care services through military health care or through the Indian Health Service, or had Supplemental Social Security Income. We also excluded adult females from the Sample Adult file who reported being pregnant. Low-income adults had any unmet medical needs if they reported that in the past 12 months they did not get needed medical care because they could not afford it; delayed seeking medical care due to worries about costs; or needed but did not get because they could not afford prescription medicines, mental health care or counseling, dental care, or eyeglasses.

For the purposes of these NHIS analyses, the 30 states and the District of Columbia that expanded their Medicaid programs prior to July 1, 2016, were classified as expansion states. The remaining 20 states were classified as non-expansion states. Health insurance classification was based on a hierarchy of mutually exclusive categories in the following order: private health insurance, Medicaid, other coverage, and uninsured. Adults with more than one coverage type were assigned the first appropriate category in the hierarchy and those with other coverage were excluded from these analyses.

The difference between all low-income adults in expansion and non-expansion states was statistically significant at $p < 0.05$. The difference between low-income adults who were uninsured in expansion and non-expansion states was statistically significant at $p < 0.05$.

Differences between low-income adults who were uninsured in expansion or non-expansion states and low-income adults who were insured—Medicaid or private health insurance—in expansion or non-expansion states were statistically significant at $p < 0.05$.

Figure 4. Percentage of Low-Income Adults in Expansion and Non-Expansion States and by Insurance Status Who Reported Any Unmet Medical Need, 2016.

**Access to Health Care: Measuring Any Unmet Medical Needs**

The National Center for Health Statistics, the federal agency that conducts the National Health Interview Survey (NHIS), developed a composite measure on any unmet medical needs, which was based on six survey questions on respondents' ability to afford different types of needed health care services. These questions asked whether in the past 12 months respondents could not afford medical care at any time; delayed seeking medical care due to worries about costs; or could not afford needed prescription drugs, mental health or counseling, dental care, or eyeglasses.

Source: GAO summary of a selected NHIS composite measure. | GAO-18-607.

## Survey Estimates Showed Low-Income Adults in Expansion States and Those Who Were Insured Were Less Likely to Report Financial Barriers to Health Care

The 2016 NHIS estimates showed that smaller percentages of low-income adults in expansion states reported financial barriers to needed health care compared with those in non-expansion states; and smaller percentages of those who were insured reported financial barriers to needed health care compared with those who were uninsured, regardless of where they lived, for example:

### Low-Income Adults in Expansion and Non-Expansion States

Nine percent of low-income adults in expansion states reported that they could not afford needed medical care, compared with 20 percent of low-income adults in non-expansion states.[20]

[20] This difference was statistically significant at $p < 0.05$.

## Low-Income Adults Who Were Insured and Uninsured

Twelve percent or less of low-income adults who had Medicaid or private health insurance in expansion or non-expansion states reported financial barriers to needed medical care, compared with 27 percent or more of those who were uninsured in expansion or non-expansion states.[21] In addition, among low- income adults who were uninsured, a smaller percentage of those who lived in expansion states reported financial barriers to two of the six needed health care services compared with those who lived in non-expansion states.[22] (See Figure 5). See Tables 10 through 13 in appendix V for estimates of all survey questions we reviewed on financial barriers to health care.

**Access to Health Care: Measuring Financial Barriers to Health Care**

The 2016 National Health Interview Survey (NHIS) asked respondents whether they did not obtain different types of needed health care services in the past 12 months because they could not afford the service. Services included:

- medical care,
- specialty care,
- prescription medications,
- mental health care or counseling,
- dental care, and
- eyeglasses.

Source: GAO summary of selected NHIS questions. | GAO-18-607.

The 2016 NHIS also collected information on non-financial barriers to health care.

Specifically, the survey asked whether respondents had delayed health care due to non-financial reasons, such as they lacked transportation, were

[21] These differences were statistically significant at $p < 0.05$.

[22] For financial barriers to medical care and prescription drugs, differences were statistically significant at $p < 0.05$. For mental health care, dental care, specialty care, and eyeglasses, differences were not statistically significant at $p < 0.05$.

unable to get through on the phone, were unable to get a timely appointment, experienced long wait time at the doctor's office, or were not able to get to a clinic or doctor's office when it was open.[23] The 2016 NHIS showed that the same or similar percentages of low-income adults in expansion and non-expansion states reported delaying care due to a lack of transportation or other non-financial reasons.[24] Further, generally similar or larger percentages of low-income adults with insurance reported delaying care due to non-financial reasons, compared with those who were uninsured.[25] See Tables 14 and 15 in appendix V for estimates of low-income adults in expansion and non-expansion states and by insurance status on non-financial barriers to health care.

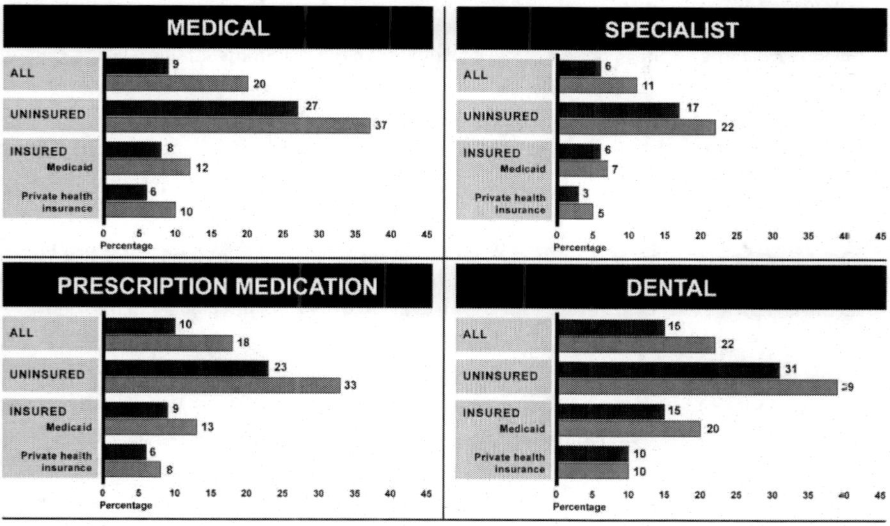


Figure 5. (Continued)

[23] NCHS developed a composite measure on any non-financial barriers to health care, which was based on these five survey questions.

[24] Any differences in the percentage of low-income adults in expansion and non-expansion states that reported delaying care due to a lack of transportation, long wait times at the doctor's office, or other non-financial reason were not statistically significant at $p < 0.05$.

[25] Estimates were not available for all insured and uninsured low-income adult populations for all survey questions on non-financial barriers we reviewed, because estimates did not meet NCHS's standards for accuracy and precision. See Table 15 in appendix V.

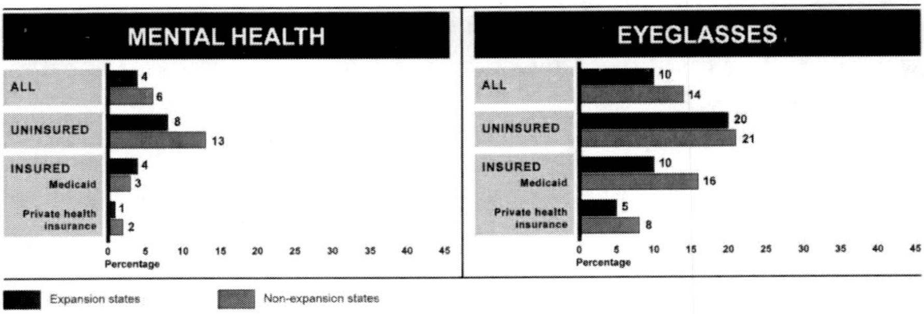


Source: GAO summary of the 2016 NHIS estimates produced by the National Center for Health Statistics. | GAO-18-607.

Notes: Estimates are for selected questions, which were from the Access to Health Care and Utilization sections of the Family and Sample Adult Core components of the 2016 National Health Interview Survey (NHIS). For the purposes of these NHIS analyses, low-income adults are individuals ages 19 to 64, with family incomes that did not exceed 138 percent of the federal poverty level. These analyses excluded low-income adults who were noncitizens, were covered by Medicare, only received health care services through military health care or through the Indian Health Service, or had Supplemental Social Security Income. We also excluded adult females from the Sample Adult file who reported being pregnant.

For the purposes of these NHIS analyses, the 30 states and the District of Columbia that expanded their Medicaid programs prior to July 1, 2016, were classified as expansion states. The remaining 20 states were classified as non-expansion states.

Health insurance classification was based on a hierarchy of mutually exclusive categories in the following order: private health insurance, Medicaid, other coverage, and uninsured. Adults with more than one coverage type were assigned the first appropriate category in the hierarchy and those with other coverage were excluded from these analyses.

For all six service types, the difference between all low-income adults in expansion and non-expansion states was statistically significant at $p < 0.05$. For two of the six service types—medical care and prescription medications—the difference between low-income adults who were uninsured in expansion and non-expansion states was statistically significant at $p < 0.05$.

For all six service types, with four exceptions, differences between low-income adults who were uninsured in expansion or non-expansion states and low-income adults who were insured—Medicaid or private health insurance—in expansion or non-expansion states were statistically significant at $p < 0.05$. For mental health care, differences between low-income adults who were uninsured in expansion states and low-income adults who had Medicaid in expansion or non-expansion states were not statistically significant at $p < 0.05$. For eyeglasses, differences between low-income adults who were uninsured in expansion or non-expansion states and those who had Medicaid in non-expansion states were not statistically significant at $p < 0.05$.

Figure 5. Percentage of Low-Income Adults in Expansion and Non-Expansion States and by Insurance Status Who Reported Financial Barriers to Different Types of Needed Health Care Services, 2016.

## Survey Estimates Showed Low-Income Adults in Expansion States and Those Who Were Insured Were Generally More Likely to Report Having a Usual Place of Care and Receiving Selected Health Care Services

The 2016 NHIS estimates showed that a larger percentage of low-income adults in expansion states reported having a usual place of care compared with those in non-expansion states; and larger percentages of those who were insured reported having a usual place of care compared with those who were uninsured, regardless of where they lived, for example:[26]

### Low-Income Adults in Expansion and Non-Expansion States

Eighty-two percent of the low-income adults in expansion states reported having a usual place of care when they were sick or needed advice about their health, compared with 68 percent of those in non-expansion states.[27]

### Low-Income Adults Who Were Insured and Uninsured

Seventy-eight percent or more of those who had Medicaid or private health insurance in expansion or non-expansion states reported having a usual place of care, compared with 46 percent or less of those who were uninsured in expansion or non-expansion states.[28]

---

[26] Low-income adults who reported the emergency department as their usual place of care were considered to not have a usual place of care.

[27] This difference was statistically significant at $p < 0.05$.

[28] These differences were statistically significant at $p < 0.05$.

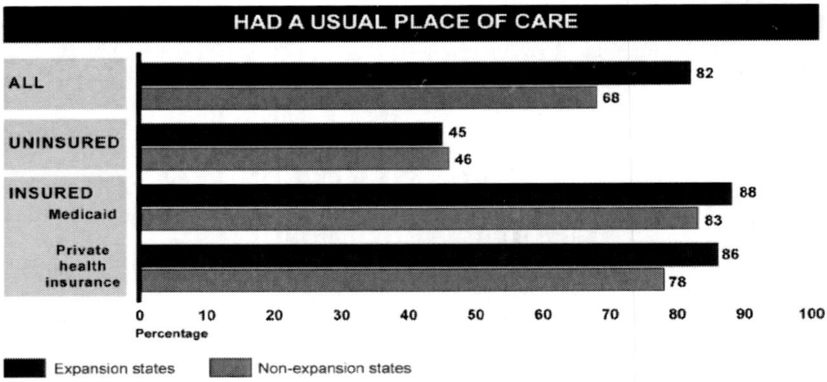


Source: GAO summary of the 2016 NHIS estimates produced by the National Center for Health Statistics. | GAO-18-607.

Notes: Estimates are for a selected survey question, which was from the Health Care Access and Utilization section of the Sample Adult Core component of the 2016 National Health Interview Survey (NHIS). For the purposes of these NHIS analyses, low-income adults are individuals ages 19 to 64, with family incomes that did not exceed 138 percent of the federal poverty level. These analyses excluded low-income adults who were noncitizens, were covered by Medicare, only received health care services through military health care or through the Indian Health Service, or had Supplemental Social Security Income. We also excluded adult females from the Sample Adult file who reported being pregnant. Low-income adults who reported the emergency department as their usual place of care were considered to not have a usual place of care.

For the purposes of these NHIS analyses, the 30 states and the District of Columbia that expanded their Medicaid programs prior to July 1, 2016, were classified as expansion states. The remaining 20 states were classified as non-expansion states.

Health insurance classification was based on a hierarchy of mutually exclusive categories in the following order: private health insurance, Medicaid, other coverage, and uninsured. Adults with more than one coverage type were assigned the first appropriate category in the hierarchy and those with other coverage were excluded from these analyses.

The difference between all low-income adults in expansion and non-expansion states is statistically significant at $p < 0.05$.

Differences between low-income adults who were uninsured in expansion or non-expansion states and low-income adults who were insured—Medicaid or private health insurance—in expansion or non-expansion states were statistically significant at $p < 0.05$.

Figure 6. Percentage of Low-Income Adults in Expansion and Non-Expansion States and by Insurance Status Who Reported Having a Usual Place of Care, 2016.

Among the uninsured, similar percentages of low-income adults in expansion and non-expansion states reported having a usual place of care.[29] (See Figure 6). See Tables 16 through 19 in appendix VI for estimates of all survey questions we reviewed on having a usual place of care.

**Access to Health Care: Having a Usual Place of Care**

The 2016 National Health Interview Survey (NHIS) asked respondents about whether they had a place they usually go when sick or need advice about their health.

Source: GAO summary of selected NHIS questions. | GAO-18-607.

## Survey Estimates Showed Low-Income Adults in Expansion States and Those Who Were Insured Were Generally More Likely to Report Receiving Selected Services

The 2016 estimates showed that larger percentages of low-income adults in expansion states reported receiving selected health care services, such as a flu vaccine, compared with those in non-expansion states; and larger percentages of those with insurance reported receiving selected health care services compared with those who were uninsured, regardless of where they lived, for example:

## Low-Income Adults in Expansion and Non-Expansion States

Thirty-one percent of low-income adults in expansion states reported receiving flu vaccinations, compared with 24 percent of those in non-expansion states.[30]

---

[29] This difference was not statistically significant at $p < 0.05$.

[30] This difference was statistically significant at $p < 0.05$. Differences between percentages of low-income adults in expansion states and those in non-expansion states who reported receiving other selected services, such as having their blood sugar checked, were not statistically significant at $p < 0.05$.

## Low-Income Adults Who Were Insured and Uninsured

Forty-three percent or more of low-income adults who had Medicaid or private health insurance in expansion or non-expansion states reported receiving blood cholesterol checks, compared with 28 percent or less of low-income adults who were uninsured in expansion or non-expansion states.[31] Among the uninsured, generally similar percentages of low-income adults in expansion and non-expansion states reported blood cholesterol checks, flu vaccines, and other selected services.[32] (See Figure 7). See Tables 20 and 21 in appendix VI for estimates of all survey questions we reviewed on selected health care services.

**Access to Health Care: Measuring Receipt of Selected Health Care Services**

The 2016 National Health Interview Survey (NHIS) asked respondents whether they had received certain health care services in the past 12 months, including:

- having their blood cholesterol checked by a doctor, nurse, or other health professional;
- having their blood pressure checked by a doctor, nurse, or other health professional;
- having a fasting test for high blood sugar or diabetes;
- getting a flu vaccine by both shot and nasal spray; and
- visiting a hospital emergency department.

Source: GAO summary of selected NHIS questions. | GAO-18-607.

[31] These differences were statistically significant at $p < 0.05$.

[32] Any differences between the percentages of low-income adults who were uninsured in expansion and non-expansion states who reported receiving selected health care services were not statistically significant at $p < 0.05$.

The 2016 NHIS also asked respondents whether they visited or had spoken to a health care professional about their health, including:

- a general doctor, such as a general practitioner, family doctor, and internist;
- a nurse practitioner, physician's assistant, or midwife; and
- a doctor who specializes in a particular disease, with the exception of obstetricians, gynecologists, psychiatrists, and ophthalmologists.

See Tables 22 and 23 in appendix VI for estimates of low-income adults in expansion and non-expansion states and by insurance status on contacting health care professionals.

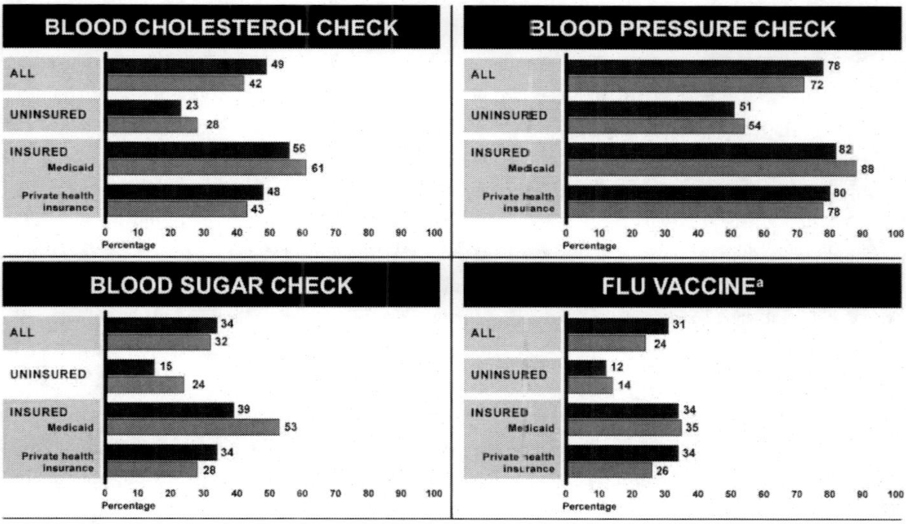


Figure 7. (Continued).

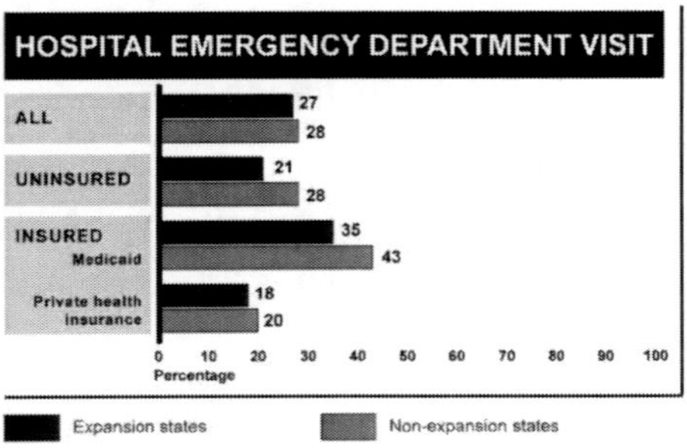


Source: GAO summary of the 2016 National Health Interview Survey estimates produced by the National Center for Health Statistics. | GAO-18-607.

Notes: Estimates are based on selected survey questions, which were from the Access to Health Care and Utilization sections of the Sample Adult Core component of the 2016 National Health Interview Survey (NHIS). For the purposes of these NHIS analyses, low-income adults are individuals ages 19 to 64, with family incomes that did not exceed 138 percent of the federal poverty level. These analyses excluded low-income adults who were noncitizens, were covered by Medicare, only received health care services through military health care or through the Indian Health Service, or had Supplemental Social Security Income. We also excluded adult females from the Sample Adult file who reported being pregnant.

For the purposes of these NHIS analyses, the 30 states and the District of Columbia that expanded their Medicaid programs prior to July 1, 2016, were classified as expansion states. The remaining 20 states were classified as non-expansion states.

Health insurance classification was based on a hierarchy of mutually exclusive categories in the following order: private health insurance, Medicaid, other coverage, and uninsured. Adults with more than one coverage type were assigned the first appropriate category in the hierarchy and those with other coverage were excluded from these analyses.

For blood cholesterol check, blood pressure check, and flu vaccine, the differences between all low-income adults in expansion states and non-expansion states was statistically significant at $p < 0.05$.

For all five services with four exceptions, differences between low-income adults who were uninsured in expansion or non-expansion states and low-income adults who were insured—Medicaid or private health insurance—in expansion or non-expansion states were statistically significant at $p < 0.05$. For receiving a blood sugar check, the difference between low-income adults who were uninsured in non-expansion states and low-income adults who had private health insurance in non-expansion states was not statistically significant at $p < 0.05$. For visiting the hospital emergency department, the difference between low-income adults who were uninsured in non-expansion states and those who had Medicaid in expansion states was not statistically significant at $p < 0.05$, and the differences between the low-income adults who were uninsured in expansion states and those who had private health insurance in expansion or non-expansion states were not statistically significant at $p < 0.05$.

[a]Includes vaccines by both shot and nasal spray.

Figure 7. Percentage of Low-Income Adults in Expansion and Non-Expansion States and by Insurance Status Who Reported Using Selected Health Care Services, 2016.

## AGENCY COMMENTS AND OUR EVALUATION

We provided a draft of this chapter to HHS for comment. HHS provided technical comments, which we incorporated as appropriate.

As agreed with your offices, unless you publicly announce the contents of this chapter earlier, we plan no further distribution until 30 days from the report date. At that time, we will send copies of this chapter to the Secretary of Health and Human Services, the appropriate congressional committee, and other interested parties.

If you are your staff members have any questions about this chapter, please contact me. Contact points for our Offices of Congressional Relations and Public Affairs may be found on the last page of this chapter. Major contributors to this chapter are listed in appendix VII.

Sincerely yours,

Carolyn L. Yocom
Director, Health Care

## APPENDIX I: OBJECTIVES, SCOPE, AND METHODOLOGY

To describe national survey estimates of (1) the number and demographic characteristics of uninsured, low-income adults in expansion and non-expansion states; (2) unmet medical needs for low-income adults in expansion and non-expansion states and by insurance status; (3) barriers to health care for low-income adults in expansion and non-expansion states and by insurance status; and (4) having a usual place of care and receiving selected health care services for low-income adults in expansion and non-expansion states and by insurance status, we used data from the 2016 National Health Interview Survey (NHIS).[33] The 2016 NHIS were the most

[33] The estimates of demographic characteristics and access to health care from the 2016 NHIS for this study were produced by Robin A. Cohen, and Emily P. Zammitti of National Center for Health Statistics' Division of Health Interview Statistics based on the analysis plans we

recent data available when we conducted our analyses. This appendix describes the data source, study population, analyses conducted, study limitations, and data reliability assessment.

## Data Source

The NHIS collects demographic, health status, health insurance, health care access, and health care service use data for the civilian, noninstitutionalized U.S. population. It is an annual, nationally representative, cross-sectional household interview survey.[34] NHIS interviews are conducted continuously throughout the year for the National Center for Health Statistics (NCHS), which is a federal agency within the Department of Health and Human Services that compiles statistical information to help guide health policy decisions. Interviews are conducted in respondents' homes, and interviewers may conduct follow-up interviews over the telephone to complete an interview. Information about some NHIS respondents, such as information about their health status, may be obtained through an interview with another family member on behalf of the respondent.

NHIS data are organized into several data files. Estimates used for our study are based on data with the 2016 Family and Sample Adult Core components of the 2016 NHIS. Sociodemographic, insurance, and select health care access and utilization variables were defined using data collected in the Family Core component of the survey, which includes data on every

---

provided. See R.A. Cohen and E.P. Zammitti, *Coverage, Access, and Utilization by Medicaid Expansion Status: Estimates from* the *National Health Interview Survey, United States, 2016,* (Hyattsville, MD.: National Center for Health Statistics, December 2017), accessed December 12, 2017, https://www.cdc.gov/nchs/health_policy/coverage_and_access.htm; and R.A. Cohen and E.P. Zammitti, *Access and Utilization by Medicaid Expansion Status for Low-Income Adults Aged 19-64: Estimates from the National Health Interview Survey, United States, 2016*, (Hyattsville, MD.: National Center for Health Statistics, January 2018), accessed January 17, 2018, https://www.cdc.gov/nchs/health_policy/coverage_and_access.htm.

[34] Several segments of the U.S. population are not included in the NHIS. Examples of persons excluded from the survey are patients in long-term care facilities, persons on active duty with the Armed Forces (although their dependents are included), persons incarcerated in the prison system, and U.S. nationals living in foreign countries.

household member for the families participating in NHIS. Other measures of health care access and utilization examined in this study are based on data collected in the Sample Adult Core component. In this component, the respondent (i.e., the sample adult) is randomly selected from among all adults aged ≥18 years in the family. A proxy respondent might respond for the sample adult if, because of health reasons, the sample adult is physically or mentally unable to respond themselves. The 2016 imputed income files were used to define poverty thresholds, which is based on reported and imputed family income. The NHIS publicly released data files for 2016 include data for 40,220 households containing 97,169 persons, and the total household response rate was 67.9 percent.

## Study Population

For this study we asked NCHS to provide estimates of low-income, non-elderly adults, which we defined as individuals ages 19 to 64, with family incomes that did not exceed 138 percent of the federal poverty level (FPL).[35] We also requested that estimates be provided separately for respondents based on whether they resided in an expansion or non-expansion state, and whether they were covered by private health insurance, Medicaid, or had no insurance. We gave NCHS specifications for the definition of low-income, non-elderly adults; the states that should be classified as expansion or non-expansion states in calendar year 2016; and the respondents who should be classified as having private health insurance, Medicaid, or no insurance.

[35] We chose this definition because under the Patient Protection and Affordable Care Act (PPACA), states may opt to expand their Medicaid programs to cover non-elderly, nonpregnant adults who are not eligible for Medicare, and whose income does not exceed 133 percent of the FPL beginning January 1, 2014. Pub. L. No. 111-148, 124 Stat. 119 (2010), as amended by the Health Care and Education Reconciliation Act of 2010, Pub. L. No. 111-152, 124 Stat. 1029 (2010). PPACA also provides for a 5 percent disregard when calculating income for determining Medicaid eligibility, which effectively increases income eligibility from 133 percent of FPL to 138 percent of FPL. The FPL is based on family income and family size, using the U.S. Census Bureau's poverty thresholds. In 2016, 138 percent of FPL for an individual was $17,231 and for a family of four was $33,897. PPACA also permitted an early expansion option, whereby states could expand eligibility for this population, or a subset of this population, starting on April 1, 2010.

## Table 2. States Classified as Expansion States and Non-Expansion States for this Study

| Expansion states (date of expansion) | Non-expansion states |
|---|---|
| Alaska (September 1, 2015)[a] | Alabama |
| Arizona (January 1, 2014) | Florida |
| Arkansas (January 1, 2014) | Georgia |
| California (January 1, 2014) | Idaho |
| Colorado (January 1, 2014) | Kansas |
| Connecticut (January 1, 2014) | Louisiana[b] |
| Delaware (January 1, 2014) | Maine |
| District of Columbia (January 1, 2014) | Mississippi |
| Hawaii (January 1, 2014) | Missouri |
| Illinois (January 1, 2014) | Nebraska |
| Indiana (February 1, 2015) | North Carolina |
| Iowa (January 1, 2014) | Oklahoma |
| Kentucky (January 1, 2014) | South Carolina |
| Maryland (January 1, 2014) | South Dakota |
| Massachusetts (January 1, 2014) | Tennessee |
| Michigan (April 1, 2014) | Texas |
| Minnesota (January 1, 2014) | Utah |
| Montana (January 1, 2016)[c] | Virginia |
| Nevada (January 1, 2014) | Wisconsin |
| New Hampshire (August 15, 2014) | Wyoming |
| New Jersey (January 1, 2014) | n/a |
| New Mexico (January 1, 2014) | n/a |
| New York (January 1, 2014) | n/a |
| North Dakota (January 1, 2014) | n/a |
| Ohio (January 1, 2014) | n/a |
| Oregon (January 1, 2014) | n/a |
| Pennsylvania (January 1, 2015) | n/a |
| Rhode Island (January 1, 2014) | n/a |
| Vermont (January 1, 2014) | n/a |
| Washington (January 1, 2014) | n/a |
| West Virginia (January 1, 2014) | n/a |

Source: GAO summary of Kaiser Family Foundation's data | GAO-18-607

Note: For this study we classified the 30 states and the District of Columbia that expanded their Medicaid programs before July 1, 2016, as expansion states. We classified the remaining 20 states as non-expansion states.

[a]We excluded individuals interviewed in Alaska from January through February 2016 to allow for a 6- month time period for the effects of the expansion to take place.

[b]We only included individuals interviewed in Louisiana from January through June 2016 (the 6-month period before Louisiana expanded Medicaid on July 1, 2016), and classified Louisiana as a non-expansion state.

[c]We excluded individuals interviewed in Montana from January through June 2016 to allow for a 6- month time period for the effects of the expansion to take place.

**Table 3. Sample Sizes and Population Estimates of Low-Income Adults by State Expansion Status**

| n/a | Expansion states | | Non-expansion states | | All states | |
|---|---|---|---|---|---|---|
| n/a | Sample size | Population estimate (thousands) | Sample size | Population estimate (thousands) | Sample size | Population estimate (thousands) |
| Low-Income adults | 2,027 | 14,564 | 1,476 | 9,459 | 3,503 | 24,023 |

Source: GAO summary of 2016 NHIS estimates produced by National Center for Health Statistics. | GAO-18-607.

Notes: Estimates are from the Family Core and Sample Adult components of the 2016 National Health Interview Survey (NHIS). For the purposes of these NHIS analyses, low-income adults are individuals ages 19 through 64, with family incomes that did not exceed 138 percent of the federal poverty level. These analyses excluded low-income adults who were noncitizens, were covered by Medicare, only received health care services through military health care or through the Indian Health Service, or had Supplemental Social Security Income. We also excluded adult females from the Sample Adult file who reported being pregnant.

For the purposes of these NHIS analyses, the 30 states and the District of Columbia that expanded their Medicaid programs before July 1, 2016, were classified as expansion states. The remaining 20 states were classified as non-expansion states.

We asked NCHS to exclude respondents who were noncitizens, were covered by Medicare, only received health care services through military health care or through the Indian Health Service, or had Supplemental Social Security Income. We also excluded adult females from the Sample Adult file who responded they were pregnant at the time of the interview. In addition, we asked NCHS to exclude individuals for which information was missing—not recorded or not provided during the interview—on health insurance coverage (Medicaid, private health insurance, Indian Health Service, military health care, or no health insurance), receipt of Supplemental Social Security Income, and U.S. citizenship.

We classified individuals in our study population as residing in an expansion or non-expansion state based on their state of residence when they were interviewed for the 2016 NHIS. We classified the 30 states and the District of Columbia that expanded their Medicaid eligibility before July 1, 2016, as expansion states. The remaining 20 states were classified as non-expansion states. Louisiana expanded Medicaid coverage on July 1, 2016; therefore, we classified it as a non-expansion state. We decided not to classify Louisiana as an expansion state because we allowed a 6- month period for the effects of expansion to appear. Therefore, for Louisiana we only included NHIS respondents interviewed from January through June 2016 when Louisiana was a non-expansion state. Similarly, for two expansion states—Alaska and Montana—we only included individuals who were interviewed March through December 2016 and July through December 2016, respectively, after the state expanded Medicaid to allow for a 6-month time period for the effect of expansion to take place. (See Table 2).

Table 3 illustrates the sample size and population estimates of low-income sample adults by expansion state, non-expansion state, and national total.

We classified NHIS respondents as having private health insurance, Medicaid, or no insurance based on the health insurance classification approach used by NCHS for NHIS. NCHS assigned NHIS respondents' health insurance classification based on a hierarchy of mutually exclusive categories in the following order: private health insurance, Medicaid, other coverage, and uninsured.[36] Low-income adults with more than one coverage type were assigned to the first appropriate category in the hierarchy. Respondents were classified as having private health insurance if they reported that they were covered by any comprehensive private health insurance plan (including health maintenance and preferred provider organizations). Private coverage excluded plans that pay for one type of service, such as accidents or dental care. Respondents were classified as having Medicaid if they reported they were covered by Medicaid or by a state-sponsored health plan with no premiums or it was not known whether a premium was charged. Respondents were classified as being uninsured if they did not report having any private health insurance, Medicare, Medicaid, Children's Health Insurance Program, state-sponsored or other government-sponsored health plan, or military health plan. Respondents were also

[36] Our study excludes NHIS respondents classified in NCHS's health insurance hierarchy as having "other coverage." NCHS defines other coverage as insurance coverage with the Children's Health Insurance Program, government sponsored-health plans, Medicare, or other state sponsored health plans with a premium.

classified as being uninsured if they only had insurance coverage with a private plan that paid for one type of service, such as accidents or dental care.

## Analyses Conducted

We gave NCHS officials specifications to calculate estimates from the 2016 NHIS for demographic characteristics, access to care, as well as composite measures of access to health care based on selected survey questions. Composite measures are NCHS-developed measures based on responses to NHIS questions covering related topics. The analysis included two composite measures:

1. any unmet medical needs, which is based on responses to six underlying survey questions that asked respondents about whether during the past 12 months they needed medical care but did not get it because they could not afford it; delayed seeking medical care because of worry about the cost, or did not get prescription medicines, mental health care or counseling, eyeglasses, or dental care due to cost; and
2. any non-financial barriers to health care, which is based on five underlying questions that asked respondents whether they delayed care in the past 12 months for any of the following reasons: could not get through on the telephone; could not get an appointment soon enough; waited too long to see the doctor after arriving at the doctor's office; the clinic/doctor's office was not open when respondent could get there; and did not have transportation.

NCHS officials calculated our requested estimates of groups within our study population based on whether respondents resided in an expansion or non-expansion state and whether they had private health insurance, Medicaid, or were uninsured at the time of the interview. For each comparison—such as comparisons of access to health care for respondents in expansion versus non-expansion states—we asked NCHS to test for statistically significant differences. We identified a statistically significant difference when the p-value from a t-test of the difference in the estimated proportions between two study subgroups had a value of less than 0.05.

To describe the number and demographic characteristics of uninsured, low-income adults, we compared estimates of selected demographic characteristics (race and ethnicity, gender, poverty status, and employment status) and reported health status for this group in expansion and non-expansion states.[37] These and other estimates of demographic characteristics and reported health status from the 2016 NHIS for uninsured, low-income adults by expansion states, non-expansion states, and all states are provided in Tables 6 and 7 in appendix III.

To describe unmet medical needs, barriers to health care, and having a usual place of care and receiving selected services for all low-income adults in expansion and non-expansion states and by insurance status, we asked NCHS to calculate estimates based on responses to selected NHIS questions and NCHS composite measures. We selected these survey questions and composite measures from the Family and Adult Access to Health Care and Utilization and Adult Health Behaviors sections of the 2016 NHIS. To summarize estimates of low-income adults in expansion and non-expansion states and by insurance status, responses to selected survey questions and composite measures were calculated as an estimated percentage of the relevant group's total population for eight groups of low-income adults: (1) those in expansion states, (2) those in non-expansion states, (3) those who had Medicaid in expansion states, (4) those who had Medicaid in non-expansion states, (5) those who had private health insurance in expansion states, (6) those who had private health insurance in non-expansion states, (7) those who were uninsured in expansion states, and (8) those who were uninsured in non-expansion states.

We asked NCHS to test for statistically significant differences for the estimates of access to care between selected groups of low-income adults.

[37] We tested for statistically significant differences between uninsured, low-income adults in expansion and non-expansion states.

(See Table 4). The results of the tests for statistically significant differences for these comparison groups are in appendixes IV through VI.

**Table 4. Comparison Groups of Low-Income Adults for Tests of Statistically Significant Differences in Selected Measures of Access to Care**

| Comparison Groups of Low-Income Adults | | |
|---|---|---|
| **Category one** | **Comparison text** | **Category two** |
| All in expansion states | versus | All in non-expansion states |
| Uninsured in expansion states | versus | Uninsured in non-expansion states |
| Medicaid in expansion states | versus | Medicaid in non-expansion states |
| Private health insurance in expansion states | versus | Private health insurance in non-expansion states |
| Uninsured in expansion states | versus | Medicaid in expansion states |
| Uninsured in expansion states | versus | Medicaid in non-expansion states |
| Uninsured in expansion states | versus | Private health insurance in expansion states |
| Uninsured in expansion states | versus | Private health insurance in non-expansion states |
| Uninsured in non-expansion states | versus | Medicaid in expansion states |
| Uninsured in non-expansion states | versus | Medicaid in non-expansion states |
| Uninsured in non-expansion states | versus | Private health insurance in expansion states |
| Uninsuredin non-expansion states | versus | Private health insurance in non-expansion states |

Source: GAO. | GAO-18-607.

Notes: Tests for statistically significant differences of estimates of access to care for selected subgroups of low-income adults were produced by the National Center for Health Statistics using data from the 2016 National Health Interview Survey (NHIS).

For the purposes of these NHIS analyses, low-income adults were individuals ages 19 through 64, with family incomes that did not exceed 138 percent of the federal poverty level. These analyses excluded low-income adults who were noncitizens, were covered by Medicare, only received health care services through military health care or through the Indian Health Service, or had Supplemental Social Security Income. We also excluded adult females from the Sample Adult file who reported being pregnant.

For the purposes of these NHIS analyses, the 30 states and the District of Columbia that expanded their Medicaid programs before July 1, 2016, were classified as expansion states. The remaining 20 states were classified as non-expansion states.

## Study Limitations and Data Reliability Assessment

Our study has some limitations. First, our study did not examine whether statistically significant differences in estimates of access to health care between respondents in expansion and non-expansion states were associated with the choice to expand Medicaid.[38] Second, NHIS data are based on respondent-reported data, which may be subject to potential biases and recall of participants' use of health services and may be less accurate than administrative data or clinical data. Third, we could not report estimates of access to health care that did not meet NCHS's standards of reliability or precision.[39]

We assessed the reliability of NHIS data by reviewing NHIS data documentation; interviewing knowledgeable NCHS officials and academic researchers; and examining the data for logical errors, missing values, and values outside of expected ranges. We determined that the data were sufficiently reliable for the purposes of these analyses.

# APPENDIX II: STATUS OF MEDICAID ELIGIBILITY EXPANSION BY STATES, AS OF 2017

Under the Patient Protection and Affordable Care Act (PPACA), states may opt to expand their Medicaid programs' eligibility to cover certain low-income adults beginning January 2014.[40] As of December 2017, 31 states

---

[38] To examine whether differences in access to health care between respondents in expansion and non-expansion states were associated with Medicaid expansion, we would need to simultaneously examine multiple factors—such as demographics, health status, community characteristics, and other factors—that may differ between respondents in expansion and non-expansion states. Examining whether estimated differences in access to health care between respondents in expansion states and non-expansion states were associated with expansion would require other analysis methods—such as regression analysis. Regression analysis is a statistical technique in which the functional relationship between a dependent variable (such as whether a respondent had a usual place of care) and one or more independent variables (such as whether the respondent resided in an expansion state or the respondent's level of education) can be estimated. We did not conduct a regression analysis for this study.

[39] For example, estimates for four survey questions about non-financial barriers to care for uninsured, low-income adults in expansion states did not meet NCHS standards. HHS officials suggest that for more information about NCHS's standards of reliability or precision, see Parker JD, Talih M, Malec DJ, Beresovsky V, Carroll M, Gonzalez JF, et al. National Center for Health Statistics Data Presentation Standards for Proportions. National Center for Health Statistics. Vital Health Stat 2(175). 2017. Available from: https://www.cdc.gov/nchs /data/series/sr_02/sr02_175.pdf.

[40] Specifically, states may opt to expand their Medicaid programs to cover non-elderly, non-pregnant adults who are not eligible for Medicare and whose income does not exceed 133

and the District of Columbia had expanded their Medicaid programs as permitted under PPACA and 19 states had not.[41] Table 5 lists the states that expanded Medicaid eligibility and those that did not. It also includes state population and other Medicaid data, which is presented in the roll-over information in interactive Figure 2.

**Table 5. Status of Medicaid Eligibility Expansion, by State, as of 2017**

| State | Status of Medicaid expansion | Date of Medicaid expansion | State population (as of July 2017) | Medicaid enrollment (calendar year 2017) |
|---|---|---|---|---|
| Alabama | Non-expansion | None | 4,874,747 | 1,018,770 |
| Alaska | Expansion | September 1, 2015 | 739,795 | 187,461 |
| Arizona | Expansion | January 1, 2014 | 7,016,270 | 1,936,263 |
| Arkansas | Expansion | January 1, 2014 | 3,004,279 | 940,776 |
| California | Expansion | January 1, 2014 | 39,536,653 | 11,517,800 |
| Colorado | Expansion | January 1, 2014 | 5,607,154 | 1,347,895 |
| Connecticut | Expansion | January 1, 2014 | 3,588,184 | 898,660 |
| Delaware | Expansion | January 1, 2014 | 961,939 | 208,695 |
| District of Columbia | Expansion | January 1, 2014 | 693,972 | 259,057 |
| Florida | Non-expansion | None | 20,984,400 | 4,030,767 |
| Georgia | Non-expansion | None | 10,429,379 | 1,865,535 |
| Hawaii | Expansion | January 1, 2014 | 1,427,538 | 329,675 |
| Idaho | Non-expansion | None | 1,716,943 | 319,739 |
| Illinois | Expansion | January 1, 2014 | 12,802,023 | 2,865,435 |
| Indiana | Expansion | February 1, 2015 | 6,666,818 | 1,346,668 |
| Iowa | Expansion | January 1, 2014 | 3,145,711 | 594,586 |
| Kansas | Non-expansion | None | 2,913,123 | 373,437 |
| Kentucky | Expansion | January 1, 2014 | 4,454,189 | 1,340,826 |
| Louisiana[a] | Expansion | July 1, 2016 | 4,684,333 | 1,637,972 |
| Maine | Non-expansion | None | 1,335,907 | 258,710 |
| Maryland | Expansion | January 1, 2014 | 6,052,177 | 1,172,931 |

percent of the federal poverty level (FPL). PPACA also provides for a 5 percent disregard when calculating income for determining Medicaid eligibility, which effectively increases income eligibility from 133 percent of FPL to 138 percent of FPL. PPACA also permitted an early expansion option, whereby states could expand eligibility for this population, or a subset of this population, starting on April 1, 2010.

[41] Louisiana expanded Medicaid eligibility on July 1, 2016. For the purposes of these NHIS analyses, Louisiana was classified as a non-expansion state and we only included low-income adults interviewed from January through June 2016 when Louisiana was a non-expansion state.

**Table 5. (Continued)**

| State | Status of Medicaid expansion | Date of Medicaid expansion | State population (as of July 2017) | Medicaid enrollment (calendar year 2017) |
|---|---|---|---|---|
| Massachusetts | Expansion | January 1, 2014 | 6,859,819 | 1,787,828 |
| Michigan | Expansion | April 1, 2014 | 9,962,311 | 2,136,440 |
| Minnesota | Expansion | January 1, 2014 | 5,576,606 | 1,116,804 |
| Mississippi | Non-expansion | None | 2,984,100 | 709,656 |
| Missouri | Non-expansion | None | 6,113,532 | 978,801 |
| Montana | Expansion | January 1, 2016 | 1,050,493 | 238,793 |
| Nebraska | Non-expansion | None | 1,920,076 | 227,531 |
| Nevada | Expansion | January 1, 2014 | 2,998,039 | 603,094 |
| New Hampshire | Expansion | August 15, 2014 | 1,342,795 | 194,606 |
| New Jersey | Expansion | January 1, 2014 | 9,005,644 | 1,694,461 |
| New Mexico | Expansion | January 1, 2014 | 2,088,070 | 885,472 |
| New York | Expansion | January 1, 2014 | 19,849,399 | 1,523,749 |
| North Carolina | Non-expansion | None | 10,273,419 | 1,678,020 |
| North Dakota | Expansion | January 1, 2014 | 755,393 | 69,169 |
| Ohio | Expansion | January 1, 2014 | 11,658,609 | 3,002,378 |
| Oklahoma | Non-expansion | None | 3,930,864 | 671,524 |
| Oregon | Expansion | January 1, 2014 | 4,142,776 | 987,823 |
| Pennsylvania | Expansion | January 1, 2015 | 12,805,537 | 2,795,591 |
| Rhode Island | Expansion | January 1, 2014 | 1,059,639 | 308,038 |
| South Carolina | Non-expansion | None | 5,024,369 | 1,248,324 |
| South Dakota | Non-expansion | None | 869,666 | 101,921 |
| Tennessee | Non-expansion | None | 6,715,984 | 1,615,817 |
| Texas | Non-expansion | None | 28,304,596 | 4,331,612 |
| Utah | Non-expansion | None | 3,101,833 | 302,445 |
| Vermont | Expansion | January 1, 2014 | 623,657 | 182,041 |
| Virginia | Non-expansion | None | 8,470,020 | 1,029,118 |
| Washington | Expansion | January 1, 2014 | 7,405,743 | 1,822,796 |
| West Virginia | Expansion | January 1, 2014 | 1,815,857 | 552,292 |
| Wisconsin | Non-expansion | None | 5,795,483 | 1,188,306 |
| Wyoming | Non-expansion | None | 579,315 | 61,303 |

Source: GAO summary of U.S. Census Bureau, Centers for Medicare & Medicaid Services, and Kaiser Family Foundation's data | GAO-18-607.

Note: Census population estimates are as of July 1, 2017. Medicaid enrollment numbers come from CMS-64 enrollment data and may differ from other data sources. Average monthly enrollment was tabulated from the CMS-64 enrollment report for calendar year 2017 that was accessed April 4, 2018.

[a]Louisiana expanded Medicaid eligibility on July 1, 2016. For the purposes of these NHIS analyses, Louisiana was classified as a non-expansion state and we only included low-income adults interviewed from January through June 2016 when Louisiana was a non-expansion state.

# Appendix III: Estimates of Demographic Characteristics and Health Status in Expansion and Non-Expansion States

This appendix provides additional 2016 National Health Interview Survey (NHIS) estimates we obtained from the National Center for Health Statistics (NCHS).[42] Table 6 presents estimates of selected demographic characteristics for low-income adults who were uninsured at the time of the survey interview.[43] The table provides estimates for these adults based on whether they resided in states that expanded Medicaid eligibility as permitted under the Patient Protection and Affordable Care Act (PPACA) (referred to as expansion states) or states that did not (referred to as non-expansion states).[44] We report statistically significant differences when comparing the responses of uninsured, low-income adults in expansion and non-expansion states.

---

[42] NCHS provides additional estimates on its website of reported demographic characteristics and selected health conditions for individuals ages 19 to 64 who were uninsured at the time of the interview and had family incomes less than or equal to 138 percent of the federal poverty level (FPL). See R.A. Cohen and E.P. Zammitti, *Coverage, Access, and Utilization by Medicaid Expansion Status: Estimates from the National Health Interview Survey, United States, 2016*, (Hyattsville, Md.: National Center for Health Statistics, December 2017), accessed December 12, 2017, https://www.cdc.gov/nchs/health_policy/coverage_and_access.htm.

[43] In this report, low income adults are individuals ages 19 to 64, with family incomes that did not exceed 138 percent of FPL. FPL is based on family income and size, using the U.S. Census Bureau's poverty thresholds. In 2016, 138 percent of FPL for an individual was $17,231 and for a family of four was $33,897. These analyses excluded those who were covered by Medicare, had only military health care, had only Indian Health Service, were noncitizens, or had Supplemental Social Security Income. We also excluded adult females from the Sample Adult file who reported being pregnant. An individual is defined as uninsured if they did not have any private health insurance, Medicare, Medicaid, Children's Health Insurance Program, state-sponsored or other government-sponsored health plan, or military plan. An individual is also defined as uninsured if they had only a private plan that paid for one type of service, such as accidents or dental care.

[44] Historically, Medicaid eligibility has been limited to certain categories of low-income individuals such as children, parents, pregnant women, persons with disabilities, and individuals ages 65 and older. Under PPACA, states may opt to expand their Medicaid programs to cover non-elderly, non-pregnant adults who are not eligible for Medicare and whose income does not exceed 133 percent of FPL. PPACA also provides for a 5 percent disregard when calculating income for determining Medicaid eligibility, which effectively increases income eligibility from 133 percent of FPL to 138 percent of FPL.

## Table 6. Demographic Characteristics of Uninsured, Low-Income Adults in Expansion and Non-Expansion States, 2016

| n/a | Expansion states | Non-expansion states | All states |
|---|---|---|---|
| Demographic characteristics | Percent (standard error) N = 1,915,000 | Percent (standard error) N = 3,721,000 | Percent (standard error) N = 5,639,000 |
| Age group: 19-34 years | 53.7 (2.96) | 47.7 (1.82) | 49.8 (1.60) |
| Age group: 35-49 years | 23.3 (2.29) | 28.2 (1.60) | 26.5 (1.33) |
| Age group: 50-64 years | 23.0 (2.31) | 24.1 (1.67) | 23.7 (1.36) |
| Poverty status[a]: Less than 100% FPL | 58.5 (3.28)[b] | 68.5 (2.05)[b] | 65.1 (1.81) |
| Poverty status[a]: 100% to less than or equal to 138% FPL | 41.5 (3.28)[b] | 31.5 (2.05)[b] | 34.9 (1.81) |
| Sex: Male | 62.7 (2.33)[b] | 50.6 (1.49)[b] | 54.7 (1.31) |
| Sex: Female | 37.3 (2.33)[b] | 49.4 (1.49)[b] | 45.3 (1.31) |
| Race and ethnicity: Hispanic | 21.9 (2.64) | 19.7 (3.26) | 20.4 (2.30) |
| Race and ethnicity: Non-Hispanic, white only | 53.3 (3.40) | 45.0 (2.70) | 47.9 (2.14) |
| Race and ethnicity: Non-Hispanic, black only | 17.4 (2.47)[b] | 29.8 (2.32)[b] | 25.6 (1.73) |
| Race and ethnicity: Non-Hispanic, Asian only | NA | 1.3 (0.57) | 2.2 (0.60) |
| Race and ethnicity: Non-Hispanic, other | 3.2 (1.02) | 4.3 (0.98) | 3.9 (0.73) |
| Marital status: Married | 26.3 (3.00) | 28.3 (1.76) | 27.6 (1.54) |
| Marital status: Widowed | 1.3 (0.48) | 2.4 (0.56) | 2.1 (0.40) |
| Marital status: Divorced or separated | 12.3 (1.79) | 16.1 (1.21) | 14.8 (1.02) |
| Marital status: Living with a partner | 16.9 (2.04) | 14.4 (1.63) | 15.2 (1.28) |
| Marital status: Never married | 43.2 (3.10) | 38.8 (2.08) | 40.3 (1.74) |
| Number of family members: 1 | 23.4 (2.30) | 18.7 (1.63) | 20.3 (1.34) |
| Number of family members: 2-4 | 56.2 (2.88) | 60.9 (2.08) | 59.3 (1.68) |
| Number of family members: 5 or more | 20.4 (2.77) | 20.4 (1.73) | 20.4 (1.49) |
| Employment status: Employed | 63.8 (2.43) | 55.7 (1.60) | 58.4 (1.37) |
| Employment status: Unemployed | 14.3 (1.85) | 16.8 (1.35) | 15.9 (1.10) |
| Employment status: Not in workforce | 22.0 (2.17)[b] | 27.5 (1.60)[b] | 25.7 (1.30) |
| Education status: Less than high school | 29.5 (2.84) | 29.1 (1.73) | 29.3 (1.50) |
| Education status: High school diploma or GED[c] | 34.6 (2.65) | 40.7 (1.87) | 38.7 (1.52) |

| n/a | Expansion states | Non-expansion states | All states |
|---|---|---|---|
| Education status: Some college | 28.1 (2.49) | 25.8 (1.69) | 26.5 (1.39) |
| n/a | Expansion states | Non-expansion states | All states |
| Demographic characteristics | Percent (standard error) N = 1,915,000 | Percent (standard error) N = 3,721,000 | Percent (standard error) N = 5,639,000 |
| Education status: Bachelor's degree or more | 7.8 (1.71) | 4.4 (0.78) | 5.5 (0.79) |

Legend: NA = Not available because of estimates did not meet the National Center for Health Statistics' (NCHS) standards for accuracy and precision.

Source: GAO summary of 2016 NHIS estimates produced by NCHS. | GAO-18-607

Notes: Estimates reflect questions included in the Family Core component of the National Health Interview Survey (NHIS). Estimates are based on household interviews of a sample of the civilian, noninstitutionalized U.S. population. Estimates were not available when they did not meet NCHS's standards for accuracy and precision.

For the purposes of these NHIS analyses, low-income adults are individuals ages 19 through 64, with family incomes that did not exceed 138 percent of the federal poverty level. These analyses excluded low-income adults who were noncitizens, were covered by Medicare, only received health care services through military health care or through the Indian Health Service, or had Supplemental Social Security Income. We also excluded adult females from the Sample Adult file who reported being pregnant. An individual was defined as uninsured if they did not have any private health insurance, Medicare, Medicaid, Children's Health Insurance Program, state-sponsored or other government-sponsored health plan, or military plan. An individual was also defined as uninsured if they had only a private plan that paid for one type of service, such as accidents or dental care.

For the purposes of these NHIS analyses, the 30 states and the District of Columbia that expanded their Medicaid programs prior to July 1, 2016, were classified as expansion states. The remaining 20 states were classified as non-expansion states. See R.A. Cohen and E.P. Zammitti, Coverage, Access, and Utilization by Medicaid Expansion Status: Estimates from the National Health Interview Survey, United States, 2016, (Hyattsville, Md.: National Center for Health Statistics, December 2017), accessed December 12, 2017, https://www.cdc.gov/nchs/health_policy/coverage_and_access.htm.

[a]The FPL is based on family income and family size, using the U.S. Census Bureau's poverty thresholds. The 2016 NHIS imputed income files were used to help create the poverty variable, and this variable is based on reported and imputed family information. See https://www.cdc.gov/nchs/nhis/nhis_2016_data_release.htm.

[b]Difference between expansion and non-expansion states was statistically significant at $p < 0.05$.

[c]General Educational Development (GED) is General Educational Development high school equivalency diploma.

Table 7 shows estimates of the reported health status of uninsured, low-income adults based on whether they resided in an expansion or non-expansion state. The table provides the number and percent of these adults who reported that at the time of the interview their health status was excellent or very good; good; or fair or poor. The table also shows the extent to which these adults reported whether their health status was different at the time of the interview compared to the previous year. We report statistically significant differences when comparing the responses of uninsured, low-income adults in expansion and non-expansion states.

### Table 7. Health Status of Uninsured, Low-Income Adults in Expansion and Non-Expansion Status, 2016

| n/a | Expansion states | Non-expansion states | All states |
|---|---|---|---|
| Health status | Percent (standard error) N = 1,834,000 | Percent (standard error) N = 3,382,000 | Percent (standard error) N = 5,219,000 |
| Health status: Excellent or very good | 47.1 (4.33) | 49.9 (2.79) | 49.0 (2.37) |
| Health status: Good | 40.0 (4.52)[a] | 28.0 (2.46)[a] | 32.2 (2.30) |
| Health status: Fair or poor | 12.9 (3.04)[a] | 22.0 (2.29)[a] | 18.8 (1.85) |
| Health status compared to previous year: Better | 15.7 (3.05) | 17.0 (2.04) | 16.5 (1.70) |
| Health status compared to previous year: Same | 75.2 (4.03) | 66.5 (2.49) | 69.6 (2.15) |
| Health status compared to previous year: Worse | NA | 16.5 (2.07) | 13.9 (1.75) |

Legend: NA = Not available because of estimates did not meet the National Center for Health Statistics' (NCHS) standards for accuracy and precision.

Source: GAO summary of 2016 NHIS estimates produced by NCHS. | GAO-18-607.

Notes: Estimates reflect questions included in the Family Core and Sample Adult Core components of the National Health Interview Survey (NHIS). Estimates are based on household interviews of a sample of the civilian, noninstitutionalized U.S. population. Estimates were not available when they did not meet NCHS's standards for accuracy and precision. For the purposes of these NHIS analyses, low-income adults are individuals ages 19 through 64, with family incomes that did not exceed 138 percent of the federal poverty level. These analyses excluded low-income adults who were noncitizens, were covered by Medicare, only received health care services through military health care or through the Indian Health Service, or had Supplemental Social Security Income. We also excluded adult females from the Sample Adult file who reported being pregnant. An individual was defined as uninsured if they did not have any private health insurance, Medicare, Medicaid, Children's Health Insurance Program, state-sponsored or other government-sponsored health plan, or military plan. An individual was also defined as uninsured if they had only a private plan that paid for one type of service, such as accidents or dental care. For the purposes of these NHIS analyses, the 30 states and the District of Columbia that expanded their Medicaid programs prior to July 1, 2016, were classified as expansion states. The remaining 20 states were classified as non-expansion states. See R.A. Cohen and E.P. Zammitti, Coverage, Access, and Utilization by Medicaid Expansion Status: Estimates from the National Health Interview Survey, United States, 2016, (Hyattsville, Md.: National Center for Health Statistics, December 2017), accessed December 12, 2017, https://www.cdc.gov/nchs/health_policy/coverage_and_access.htm.

[a]For Good and for Fair or Poor, the difference between expansion and non-expansion states was statistically significant at $p < 0.05$.

# APPENDIX IV: ESTIMATES OF ANY UNMET MEDICAL NEEDS IN EXPANSION AND NON-EXPANSION STATES AND BY INSURANCE STATUS

This appendix provides estimates of any unmet medical needs for low-income adults—individuals ages 19 to 64, with family incomes that did not exceed 138 percent of the federal poverty level (FPL)—from the 2016 National Health Interview Survey (NHIS), which were produced by the National Center for Health Statistics (NCHS).[45] Estimates are based on a composite measure of any unmet medical needs. Table 8 shows estimates of all low-income adults in expansion and non-expansion states.[46] We also

---

[45] Estimates are based on selected survey questions, which were from the Access to Health Care and Utilization and Health Behaviors sections of the Family and Sample Adult Core components of the 2016 National Health Interview Survey (NHIS). For the purposes of these NHIS analyses, low-income adults are individuals ages 19 through 64, with family incomes that did not exceed 138 percent of the federal poverty level. These analyses excluded low-income adults who were noncitizens, were covered by Medicare, only received health care services through military health care or through the Indian Health Service, or had Supplemental Social Security Income. We also excluded adult females from the Sample Adult file who reported being pregnant. NCHS provides additional estimates of access to care and utilization for low-income adults on its website. See R.A. Cohen and E.P. Zammitti, *Access and Utilization by Medicaid Expansion Status for Low-Income Adults Aged 19-64: Estimates from the National Health Interview Survey, United States, 2016*, (Hyattsville, MD.: National Center for Health Statistics, January 2018), accessed January 17, 2018, https://www.cdc.gov/nchs/health_policy/coverage_and_access.htm; and R.A. Cohen and E.P. Zammitti, *Coverage, Access, and Utilization by Medicaid Expansion Status: Estimates from the National Health Interview Survey, United States, 2016,* (Hyattsville, Md.: National Center for Health Statistics, December 2017), accessed December 12, 2017, https://www.cdc.gov/nchs/health_policy/coverage_and_access.htm.

[46] We classified the 30 states and the District of Columbia that expanded their Medicaid program prior to July 1, 2016 as expansions states, and the remaining 20 states were classified as non-expansion states. States classified as expansion states were Alaska, Arizona, Arkansas, California, Colorado, Connecticut, Delaware, Hawaii, Illinois, Indiana, Iowa, Kentucky, Maryland, Massachusetts, Michigan, Minnesota, Montana, Nevada, New Hampshire, New Jersey, New Mexico, New York, North Dakota, Ohio, Oregon, Pennsylvania, Rhode Island, Vermont, Washington, and West Virginia. The 20 non-expansion states are Alabama, Florida, Georgia, Idaho, Kansas, Louisiana, Maine, Mississippi, Missouri, Nebraska, North Carolina, Oklahoma, South Carolina, South Dakota, Tennessee, Texas, Utah, Virginia, Wisconsin, and Wyoming. For 3 states, we only included NHIS respondents for part of calendar year 2016. Specifically, we excluded respondents who were surveyed during the first 6 months after a state expanded Medicaid to allow for the effect of expansion to take place. Two of the 3 states—Alaska and Montana—were classified as expansion states and the third state, Louisiana, was classified as non-expansion. For Alaska, which expanded Medicaid on September 1, 2015, we excluded responses from those surveyed in January 2016 and February

report statistically significant differences between low-income adults in expansion and non-expansion states.

### Table 8. Percentage of Low-Income Adults in Expansion and Non-Expansion States Who Reported Any Unmet Medical Needs, 2016

| n/a | Expansion states (standard error) N =14,913,000 | Non-expansion states (standard error) N =9,627,000 |
|---|---|---|
| Any unmet medical needs | 26.4 (1.40)[a] | 40.1 (1.91)[a] |

Source: GAO summary of 2016 NHIS estimates produced by the National Center for Health Statistics. | GAO-18-607.

Notes: Estimates are for a composite measure, which was based on responses to questions from the Access to Health Care and Utilization sections of the Family and Sample Adult Core components of the 2016 National Health Interview Survey (NHIS). For the purposes of these NHIS analyses, low-income adults are individuals ages 19 through 64, with family incomes that did not exceed 138 percent of the federal poverty level. These analyses excluded low-income adults who were noncitizens, were covered by Medicare, only received health care services through military health care or through the Indian Health Service, or had Supplemental Social Security Income. We also excluded adult females from the Sample Adult file who reported being pregnant. Low-income adults had any unmet medical needs if they reported that in the past 12 months they did not get needed medical care because they could not afford it; delayed seeking medical care due to worries about costs; or needed but did not get because they could not afford prescription medicines, mental health care or counseling, dental care, or eyeglasses.

For the purposes of these NHIS analyses, the 30 states and the District of Columbia that expanded their Medicaid programs prior to July 1, 2016, were classified as expansion states. The remaining 20 states were classified as non-expansion states. See R.A. Cohen and E.P. Zammitti, Access and Utilization by Medicaid Expansion Status for Low-Income Adults Aged 19-64: Estimates from the National Health Interview Survey, United States, 2016, (Hyattsville, MD.: National Center for Health Statistics, January 2018), accessed January 17, 2018, https://www.cdc.gov/nchs/health_policy/coverage_and_access.htm.

[a]Difference between low-income adults in expansion and non-expansion states was statistically significant at $p < 0.05$.

Table 9 shows estimates of six groups of low-income adults: (1) low-income adults who were uninsured in expansion states; (2) low-income adults who were uninsured in non-expansion states; (3) low-income adults who had Medicaid in expansion states; (4) low-income adults who had

2016. For Montana, which expanded Medicaid on January 1, 2016, we excluded responses from those surveyed from January through June 2016. Because we classified Louisiana as a non-expansion state, we excluded all responses from those surveyed after the state expanded Medicaid on July 1, 2016.

Medicaid in non-expansion states; (5) low-income adults who had private health insurance in expansion states; and (6) low-income adults who had private health insurance in non-expansion states.[47] We also report any statistically significant differences when comparing the six groups of low-income adults, specifically:

- low-income adults who were uninsured in expansion states compared with each of the four groups of low-income adults who were insured— low-income adults who had Medicaid in expansion states, low-income adults who had Medicaid in non-expansion states, low-income adults who had private health insurance in expansion states, and low-income adults who had private insurance in non-expansion states;
- low-income adults who were uninsured in non-expansion states compared with each of the four groups of low-income adults who were insured;
- low-income adults who were uninsured in expansion states compared with low-income adults who were uninsured in non-expansion states;
- low-income adults who had Medicaid in expansion states compared with low-income adults who had Medicaid in non-expansion states; and

[47] Health insurance classification was based on a hierarchy of mutually exclusive categories in the following order: private health insurance, Medicaid, other coverage, and uninsured. Low-income adults with more than one coverage type were assigned the first appropriate category in the hierarchy, and those with other coverage were excluded from these analyses. Low-income adults were classified as having private health insurance if they reported that they were covered by any comprehensive private health insurance plan, including health maintenance and preferred provider organization plans. Private health insurance excludes plans that pay for only one type of service, such as accidents or dental care. Low-income adults were classified as having Medicaid if they reported that they were covered by Medicaid or by state-sponsored health plans with no premiums or if it is not known if a premium is charged. Low-income adults were classified as uninsured if they did not have any private health insurance or were not enrolled in Medicare, Medicaid, the Children's Health Insurance Program, a state-sponsored or other government-sponsored health plan, or a military plan. An adult was also defined as uninsured if they had only a private plan that paid for one type of service, such as accidents or dental care.

## Table 9. Percentage of Low-Income Adults in Expansion and Non-Expansion States Who Reported Any Unmet Medical Needs, by Insurance Status, 2016

| n/a | Uninsured | | Medicaid | | Private health insurance | |
|---|---|---|---|---|---|---|
| n/a | Expansion states (standard error) N = 1,834,000 | Non-expansion states (standard error) N = 3,382,000 | Expansion states (standard error) N = 7,671,000 | Non-expansion states (standard error) N = 2,160,000 | Expansion states (standard error) N = 5,408,000 | Non-expansion states (standard error) N = 4,085,000 |
| Any unmet medical needs | 49.6 (4.53)[a,b] | 62.7 (3.00)[a,c] | 26.5 (1.85)[b,c] | 34.4 (3.75)[b,c] | 18.2 (1.85)[b,c,d] | 24.5 (2.11)[b,c,d] |

Source: GAO summary of the 2016 NHIS estimates produced by the National Center for Health Statistics. | GAO-18-607.

Notes: Estimates are for a composite measure, which was based on responses to questions from the Access to Health Care and Utilization and sections of the Family and Sample Adult Core components of the 2016 National Health Interview Survey (NHIS). For the purposes of these NHIS analyses, low-income adults are individuals ages 19 through 64, with family incomes that did not exceed 138 percent of the federal poverty level. These analyses excluded low-income adults who were noncitizens, were covered by Medicare, only received health care services through military health care or through the Indian Health Service, or had Supplemental Social Security Income. We also excluded adult females from the Sample Adult file who reported being pregnant. Adults had any unmet medical needs if they reported that in the past 12 months they did not get needed medical care because they could not afford it; delayed seeking medical care due to worries about costs; or needed but did not get because they could not afford prescription medicines, mental health care or counseling, dental care, or eyeglasses. For the purposes of these NHIS analyses, the 30 states and the District of Columbia that expanded their Medicaid programs prior to July 1, 2016, were classified as expansion states. The remaining 20 states were classified as non-expansion states. Health insurance classification was based on a hierarchy of mutually exclusive categories in the following order: private health insurance, Medicaid, other coverage, and uninsured. Low-income adults with more than one coverage type were assigned the first appropriate category in the hierarchy and those with other coverage were excluded from these analyses. See R.A. Cohen and E.P. Zammitti, Coverage, Access, and Utilization by Medicaid Expansion Status: Estimates from the National Health Interview Survey, United States, 2016, (Hyattsville, Md.: National Center for Health Statistics, December 2017), accessed December 12, 2017, https://www.cdc.gov/nchs/health_policy/coverage_and_access.htm.

[a]Difference between low-income adults who were uninsured in expansion and non-expansion states was statistically significant at $p < 0.05$.

[b]Difference between low-income adults who were uninsured in expansion states and low-income adults in expansion or non-expansion states who were insured—Medicaid or private health insurance—was statistically significant at $p < 0.05$.

[c]Difference between low-income adults who were uninsured in non-expansion states and low-income adults in expansion or non-expansion states who were insured—Medicaid or private health insurance—was statistically significant at $p < 0.05$.

[d]Difference between low-income adults who had private health insurance in expansion and non-expansion states was statistically significant at $p < 0.05$.

- low-income adults who had private health insurance in expansion states compared with low-income adults who had private health insurance in non-expansion states.[48]

# Appendix V: Estimates of Barriers to Health Care in Expansion and Non-Expansion States and by Insurance Status

This appendix provides estimates of barriers to health care for low-income adults—individuals ages 19 to 64, with family incomes that did not exceed 138 percent of the federal poverty level (FPL)—from the 2016 National Health Interview Survey (NHIS), which we obtained from the National Center for Health Statistics (NCHS).[49] Estimates of financial barriers to needed medical, specialty, and other types of health care and prescription drugs are based on selected survey questions. Estimates of non-

---

[48] We did not request that NCHS test for significant differences between low-income adults who had Medicaid in expansion or non-expansion states and low-income adults who had private health insurance in expansion or non-expansion states.

[49] Estimates are based on selected survey questions and a composite measure, which was based on responses to some of these questions. These survey questions were from the Access to Health Care and Utilization section of the Sample Adult Core component of the 2016 National Health Interview Survey (NHIS). For the purposes of these NHIS analyses, low-income adults are individuals ages 19 through 64, with family incomes that did not exceed 138 percent of FPL. These analyses excluded low-income adults who were noncitizens, were covered by Medicare, only received health care services through military health care or through the Indian Health Service, or had Supplemental Social Security Income. We also excluded adult females from the Sample Adult file who reported being pregnant. NCHS provides additional estimates of access to care and utilization for low-income adults on its website. See R.A. Cohen and E.P. Zammitti, *Access and Utilization by Medicaid Expansion Status for Low-Income Adults Aged 19-64: Estimates from the National Health Interview Survey, United States, 2016*, (Hyattsville, MD.: National Center for Health Statistics, January 2018), accessed January 17, 2018, https://www.cdc.gov/nchs/health_policy/coverage_and_access.htm; and R.A. Cohen and E.P. Zammitti, *Coverage, Access, and Utilization by Medicaid Expansion Status: Estimates from the National Health Interview Survey, United States, 2016,* (Hyattsville, Md.: National Center for Health Statistics, December 2017), accessed December 12, 2017, https://www.cdc.gov/nchs/health_policy/coverage_and_access.htm.

financial barriers to health care are based on responses to selected survey questions and a composite measure.[50] Estimates are reported for:

- All low-income adults in expansion and non-expansion states.[51] We also report statistically significant differences between low-income adults in expansion and non-expansion states.
- Six groups of low-income adults: (1) low-income adults who were uninsured in expansion states; (2) low-income adults who were uninsured in non-expansion states; (3) low-income adults who had Medicaid in expansion states; (4) low-income adults who had Medicaid in non-expansion states; (5) low-income adults who had private health insurance in expansion states; and (6) low-income adults who had private health insurance in non-expansion states.[52]

---

[50] NCHS developed a composite measure on any non-financial barrier to care based on responses to five survey questions that asked respondents whether they delayed care due to a lack of transportation, long wait times, or other non-financial reasons.

[51] We classified the 30 states and the District of Columbia that expanded their Medicaid program prior to July 1, 2016 as expansion states, and the remaining 20 states were classified as non-expansion states. States classified as expansion states were Alaska, Arizona, Arkansas, California, Colorado, Connecticut, Delaware, Hawaii, Illinois, Indiana, Iowa, Kentucky, Maryland, Massachusetts, Michigan, Minnesota, Montana, Nevada, New Hampshire, New Jersey, New Mexico, New York, North Dakota, Ohio, Oregon, Pennsylvania, Rhode Island, Vermont, Washington, and West Virginia. The 20 non-expansion states are Alabama, Florida, Georgia, Idaho, Kansas, Louisiana, Maine, Mississippi, Missouri, Nebraska, North Carolina, Oklahoma, South Carolina, South Dakota, Tennessee, Texas, Utah, Virginia, Wisconsin, and Wyoming. For 3 states, we only included NHIS respondents for part of calendar year 2016. Specifically, we excluded respondents who were surveyed during the first 6 months after a state expanded Medicaid to allow for the effect of expansion to take place. Two of the 3 states—Alaska and Montana—were classified as expansion states and the third state, Louisiana, was classified as non-expansion. For Alaska, which expanded Medicaid on September 1, 2015, we excluded responses from those surveyed in January 2016 and February 2016. For Montana, which expanded Medicaid on January 1, 2016, we excluded responses from those surveyed from January through June 2016. Because we classified Louisiana as a non-expansion state, we excluded all responses from those surveyed after the state expanded Medicaid on July 1, 2016.

[52] Health insurance classification was based on a hierarchy of mutually exclusive categories in the following order: private health insurance, Medicaid, other coverage, and uninsured. Low-income adults with more than one coverage type were assigned the first appropriate category in the hierarchy, and those with other coverage were excluded from these analyses. Low-income adults were classified as having private health insurance if they reported that they were covered by any comprehensive private health insurance plan, including health maintenance and preferred provider organization plans. Private health insurance excludes plans that pay for only one type of service, such as accidents or dental care. Low-income adults were classified as having Medicaid if they reported that they were covered by Medicaid

We also report any statistically significant differences when comparing the six groups of low-income adults, specifically:

- o low-income adults who were uninsured in expansion states compared with each of the four groups of low-income adults who were insured—low-income adults who had Medicaid in expansion states, low-income adults who had Medicaid in non-expansion states, low-income adults who had private health insurance in expansion states, and low-income adults who had private insurance in non-expansion states;
- o low-income adults who were uninsured in non-expansion states compared with each of the four groups of low-income adults who were insured;
- o low-income adults who were uninsured in expansion states compared with low-income adults who were uninsured in non-expansion states;
- o low-income adults who had Medicaid in expansion states compared with low-income adults who had Medicaid in non-expansion states; and
- o low-income adults who had private health insurance in expansion states compared with low-income adults who had private health insurance in non-expansion states.[53]

## Financial Barriers to Medical, Specialty, and Other Types of Health Care

Tables 10 and 11 present estimates and differences in estimates of responses to survey question that asked whether respondents did not obtain

---

or by state-sponsored health plans with no premiums or if it is not known if a premium is charged. Low-income adults were classified as uninsured if they did not have any private health insurance or were not enrolled in Medicare, Medicaid, the Children's Health Insurance Program, a state-sponsored or other government-sponsored health plan, or a military plan. An adult was also defined as uninsured if they had only a private plan that paid for one type of service, such as accidents or dental care.

[53] We did not request that NCHS test for significant differences between low-income adults who had Medicaid in expansion or non-expansion states and low-income adults who had private health insurance in expansion or non-expansion states.

different types of needed health care services in the past 12 months because they could not afford it.

### Table 10. Percentage of Low-Income Adults in Expansion and Non-Expansion States Who Reported Financial Barriers to Different Types of Needed Health Care Services, 2016

| Type of services low-income adults could not afford in the past 12 months | Expansion states (standard error) N =14,913,000 | Non-expansion states (standard error) N =9,627,000 |
|---|---|---|
| Did not get needed medical care due to costs | 9.4 (0.87)[a] | 19.9 (1.45)[a] |
| Delayed seeking medical care due to costs | 10.6 (0.99)[a] | 21.4 (1.61)[a] |
| Needed but could not afford prescription medication | 9.7 (0.90)[a] | 18.1 (1.42)[a] |
| Needed but could not afford mental health care | 3.5 (0.50)[a] | 5.8 (1.04)[a] |
| Needed but could not afford dental care | 15.1 (1.12)[a] | 22.3 (1.56)[a] |
| Needed but could not afford eyeglasses | 9.6 (0.90)[a] | 14.3 (1.36)[a] |
| Needed but could not afford follow-up care | 4.6 (0.66)[a] | 8.5 (1.00)[a] |
| Needed but could not afford specialist care | 6.1 (0.82)[a] | 11.2 (1.27)[a] |

Source: GAO summary of the 2016 NHIS estimates produced by the National Center for Health Statistics. | GAO-18-607.

Notes: Estimates are based on selected survey questions, which were from the Access to Health Care and Utilization sections of the Family and Sample Adult Core components of the 2016 National Health Interview Survey (NHIS). For the purposes of these NHIS analyses, low-income adults are individuals ages 19 through 64, with family incomes that did not exceed 138 percent of the federal poverty level. These analyses excluded low-income adults who were noncitizens, were covered by Medicare, only received health care services through military health care or through the Indian Health Service, or had Supplemental Social Security Income. We also excluded adult females from the Sample Adult file who reported being pregnant.

For the purposes of these NHIS analyses, the 30 states and the District of Columbia that expanded their Medicaid programs prior to July 1, 2016, were classified as expansion states. The remaining 20 states were classified as non-expansion states. See R.A. Cohen and E.P. Zammitti, Access and Utilization by Medicaid Expansion Status for Low-Income Adults Aged 19-64: Estimates from the National Health Interview Survey, United States, 2016, (Hyattsville, MD.: National Center for Health Statistics, January 2018), accessed January 17, 2018, https://www.cdc.gov/nchs/health_policy/coverage_and_access.htm.

[a]Difference between low-income adults in expansion and non-expansion states was statistically significant at $p < 0.05$.

**Table 11. Percentage of Low-Income Adults in Expansion and Non-Expansion States Who Reported Financial Barriers to Different Types of Needed Health Care Services, by Insurance Status, 2016**

| Type of service low-income adults could not afford in the past 12 months | Uninsured | | Medicaid | | Private health insurance | |
|---|---|---|---|---|---|---|
| n/a | Expansion states (standard error) N =1,834,000 | Non-expansion states (standard error) N =3,382,000 | Expansion states (standard error) N =7,671,000 | Non-expansion states (standard error) N =2,160,000 | Expansion states (standard error) N =5,408,000 | Non-expansion states (standard error) N =4,085,000 |
| Did not get medical care due to costs | 27.2 (3.63)[a,b] | 37.3 (2.64)[a,c] | 7.7 (1.21)[b,c] | 12.0 (2.30)[b,c] | 5.7 (1.01)[b,c,d] | 9.7 (1.33)[b,c,d] |
| Delayed seeking medical care due to costs | 30.6 (4.28)[b] | 40.9 (3.09)[c] | 7.2 (1.20)[b,c] | 11.7 (2.28)[b,c] | 8.7 (1.21)[b,c] | 10.5 (1.38)[b,c] |
| Needed but could not afford prescription medication | 23.0 (3.85)[a,b] | 33.2 (3.11)[a,c] | 8.8 (1.14)[b,c] | 13.2 (2.07)[b,c] | 6.3 (1.18)[b,c] | 8.3 (1.34)[b,c] |
| Needed but could not afford mental health care | 7.9 (2.31)[b] | 12.8 (2.74)[c] | 4.0 (0.75)[c] | 3.0 (0.98)[c] | 1.1 (0.33)[b,c] | 1.6 (0.44)[b,c] |
| Needed but could not afford dental care | 30.8 (4.27)[b] | 38.6 (3.55)[c] | 14.5 (1.41)[b,c] | 19.8 (3.03)[b,c] | 10.4 (1.46)[b,c] | 10.4 (1.49)[b,c] |
| Needed but could not afford eyeglasses | 20.2 (3.93)[b] | 21.1 (2.94)[c] | 10.2 (1.18)[b,c] | 15.6 (2.85) | 5.1 (0.98)[b,c] | 8.2 (1.52)[b,c] |
| Needed but could not afford follow-up care | 15.3 (3.27)[b] | 17.8 (2.66)[c] | 3.1 (0.77)[b,c] | 2.4 (1.04)[b,c] | 3.1 (0.76)b,c | 4.0 (0.98)[b,c] |

| **Type of service low-income adults could not afford in the past 12 months** | **Uninsured** | | **Medicaid** | | **Private health insurance** | |
|---|---|---|---|---|---|---|
| Needed but could not afford specialist care | 16.8 (3.65)[b] | 21.6 (3.03)[c] | 5.7 (1.19)[b,c] | 6.5 (1.87)[b,c] | 3.1 (0.71)[b,c] | 5.2 (1.25)[b,c] |

Source: GAO summary of the 2016 NHIS estimates produced by the National Center for Health Statistics. | GAO-18-607.

Notes: Estimates are based on selected survey questions, which were from the Access to Health Care and Utilization sections of the Family and Sample Adult Core components of the 2016 National Health Interview Survey (NHIS). For the purposes of these NHIS analyses, low-income adults are individuals ages 19 through 64, with family incomes that did not exceed 138 percent of the federal poverty level. These analyses excluded low-income adults who were noncitizens, were covered by Medicare, only received health care services through military health care or through the Indian Health Service, or had Supplemental Social Security Income. We also excluded adult females from the Sample Adult file who reported being pregnant.

For the purposes of these NHIS analyses, the 30 states and the District of Columbia that expanded their Medicaid programs prior to July 1, 2016, were classified as expansion states. The remaining 20 states were classified as non-expansion states.

Health insurance classification was based on a hierarchy of mutually exclusive categories in the following order: private health insurance, Medicaid, other coverage, and uninsured. Low-income adults with more than one coverage type were assigned the first appropriate category in the hierarchy and those with other coverage were excluded from these analyses. See R.A. Cohen and E.P. Zammitti, Coverage, Access, and Utilization by Medicaid Expansion Status: Estimates from the National Health Interview Survey, United States, 2016, (Hyattsville, Md.: National Center for Health Statistics, December 2017), accessed December 12, 2017, https://www.cdc.gov/nchs/health_policy/coverage_and_access.htm.

[a]Difference between low-income adults who were uninsured in expansion and non-expansion states was statistically significant at $p < 0.05$.

[b]Difference between low-income adults who were uninsured in expansion states and low-income adults in expansion or non-expansion states who were insured—Medicaid or private health insurance—was statistically significant at $p < 0.05$.

[c]Difference between low-income adults who were uninsured in non-expansion states and low-income adults in expansion or non-expansion states who were insured—Medicaid or private health insurance—was statistically significant at $p < 0.05$.

[d]Difference between low-income adults who had private health insurance in expansion and non-expansion states was statistically significant at $p < 0.05$.

## Financial Barriers to Prescription Drugs

Tables 12 and 13 present estimates and differences in estimates of survey question that asked respondents who had been prescribed medications whether they had taken actions during the past 12 months to save money on medications.

### Table 12. Percentage of Low-Income Adults in Expansion and Non-Expansion States Who Reported Taking Actions to Save Money on Prescriptions, 2016

| **Action taken to save money on prescriptions in the past 12 months** | **Expansion states (standard error) N =14,913,000** | **Non-expansion states (standard error) N =9,627,000** |
|---|---|---|
| Skipped medication doses | 5.1 (0.67)[a] | 8.3 (1.08)[a] |
| Took less medication | 5.4 (0.70)[a] | 8.3 (1.07)[a] |
| Delayed filling a prescription | 6.7 (0.85)[a] | 11.9 (1.27)[a] |
| Asked for a lower cost medication | 10.4 (0.94)[a] | 14.2 (1.20)[a] |

Source: GAO summary of the 2016 NHIS estimates produced by the National Center for Health Statistics. | GAO-18-607.

Notes: Estimates are based on selected survey questions, which were from the Access to Health Care and Utilization section of the Sample Adult Core component of the 2016 National Health Interview Survey (NHIS). For the purposes of these NHIS analyses, low-income adults are individuals ages 19 through 64, with family incomes that did not exceed 138 percent of the federal poverty level. These analyses excluded low-income adults who were noncitizens, were covered by Medicare, only received health care services through military health care or through the Indian Health Service, or had Supplemental Social Security Income. We also excluded adult females from the Sample Adult file who reported being pregnant. Low-income adults who were not prescribed medication in the past 12 months were considered to have not taken any steps to save money on prescriptions.

For the purposes of these NHIS analyses, the 30 states and the District of Columbia that expanded their Medicaid programs prior to July 1, 2016, were classified as expansion states. The remaining 20 states were classified as non-expansion states. See R.A. Cohen and E.P. Zammitti, Access and Utilization by Medicaid Expansion Status for Low-Income Adults Aged 19-64: Estimates from the National Health Interview Survey, United States, 2016, (Hyattsville, MD.: National Center for Health Statistics, January 2018), accessed January 17, 2018, https://www.cdc.gov/nchs/health_policy/coverage_and_access.htm.

[a]Difference between low-income adults in expansion and non-expansion states was statistically significant at $p < 0.05$.

## Table 13. Percentage of Low-Income Adults in Expansion and Non-Expansion States Who Reported Taking Actions to Save Money on Medications, by Insurance Status, 2016

| Action taken to save money on prescriptions in the past 12 months | Uninsured | | Medicaid | | Private health insurance | |
|---|---|---|---|---|---|---|
| | Expansion states (standard error) N = 1,834,000 | Non-expansion states (standard error) N =3,382,000 | Expansion states (standard error) N = 7,671,000 | Non-expansion states (standard error) N = 2,160,000 | Expansion states (standard error) N = 5,408,000 | Non-expansion states (standard error) N = 4,085,000 |
| Skipped medication doses | 11.8 (3.31)[a] | 13.8 (2.42)[b] | 4.6 (0.84)[a,b] | NA | 3.5 (0.86)[a,b] | 4.6 (1.03)[a,b] |
| Took less medication | 11.9 (3.31)[a] | 13.5 (2.48)[b] | 4.7 (0.86)a,[b] | 7.5 (2.22) | 4.1 (0.96)[a,b] | 4.4 (0.88)[a,b] |
| Delayed filling a prescription | 14.5 (3.61)[a] | 17.3 (2.52)[b] | 6.3 (1.17)a,[b] | 9.3 (2.61)[b] | 4.6 (0.95)[a,b,c] | 8.8 (1.37)[b,c] |
| Asked for a lower cost medication | 15.7 (3.67) | 19.6 (2.45)[b] | 9.9 (1.24)[b] | 9.8 (1.68)[b] | 9.4 (1.44)[b] | 12.1 (1.69)[b] |

Legend: NA = Not available because of estimates did not meet the NCHS's standards for accuracy and precision.

Source: GAO summary of the 2016 NHIS estimates produced by NCHS. | GAO-18-607.

Notes: Estimates are based on selected survey questions, which were from the Access to Health Care and Utilization section of the Sample Adult Core component of the 2016 National Health Interview Survey (NHIS). Estimates were not available when they did not meet the National Center for Health Statistics' (NCHS) standards for accuracy and precision. For the purposes of these NHIS analyses, low-income adults are individuals ages 19 through 64, with family incomes that did not exceed 138 percent of the federal poverty level. These analyses excluded low-income adults who were noncitizens, were covered by Medicare, only received health care services through military health care or through the Indian Health Service, or had Supplemental Social Security Income. We also excluded adult females from the Sample Adult file who reported being pregnant. Low-income adults who were not prescribed medication in the past 12 months were considered to have not taken any steps to save money on prescriptions.

For the purposes of these NHIS analyses, the 30 states and the District of Columbia that expanded their Medicaid programs prior to July 1, 2016, were classified as expansion states. The remaining 20 states were classified as non-expansion states.

Health insurance classification was based on a hierarchy of mutually exclusive categories in the following order: private health insurance, Medicaid, other coverage, and uninsured. Low-income adults with more than one coverage type were assigned the first appropriate category in the hierarchy and those with other coverage were excluded from these analyses. See R.A. Cohen and E.P. Zammitti, Coverage, Access, and Utilization by Medicaid Expansion Status: Estimates from the National

Health Interview Survey, United States, 2016, (Hyattsville, Md.: National Center for Health Statistics, December 2017), accessed December 12, 2017, https://www.cdc.gov/nchs/health_policy/coverage_and_access.htm.

[a]Difference between low-income adults who were uninsured in expansion states and low-income adults in expansion or non-expansion states who were insured—Medicaid or private health insurance—was statistically significant at $p < 0.05$.

[b]Difference between low-income adults who were uninsured in non-expansion states and low-income adults in expansion or non-expansion states who were insured—Medicaid or private health insurance—was statistically significant at $p < 0.05$.

[c]Difference between low-income adults who had private health insurance in expansion and non-expansion states was statistically significant at $p < 0.05$.

## Non-Financial Barriers to Health Care

Tables 14 and 15 present estimates and differences in estimates of the NCHS composite measure on any non-financial barriers to health care, which was based on responses to five survey questions on whether respondents delayed care in the past 12 months due to long wait times, a lack of transportation, and other non-financial reasons. Additionally, these tables present estimates and differences in estimates of responses to the composite measure's five underlying survey questions.

### Table 14. Percentage of Low-Income Adults in Expansion and Non-Expansion States Who Reported Non-Financial Barriers to Health Care, 2016

| Non-financial barrier that delayed health care in the past 12 months | Expansion states (standard error) N = 14,913,000 | | Non-expansion states (standard error) N = 9,627,000 | |
|---|---|---|---|---|
| Any[a] | 15.3 | (1.24) | 14.8 | (1.40) |
| Unable to get through on telephone | 3.6 | (0.48) | 2.5 | (0.50) |
| Unable to get an appointment soon enough | 8.0 | (0.88) | 6.2 | (0.99) |
| Wait time at doctor's office was too long | 6.4 | (0.78) | 6.4 | (1.07) |
| Clinic or doctor's office was not open when able to go | 3.3 | (0.48) | 2.4 | (0.50) |
| No transportation | 4.3 | (0.66) | 5.1 | (0.84) |

Source: GAO summary of the 2016 NHIS estimates produced by the National Center for Health Statistics. | GAO-18-607.

Notes: Estimates are based on selected survey questions and their related composite measure. These survey questions were from the Access to Health Care and Utilization section of Sample Adult Core component of the 2016 National Health Interview Survey (NHIS). For the purposes of these NHIS analyses, low-income adults are individuals ages 19 through 64, with family incomes that did not exceed 138 percent of the federal poverty level. These analyses excluded low-income adults who were noncitizens, were covered by Medicare, only received health care services through military health care or through the Indian Health Service, or had Supplemental Social Security Income. We also excluded adult females from the Sample Adult file who reported being pregnant. For the purposes of these NHIS analyses, the 30 states and the District of Columbia that expanded their Medicaid programs prior to July 1, 2016, were classified as expansion states. The remaining 20 states were classified as non-expansion states. See R.A. Cohen and E.P. Zammitti, Access and Utilization by Medicaid Expansion Status for Low-Income Adults Aged 19-64: Estimates from the National Health Interview Survey, United States, 2016, (Hyattsville, MD.: National Center for Health Statistics, January 2018), accessed January 17, 2018, https://www.cdc.gov/nchs/health_policy/coverage_and_access.htm.

[a]Low-income adults had any non-financial barrier to care if they reported delaying care in the past 12 months because they could not get through on the telephone, could not get an appointment soon enough, the wait time at the doctor's office was too long, the doctor's office or clinic was not open when they could get there, or did not have transportation.

## Table 15. Percentage of Low-Income Adults in Expansion and Non-Expansion States Who Reported Non-Financial Barriers to Health Care, by Insurance Status, 2016

| Non-financial barrier that delayed healthcare in the past 12 months | Uninsured | | Medicaid | | Private health insurance | |
|---|---|---|---|---|---|---|
| | Expansion states (standard error) N=1,834,000 | Non-expansion states (standard error) N=3,382,000 | Expansion states (standard error) N=7,671,000 | Non-expansion states (standard error) N=2,160,000 | Expansion states (standard error) N=5,408,000 | Non-expansion states (standard error) N=4,085,000 |
| Anya | 8.6 (2.28)[b] | 14.0 (2.46) | 17.6 (1.83)[b] | 19.5 (3.04)[b] | 14.2 (1.61)[b] | 12.9 (2.16) |
| Unable to get through on phone | NA | 1.7 (0.68)[c] | 4.1 (0.73)[c] | NA | 3.1 (0.75) | 2.2 (0.71) |
| Unable to get an appointment soon enough | NA | 3.0 (0.80)[c] | 9.2 (1.37)[c] | 8.4 (2.02)[c] | 7.5 (1.15)[c] | 7.6 (1.74)[c] |
| Wait time at doctor's office was too long | NA | 7.7 (2.13) | 7.9 (1.27) | 6.1 (1.42) | 4.1 (0.93) | NA |

| Non-financial barrier that delayed healthcare in the past 12 months | Uninsured | | Medicaid | | Private health insurance | |
|---|---|---|---|---|---|---|
| | Expansion states (standard error) N=1,834,000 | Non-expansion states (standard error) N=3,382,000 | Expansion states (standard error) N=7,671,000 | Non-expansion states (standard error) N=2,160,000 | Expansion states (standard error) N=5,408,000 | Non-expansion states (standard error) N=4,085,000 |
| Clinic or doctor's office was not open when able to go | NA | 1.9 (0.63)[c] | 2.5 (0.57) | 3.0 (1.08) | 4.8 (0.92)[c] | 2.4 (0.85) |
| No transportation | 1.0 (0.54)[b,d] | 6.0 (1.58)[c, d] | 6.2 (1.10)[b] | 9.9 (2.39)[b] | 2.8 (0.85) | 1.8 (0.71)[c] |

Legend: NA = Not available because of estimates did not meet the NCHS's standards for accuracy and precision.

Source: GAO summary of the 2016 NHIS estimates produced by NCHS. | GAO-18-607.

Notes: Estimates are based on selected survey questions and their related composite measure. These survey questions were from the Access to Health Care and Utilization section of the Sample Adult Core component of the 2016 National Health Interview Survey (NHIS). Estimates were not available when they did not meet the National Center for Health Statistics' (NCHS) standards for accuracy and precision. For the purposes of these NHIS analyses, low-income adults are individuals ages 19 through 64, with family incomes that did not exceed 138 percent of the federal poverty level. These analyses excluded low-income adults who were noncitizens, were covered by Medicare, only received health care services through military health care or through the Indian Health Service, or had Supplemental Social Security Income. We also excluded adult females from the Sample Adult file who reported being pregnant.

For the purposes of these NHIS analyses, the 30 states and the District of Columbia that expanded their Medicaid programs prior to July 1, 2016, were classified as expansion states. The remaining 20 states were classified as non-expansion states.

Health insurance classification was based on a hierarchy of mutually exclusive categories in the following order: private health insurance, Medicaid, other coverage, and uninsured. Low-income adults with more than one coverage type were assigned the first appropriate category in the hierarchy and those with other coverage were excluded from these analyses. See R.A. Cohen and E.P. Zammitti, Coverage, Access, and Utilization by Medicaid Expansion Status: Estimates from the National Health Interview Survey, United States, 2016, (Hyattsville, Md.: National Center for Health Statistics, December 2017), accessed December 12, 2017, https://www.cdc.gov/nchs/health_policy/coverage_and_access.htm.

[a]Low-income adults were classified as facing any non-financial barriers to care if they reported delaying care in the past 12 months because they were unable to get through on the telephone, were unable to get an appointment soon enough, the wait time at the doctor's office was too long, the doctor's office or clinic was not open when they could get there, or did not have transportation.

[b]Difference between low-income adults who were uninsured in expansion states and low-income adults in expansion or non-expansion states who were insured—Medicaid or private health insurance—was statistically significant at $p < 0.05$.

[c]Difference between low-income adults who were uninsured in non-expansion states and low-income adults in expansion or non-expansion states who were insured—Medicaid or private health insurance—was statistically significant at $p < 0.05$.

[d]Difference between low-income adults who were uninsured in expansion and non-expansion states was statistically significant at $p < 0.05$.

# APPENDIX VI: ESTIMATES ON PLACE OF CARE AND SERVICES IN EXPANSION AND NON-EXPANSION STATES AND BY INSURANCE STATUS

This appendix provides estimates on having a usual place of care and receiving selected health care services for adults—individuals ages 19 to 64, with family incomes that did not exceed 138 percent of the federal poverty level (FPL)—from the 2016 National Health Interview Survey (NHIS), which we obtained from the National Center for Health Statistics (NCHS).[54] Estimates are based on responses to selected survey questions on having a usual place of care, receiving selected health care services, and contacting health care professionals. Estimates are reported for:

---

[54] Estimates are based on selected survey questions, which were from the Access to Health Care and Utilization and Health Behavior sections of the Family and Sample Adult Core components of the 2016 National Health Interview Survey (NHIS). For the purposes of these NHIS analyses, low-income adults are individuals ages 19 through 64, with family incomes that did not exceed 138 percent of the federal poverty level. These analyses excluded low-income adults who were noncitizens, were covered by Medicare, only received health care services through military health care or through the Indian Health Service, or had Supplemental Social Security Income. We also excluded adult females from the Sample Adult file who reported being pregnant. NCHS provides additional estimates of access to care for low-income adults on its website. NCHS provides additional estimates of access to care and utilization for low-income adults on its website. See R.A. Cohen and E.P. Zammitti, *Access and Utilization by Medicaid Expansion Status for Low-Income Adults Aged 19-64: Estimates from the National Health Interview Survey, United States, 2016*, (Hyattsville, MD.: National Center for Health Statistics, January 2018), accessed January 17, 2018, https://www.cdc.gov/nchs/health_policy/coverage_and_access.htm; and R.A. Cohen and E.P. Zammitti, *Coverage, Access, and Utilization by Medicaid Expansion Status: Estimates from the National Health Interview Survey, United States, 2016,* (Hyattsville, Md.: National Center for Health Statistics, December 2017), accessed December 12, 2017, https://www.cdc.gov/nchs/health_policy/coverage_and_access.htm.

- All low-income adults in expansion and non-expansion states.[55] We also report statistically significant differences between low-income adults in expansion and non-expansion states.
- Six groups of low-income adults: (1) low-income adults who were uninsured in expansion states; (2) low-income adults who were uninsured in non-expansion states; (3) low-income adults who had Medicaid in expansion states; (4) low-income adults who had Medicaid in non-expansion states; (5) low-income adults who had private health insurance in expansion states; and (6) low-income adults who had private health insurance in non-expansion states.[56]

---

[55] We classified the 30 states and the District of Columbia that expanded their Medicaid program prior to July 1, 2016 as expansion states, and the remaining 20 states were classified as non-expansion states. States classified as expansion states were Alaska, Arizona, Arkansas, California, Colorado, Connecticut, Delaware, Hawaii, Illinois, Indiana, Iowa, Kentucky, Maryland, Massachusetts, Michigan, Minnesota, Montana, Nevada, New Hampshire, New Jersey, New Mexico, New York, North Dakota, Ohio, Oregon, Pennsylvania, Rhode Island, Vermont, Washington, and West Virginia. The 20 non-expansion states are Alabama, Florida, Georgia, Idaho, Kansas, Louisiana, Maine, Mississippi, Missouri, Nebraska, North Carolina, Oklahoma, South Carolina, South Dakota, Tennessee, Texas, Utah, Virginia, Wisconsin, and Wyoming. For 3 states, we only included NHIS respondents for part of calendar year 2016. Specifically, we excluded respondents who were surveyed during the first 6 months after a state expanded Medicaid to allow for the effect of expansion to take place. Two of the 3 states—Alaska and Montana—were classified as expansion states and the third state, Louisiana, was classified as non-expansion. For Alaska, which expanded Medicaid on September 1, 2015, we excluded responses from those surveyed in January 2016 and February 2016. For Montana, which expanded Medicaid on January 1, 2016, we excluded responses from those surveyed from January through June 2016. Because we classified Louisiana as a non-expansion state, we excluded all responses from those surveyed after the state expanded Medicaid on July 1, 2016.

[56] Health insurance classification was based on a hierarchy of mutually exclusive categories in the following order: private health insurance, Medicaid, other coverage, and uninsured. Low-income adults with more than one coverage type were assigned the first appropriate category in the hierarchy, and those with other coverage were excluded from this analysis. Low-income adults were classified as having private health insurance if they reported that they were covered by any comprehensive private health insurance plan, including health maintenance and preferred provider organization plans. Private health insurance excludes plans that pay for only one type of service, such as accidents or dental care. Low-income adults were classified as having Medicaid if they reported that they were covered by Medicaid or by state-sponsored health plans with no premiums or if it is not known if a premium is charged. Low-income adults were classified as uninsured if they did not have any private health insurance or were not enrolled in Medicare, Medicaid, the Children's Health Insurance Program, a state-sponsored or other government-sponsored health plan, or a military plan. An adult was also defined as uninsured if they had only a private plan that paid for one type of service, such as accidents or dental care.

We also report any statistically significant differences when comparing the six groups of low-income adults, specifically:

- low-income adults who were uninsured in expansion states compared with each of the four groups of low-income adults who were insured—low-income adults who had Medicaid in expansion states, low-income adults who had Medicaid in non-expansion states, low-income adults who had private health insurance in expansion states, and low-income adults who had private insurance in non-expansion states;
- low-income adults who were uninsured in non-expansion states compared with each of the four groups of low-income adults who were insured;
- low-income adults who were uninsured in expansion states compared with low-income adults who were uninsured in non-expansion states;
- low-income adults who had Medicaid in expansion states compared with low-income adults who had Medicaid in non-expansion states; and
- low-income adults who had private health insurance in expansion states compared with low-income adults who had private health insurance in non-expansion states.[57]

## Having a Usual Place of Care

Tables 16 through 19 present estimates and differences in estimates of survey questions that asked respondents about the place of care they usually go to when sick or need advice about their health and the type of place that respondents most often went.

---

[57] We did not request that NCHS test for significant differences between low-income adults who had Medicaid in expansion or non-expansion states and low-income adults who had private health insurance in expansion or non-expansion states.

## Table 16. Percentage of Low-Income Adults in Expansion and Non-Expansion States Who Reported Having a Usual Place of Care, 2016

| **n/a** | **Expansion states (standard error) N =14,913,000** | **Non-expansion states (standard error) N =9,627,000** |
|---|---|---|
| Had a usual place of care | 81.6 (1.24)[a] | 68.1 (1.68)[a] |

Source: GAO summary of the 2016 NHIS estimates produced by the National Center for Health Statistics. | GAO-18-607.

Notes: Estimates are based on a selected survey question, which was from the Health Care Access and Utilization section of the Sample Adult Core component of the 2016 National Health Interview Survey (NHIS). For the purposes of these NHIS analyses, low-income adults are individuals ages 19 through 64, with family incomes that did not exceed 138 percent of the federal poverty level. These analyses excluded low-income adults who were noncitizens, were covered by Medicare, only received health care services through military health care or through the Indian Health Service, or had Supplemental Social Security Income. We also excluded adult females from the Sample Adult file who reported being pregnant. Low-income adults who reported that in the past 12 months the emergency department was their usual place of care were considered to not have a usual place of care.

For the purposes of these NHIS analyses, the 30 states and the District of Columbia that expanded their Medicaid programs prior to July 1, 2016, were classified as expansion states. The remaining 20 states were classified as non-expansion states. See R.A. Cohen and E.P. Zammitti, Access and Utilization by Medicaid Expansion Status for Low-Income Adults Aged 19-64: Estimates from the National Health Interview Survey, United States, 2016, (Hyattsville, MD.: National Center for Health Statistics, January 2018), accessed January 17, 2018, https://www.cdc.gov/nchs/health_policy/coverage_and_access.htm.

[a]Difference between low-income adults in expansion and non-expansion states was statistically significant at $p < 0.05$.

## Table 17. Percentage of Low-Income Adults in Expansion and Non-Expansion States Who Reported Having a Usual Place of Care, by Insurance Status, 2016

| n/a | **Uninsured** | | **Medicaid** | | **Private health insurance** | |
|---|---|---|---|---|---|---|
| | Expansion states (standard error) N =1,834,000 | Non-expansion states (standard error) N =3,382,000 | Expansion states (standard error) N =7,671,000 | Non-expansion states (standard error) N =2,160,000 | Expansion states (standard error) N =5,408,000 | Non-expansion states (standard error) N =4,085,000 |
| Had a usual place of care | 45.3 (4.20)[a] | 46.0 (2.91)[b] | 87.5 (1.54)[a,b] | 83.2 (3.38)[a,b] | 85.5 (1.69)[a,b,c] | 78.2 (2.16)[a,b,c] |

Source: GAO summary of the 2016 NHIS estimates produced by the National Center for Health Statistics. | GAO-18-607.

Notes: Estimates are based on a selected survey question, which was from the Health Behaviors section of the Sample Adult Core component of the 2016 National Health Interview Survey (NHIS). For the purposes of these NHIS analyses, low-income adults are individuals ages 19 through 64, with family incomes that did not exceed 138 percent of the federal poverty level. These analyses excluded low-income adults who were noncitizens, were covered by Medicare, only received health care services through military health care or through the Indian Health Service, or had Supplemental Social Security Income. We also excluded adult females from the Sample Adult file who reported being pregnant. Low-income adults who reported that in the past 12 months the emergency department was their usual place of care were considered to not have a usual place of care.

For the purposes of these NHIS analyses, the 30 states and the District of Columbia that expanded their Medicaid programs prior to July 1, 2016, were classified as expansion states. The remaining 20 states were classified as non-expansion states.

Health insurance classification was based on a hierarchy of mutually exclusive categories in the following order: private health insurance, Medicaid, other coverage, and uninsured. Low-income adults with more than one coverage type were assigned the first appropriate category in the hierarchy and those with other coverage were excluded from these analyses. See R.A. Cohen and E.P. Zammitti, Coverage, Access, and Utilization by Medicaid Expansion Status: Estimates from the National Health Interview Survey, United States, 2016, (Hyattsville, Md.: National Center for Health Statistics, December 2017), accessed December 12, 2017, https://www.cdc.gov/nchs/health_policy/coverage_and_access.htm.

[a]Difference between low-income adults who were uninsured in expansion states and low-income adults in expansion or non-expansion states who were insured—Medicaid or private health insurance—was statistically significant at $p < 0.05$.

[b]Difference between low-income adults who were uninsured in non-expansion states and low-income adults in expansion or non-expansion states who were insured—Medicaid or private health insurance—was statistically significant at $p < 0.05$.

[c]Difference between low-income adults who had private health insurance in expansion and non-expansion states was statistically significant at $p < 0.05$.

## Table 18. Percentage of Low-Income Adults in Expansion and Non-Expansion States Who Had a Usual Place of Care by the Type of Place They Usually Went for Care, 2016

| Usual place of care | Expansion states (standard error) N =12,164,000 | Non-expansion states (standard error) N =6,554,000 |
|---|---|---|
| Clinic or health center | 30.7 (1.58)[a] | 42.7 (2.13)[a] |
| Doctor's office or health maintenance organization | 64.9 (1.69)[a] | 52.8 (2.21)[a] |
| Other | 4.5 (0.84) | 4.5 (0.88) |

Source: GAO summary of the 2016 NHIS estimates produced by the National Center for Health Statistics. | GAO-18-607.

Notes: Estimates are based on a selected survey question, which was from the Access to Health Care and Utilization section of the Sample Adult Core component of the 2016 National Health Interview Survey (NHIS). For the purposes of these NHIS analyses, low-income adults are individuals ages 19 through 64, with family incomes that did not exceed 138 percent of the federal poverty level. These analyses excluded low-income adults who were noncitizens, were covered by Medicare, only received health care services through military health care or through the Indian Health Service, or had Supplemental Social Security Income. Low-income adults who reported that in the past 12 months the emergency department was their usual place of care were considered to not have a usual place of care.

For the purposes of these NHIS analyses, the 30 states and the District of Columbia that expanded their Medicaid programs prior to July 1, 2016 and were classified as expansion states. The remaining 20 states were classified as non-expansion states. See R.A. Cohen and E.P. Zammitti, Access and Utilization by Medicaid Expansion Status for Low-Income Adults Aged 19-64: Estimates from the National Health Interview Survey, United States, 2016, (Hyattsville, MD.: National Center for Health Statistics, January 2018), accessed January 17, 2018, https://www.cdc.gov/nchs/health_policy/coverage_and_access.htm.

[a]Difference between low-income adults in expansion and non-expansion states was statistically significant at $p < 0.05$.

## Table 19. Percentage of Low-Income Adults in Expansion and Non-Expansion States with a Usual Place of Care by the Type of Place They Usually Went for Care, by Insurance Status, 2016

| Place that low-income adults reported going to most often for care in the past 12 | Uninsured | | Medicaid | | Private health insurance | |
|---|---|---|---|---|---|---|
| | Expansion states (standard error) N =831,000 | Non-expansion states (standard error) N =1,557,000 | Expansion states (standard error) N =6,709,000 | Non-expansion states (standard error) N =1,798,000 | Expansion states (standard error) N =4,626,000 | Non-expansion states (standard error) N =3,196.000 |
| Clinic or health center | 34.2 (5.86)[a] | 59.6 (4.32)[a,b] | 30.4 (2.16)[b,c] | 41.2 (4.05)[b,c] | 30.4 (2.55)[b] | 35.4 (2.81)[b] |
| Doctor's office or health maintenance organization | 52.1 (6.78)[a] | 29.4 (3.99)[a,b] | 65.6 (2.26)[b] | 58.2 (4.05)[b] | 66.1 (2.70)[b] | 61.1 (2.96)[b] |
| Other | NA | 11.0 (2.93)[b] | 4.0 (1.08)[b,c] | 0.6 (0.50)[b,c] | NA | 3.6 (0.98)[b] |

Legend: NA = Not available because of estimates did not meet the NCHS's standards for accuracy and precision.
Source: GAO summary of the 2016 NHIS estimates produced by NCHS. | GAO-18-607.

Notes: Estimates are based on a selected survey question, which was from the Access to Health Care and Utilization section of the Sample Adult Core component of the 2016 National Health Interview Survey (NHIS). Estimates were not available when they did not meet the National Center for Health Statistics' (NCHS) standards for accuracy and precision. For the purposes of these NHIS analyses, low-income adults are individuals ages 19 through 64, with family incomes that did not exceed 138 percent of the federal poverty level. These analyses excluded low-income adults who were noncitizens, were covered by Medicare, only received health care services through military health care or through the Indian Health Service, or had Supplemental Social Security Income. We also excluded adult females from the Sample Adult file who reported being pregnant. Low-income adults who reported that in the past 12 months the emergency department was their usual place of care were considered to not have a usual place of care.

For the purposes of these NHIS analyses, the 30 states and the District of Columbia that expanded their Medicaid programs prior to July 1, 2016, were classified as expansion states. The remaining 20 states were classified as non-expansion states.

Health insurance classification was based on a hierarchy of mutually exclusive categories in the following order: private health insurance, Medicaid, other coverage, and uninsured. Low-income adults with more than one coverage type were assigned the first appropriate category in the hierarchy and those with other coverage were excluded from these analyses. See R.A. Cohen and E.P. Zammitti, Coverage, Access, and Utilization by Medicaid Expansion Status: Estimates from the National Health Interview Survey, United States, 2016, (Hyattsville, Md.: National Center for Health Statistics, December 2017), accessed December 12, 2017, https://www.cdc.gov/nchs/health_policy/coverage_and_access.htm.

[a]Difference between low-income adults who were uninsured in expansion and non-expansion states was statistically significant at $p < 0.05$.

[b]Difference between low-income adults who were uninsured in non-expansion states and low-income adults in expansion or non-expansion states who were insured—Medicaid or private health insurance—was statistically significant at $p < 0.05$.

[c]Difference between low-income adults who had Medicaid in expansion and non-expansion states was statistically significant at $p < 0.05$.

## Receiving Selected Health Care Services

### Table 20. Percentage of Low-Income Adults in Expansion and Non-Expansion States Who Reported Receiving Selected Health Care Services, 2016

| Health care service received in past 12 months | Expansion states (standard error) N = 14,913,000 | Non-expansion states (standard error) N = 9,627,000 |
|---|---|---|
| Blood cholesterol check | 49.2 (1.72)[a] | 41.7 (1.93)[a] |
| Blood pressure check | 77.5 (1.51)[a] | 71.8 (1.67)[a] |
| Blood sugar check | 34.2 (1.68) | 32.0 (1.81) |
| Flu vaccine[b] | 30.9 (1.47)[a] | 23.9 (1.43)[a] |
| Colon cancer test[c] | 19.1 (2.54) | 17.9 (2.74) |
| Mammogram[d] | 46.3 (3.89) | 40.6 (5.10) |
| Overnight hospitalization | 8.9 (0.88) | 8.8 (0.96) |
| Hospital emergency department visit | 27.1 (1.35) | 27.9 (1.66) |

Source: GAO summary of the 2016 NHIS estimates produced by the National Center for Health Statistics. | GAO-18-607.

Notes: Estimates are based on selected survey questions, which were from the Access to Health Care and Utilization sections of the Family and Sample Adult Core components of the 2016 National Health Interview Survey (NHIS). For the purposes of these NHIS analyses, low-income adults are individuals ages 19 through 64, with family incomes that did not exceed 138 percent of the federal poverty level.

These analyses excluded low-income adults who were noncitizens, were covered by Medicare, only received health care services through military health care or through the Indian Health Service, or had Supplemental Social Security Income. We also excluded adult females from the Sample Adult file who reported being pregnant.

For the purposes of these NHIS analyses, the 30 states and the District of Columbia that expanded their Medicaid programs prior to July 1, 2016, were classified as expansion states. The remaining 20 states were classified as non-expansion states. See R.A. Cohen and E.P. Zammitti, Access and Utilization by Medicaid Expansion Status for Low-Income Adults Aged 19-64: Estimates from the National Health Interview Survey, United States, 2016, (Hyattsville, MD.: National Center for Health Statistics, January 2018), accessed January 17, 2018, https://www.cdc.gov/nchs/health_policy/coverage_and_access.htm.

[a]Difference between low-income adults in expansion and non-expansion states was statistically significant at $p < 0.05$.

[b]Includes vaccines by both shot and nasal spray.

[c]Limited to adults ages 50 to 64 years.

[d]Limited to female adults ages 50 to 64 years.

Tables 20 and 21 present estimates and differences in estimates of survey questions that asked respondents whether they had received a blood cholesterol check, flu vaccine, or other selected services.

## Table 21. Percentage of Low-Income Adults in Expansion and Non-Expansion States Who Reported Receiving Selected Health Care Services, by Insurance Status, 2016

| **Health care service received in past 12 months** | **Uninsured** | | **Medicaid** | | **Private health insurance** | |
|---|---|---|---|---|---|---|
| | Expansion states (standard error) N =1,834,000 | Non-expansion states (standard error) N =3,382,000 | Expansion states (standard error) N =7,671,000 | Non-expansion states (standard error) N =2,160,000 | Expansion states (standard error) N =5,408,000 | Non-expansion states (standard error) N =4,085 000 |
| Blood cholesterol check | 23.3 (4.09)[a] | 27.6 (2.84)[b] | 56.0 (2.44)[a,b] | 61.4 (4.07)[a,b] | 47.9 (2.81)[a,b] | 43.2 (2.91)[a,b] |
| Blood pressure check | 51.2 (4.23)[a] | 54.1 (3.25)[b] | 82.0 (2.01)[a,b] | 87.8 (2.25)[a,b] | 80.1 (2.26)[a,b] | 77.8 (2.13)[a,b] |
| Blood sugar check | 15.3 (3.52)[a] | 23.8 (3.00)[b] | 39.2 (2.22)[a,b,c] | 52.7 (4.04)[a,b,c] | 33.8 (2.78)[a,b] | 27.9 (2.37)[a] |
| Flu vaccine[d] | 11.8 (2.74)[a] | 14.0 (1.96)[b] | 33.5 (2.19)[a,b] | 35.3 (3.93)[a,b] | 33.8 (2.37)[a,b,e] | 25.9 (2.22)[a,b,e] |

## Table 21. (Continued)

| Health care service received in past 12 months | Uninsured | | Medicaid | | Private health insurance | |
|---|---|---|---|---|---|---|
| | Expansion states (standard error) N =1,834,000 | Non-expansion states (standard error) N =3,382,000 | Expansion states (standard error) N =7,671,000 | Non-expansion states (standard error) N =2,160,000 | Expansion states (standard error) N =5,408,000 | Non-expansion states (standard error) N =4,085,000 |
| Colon cancer test[f] | NA | NA | 24.3 (4.09) | NA | 18.1 (4.40) | 24.0 (5.06) |
| Mammo-gram[g] | NA | 21.2 (6.12)[b] | 45.5 (5.43)[b] | NA | 60.2 (7.00)[b] | 51.5 (6.67)[b] |
| Overnight hospitaliz-ation | NA | 7.3 (1.41)b | 11.6 (1.36)b | 16.8 (2.58)b | 7.2 (1.30) | 5.9 (1.28) |
| Hospital emergency department visit | 20.9 (3.65)a | 28.2 (2.98)b | 35.2 (2.14)a | 43.4 (3.65)a,b | 17.6 (1.77)b | 19.6 (2.12)b |

Legend: NA = Not available because of estimates did not meet the NCHS's standards for accuracy and precision.

Source: GAO summary of the 2016 NHIS estimates produced by NCHS. | GAO-18-607.

Notes: Estimates are based on selected survey questions, which were from the Access to Health Care and Utilization sections of the Family and Sample Adult Core components of the 2016 National Health Interview Survey (NHIS). Estimates were not available when they did not meet the National Center for Health Statistics' (NCHS) standards for accuracy and precision. For the purposes of these NHIS analyses, low-income adults are individuals ages 19 through 64, with family incomes that did not exceed 138 percent of the federal poverty level. These analyses excluded low-income adults who were noncitizens, were covered by Medicare, only received health care services through military health care or through the Indian Health Service, or had Supplemental Social Security Income. We also excluded adult females from the Sample Adult file who reported being pregnant.

For the purposes of these NHIS analyses, the 30 states and the District of Columbia that expanded their Medicaid programs prior to July 1, 2016, were classified as expansion states. The remaining 20 states were classified as non-expansion states.

Health insurance classification was based on a hierarchy of mutually exclusive categories in the following order: private health insurance, Medicaid, other coverage, and uninsured. Low-income adults with more than one coverage type were assigned the first appropriate category in the hierarchy and those with other coverage were excluded from these analyses. See R.A. Cohen and E.P. Zammitti, Coverage, Access, and Utilization by Medicaid Expansion Status: Estimates from the National Health Interview Survey, United States, 2016, (Hyattsville, Md.: National Center for Health Statistics, December 2017), accessed December 12, 2017, https://www.cdc.gov/nchs/health_policy/coverage_and_access.htm.

[a]Difference between low-income adults who were uninsured in expansion states and low-income adults in expansion or non-expansion states who were insured—Medicaid or private health insurance—was statistically significant at $p < 0.05$.

[b]Difference between low-income adults who were uninsured in non-expansion states and low-income adults in expansion or non-expansion states who were insured—Medicaid or private health insurance—was statistically significant at $p < 0.05$.

[c]Difference between low-income adults who had Medicaid in expansion and non-expansion states was statistically significant at $p < 0.05$.

[d]Includes vaccines by both shot and nasal spray.

[e]Difference between low-income adults who had private health insurance in expansion and non-expansion states was statistically significant at $p < 0.05$.

[f]Limited to adults ages 50 to 64 years.

[g]Limited to female adults ages 50 to 64 years.

## Contacting Health Care Professionals

Tables 22 and 23 present estimates and differences in estimates of survey questions that asked respondents whether they had visited or spoken to a general doctor, specialist, or other health care professionals about their health in the past 12 months.

### Table 22. Percentage of Low-Income Adults in Expansion and Non-Expansion States Who Reported Visiting or Speaking to a Health Care Professional about their Health, 2016

| Type of health care professional visited or spoken to in past 12 months | Expansion states (standard error) N =14,913,000 | Non-expansion states (standard error) N =9,627,000 |
|---|---|---|
| Any | 79.0 (1.43)[a] | 73.0 (1.47)[a] |
| General doctor[b] | 64.3 (1.66)[a] | 50.9 (1.98)[a] |
| Nurse practitioner, physician assistant, or midwife | 23.7 (1.35)[a] | 17.9 (1.36)[a] |
| Medical specialist[c] | 18.2 (1.11)[a] | 13.2 (1.14)[a] |

Source: GAO summary of the 2016 NHIS estimates produced by the National Center for Health Statistics. | GAO-18-607.

Notes: Estimates are based on selected survey questions, which were from the Access to Health Care and Utilization section of the Sample Adult Core components of the 2016 National Health Interview

Survey (NHIS). For the purposes of these NHIS analyses, low-income adults are individuals ages 19 through 64, with family incomes that did not exceed 138 percent of the federal poverty level. These analyses excluded low-income adults who were noncitizens, were covered by Medicare, only received health care services through military health care or through the Indian Health Service, or had Supplemental Social Security Income. We also excluded adult females from the Sample Adult file who reported being pregnant.

For the purposes of these NHIS analyses, the 30 states and the District of Columbia that expanded their Medicaid programs prior to July 1, 2016, were classified as expansion states; the remaining 20 states were classified as non-expansion states. See R.A. Cohen and E.P. Zammitti, Access and Utilization by Medicaid Expansion Status for Low-Income Adults Aged 19-64: Estimates from the National Health Interview Survey, United States, 2016, (Hyattsville, MD.: National Center for Health Statistics, January 2018), accessed January 17, 2018, https://www.cdc.gov/nchs/health_policy/coverage_and_access.htm.

[a]Difference between low-income adults in expansion and non-expansion states was statistically significant at $p < 0.05$.

[b]General doctors are general practitioners, family doctors, and internists.

[c]Medical specialists exclude obstetricians, gynecologists, psychiatrists, and ophthalmologists.

## Table 23. Percentage of Low-Income Adults in Expansion and Non-Expansion States Who Reported Seeing or Speaking to a Health Care Provider About their Health, by Insurance Status, 2016

| **Type of health care professional visited or spoken to in past 12 months** | **Uninsured** | | **Medicaid** | | **Private health insurance** | |
|---|---|---|---|---|---|---|
| | Expansion states (standard error) N =1,834,000 | Non-expansion states (standard error) N = 3,382,000 | Expansion states (standard error) N = 7,671,000 | Non-expansion states (standard error) N = 2,160,000 | Expan sion states (standard error) N = 5,408,000 | Non-expansion states (standard error) N = 4,085,000 |
| Any | 46.0 (4.69)[a] | 53.9 (2.95)[b] | 83.9 (1.90)[a,b,c] | 90.8 (1.78)[a,b,c] | 83.5 (2.06)[a,b] | 79.3 (2.20)[a,b] |
| General doctor[d] | 35.0 (4.46)[a] | 33.0 (3.11)[b] | 68.9 (2.27)[a,b] | 62.2 (4.07)[a,b] | 67.8 (2.43)[a,b,e] | 59.7 (2.75)[a,b,e] |
| Nurse practitioner, physician assistant, or midwife | 13.0 (3.32)[a] | 10.8 (1.97)[b] | 23.4 (1.90)[a,b] | 25.5 (3.19)[a,b] | 27.8 (2.22)[a,b,e] | 19.7 (1.98)[b,e] |
| Medical specialist[f] | NA | 6.1 (1.28)[b] | 19.7 (1.58)[b] | 24.1 (3.15)[b] | 20.5 (1.98)[b,e] | 13.1 (1.79)[b,e] |

Legend: NA = Not available because of estimates did not meet the NCHS's standards for accuracy and precision.

Source: GAO summary of the 2016 NHIS estimates produced by NCHS. | GAO-18-607

Notes: Estimates are based on for selected survey questions, which were from the Access to Health Care and Utilization section of the Sample Adult Core components of the 2016 National Health Interview Survey (NHIS). Estimates were not available when they did not meet the National Center for Health Statistics' (NCHS) standards for accuracy and precision. For the purposes of these NHIS analyses, low-income adults are individuals ages 19 through 64, with family incomes that did not exceed 138 percent of the federal poverty level. These analyses excluded low-income adults who were noncitizens, were covered by Medicare, only received health care services through military health care or through the Indian Health Service, or had Supplemental Social Security Income. We also excluded adult females from the Sample Adult file who reported being pregnant.

For the purposes of these NHIS analyses, the 30 states and the District of Columbia that expanded their Medicaid programs prior to July 1, 2016, were classified as expansion states. The remaining 20 states were classified as non-expansion states.

Health insurance classification was based on a hierarchy of mutually exclusive categories in the following order: private health insurance, Medicaid, other coverage, and uninsured. Low-income adults with more than one coverage type were assigned the first appropriate category in the hierarchy and those with other coverage were excluded from these analyses. See R.A. Cohen and E.P. Zammitti, Coverage, Access, and Utilization by Medicaid Expansion Status: Estimates from the National Health Interview Survey, United States, 2016, (Hyattsville, Md.: National Center for Health Statistics, December 2017), accessed December 12, 2017, https://www.cdc.gov/nchs/health_policy/coverage_and_access.htm.

[a]Difference between low-income adults who were uninsured in expansion states and low-income adults in expansion or non-expansion states who were insured—Medicaid or private health insurance—was statistically significant at $p < 0.05$.

[b]Difference between low-income adults who were uninsured in non-expansion states and low-income adults in expansion or non-expansion states who were insured—Medicaid or private health insurance—was statistically significant at $p < 0.05$.

[c]Difference between low-income adults who had Medicaid in expansion and non-expansion states was statistically significant at $p < 0.05$.

[d]General doctors are general practitioners, family doctors, and internists.

[e]Difference between low-income adults who had private health insurance in expansion and non-expansion states was statistically significant at $p < 0.05$.

[f]Medical specialists exclude obstetricians, gynecologists, psychiatrists, and ophthalmologists.

# APPENDIX VII: GAO STAFF ACKNOWLEDGMENTS

In addition to Carolyn L. Yocom, Katherine M. Iritani (Director), Tim Bushfield (Assistant Director), Deitra H. Lee (Analyst-in-Charge), Kristin Ekelund, Laurie Pachter, Vikki Porter, Merrile Sing, and Emily Wilson made key contributions to this chapter.

# Appendix VIII: Accessible Data

## Data Tables

### Accessible Data for Low-income Adults Who Reported Having a Usual Place of Care in Expansion and Non-Expansion States and by Insurance Status, 2016

| Any Unmet Medical Need | | |
|---|---|---|
| **Category** | **Expansion** | **Non-expansion** |
| ALL | 26 | 40 |
| UNINSURED | 50 | 63 |
| INSURED: Medicaid | 27 | 34 |
| INSURED: Private health insurance | 18 | 25 |

### Accessible Data for Low-Income Adults Who Reported Financial Barriers to Needed Medical Care in Expansion and Non-Expansion States and by Insurance Status, 2016

| Financial Barriers to Medical Care | | |
|---|---|---|
| **Category** | **Expansion** | **Non-expansion** |
| ALL | 9 | 20 |
| UNINSURED | 27 | 37 |
| INSURED: Medicaid | 8 | 12 |
| INSURED: Private health insurance | 6 | 10 |

### Accessible Data for Low-income Adults Who Reported Having a Usual Place of Care in Expansion and Non-Expansion States and by Insurance Status, 2016

| Had a Usual Place of Care | | |
|---|---|---|
| **Category** | **Expansion** | **Non-expansion** |
| ALL | 82 | 68 |
| UNINSURED | 45 | 46 |
| INSURED:Medicaid | 88 | 83 |
| INSURED: Private health insurance | 86 | 78 |

## Accessible Data for Figure 1: National Medicaid Enrollment by Eligible Population, December 2017

| Category | Percentage | Number |
|---|---|---|
| Expansion enrollees[a] | 20 | 13,791,922 |
| Aged | 8 | 5,477,668 |
| Blind or Disabled | 12 | 8,366,620 |
| Children | 45 | 30,623,798 |
| Other Adults[b] | 15 | 10,237,403 |

## Accessible Data for Figure 3: Health Status of Uninsured, Low-Income Adults in Expansion and Non-Expansion States, 2016

| n/a | n/a | Expansion | Non-expansion |
|---|---|---|---|
| Health status | Excellent or very good | 47 | 50 |
| | Good | 40 | 28 |
| | Fair or poor | 13 | 22 |

## Accessible Data for Figure 4: Percentage of Low-Income Adults in Expansion and Non-Expansion States and by Insurance Status Who Reported Any Unmet Medical Need, 2016

| Any Unmet Medical Need | | |
|---|---|---|
| **Category** | **Expansion** | **Non-expansion** |
| ALL | 26 | 40 |
| UNINSURED | 50 | 63 |
| INSURED: Medicaid | 27 | 34 |
| INSURED: Private health insurance | 18 | 25 |

## Accessible Data for Figure 5: Percentage of Low-Income Adults in Expansion and Non-Expansion States and by Insurance Status Who Reported Financial Barriers to Different Types of Needed Health Care Services, 2016

| Medical | | |
|---|---|---|
| **Category** | **Expansion** | **Non-expansion** |
| ALL | 9 | 20 |
| UNINSURED | 27 | 37 |
| INSURED: Medicaid | 8 | 12 |
| INSURED: Private health insurance | 6 | 10 |

| Specialist | | |
|---|---|---|
| **Category** | **Expansion** | **Non-expansion** |
| ALL | 6 | 11 |
| UNINSURED | 17 | 22 |
| INSURED: Medicaid | 6 | 7 |
| INSURED: Private health insurance | 3 | 5 |
| **Prescription Medication** | | |
| **Category** | **Expansion** | **Non-expansion** |
| ALL | 10 | 18 |
| UNINSURED | 23 | 33 |
| INSURED: Medicaid | 9 | 13 |
| INSURED: Private health insurance | 6 | 8 |
| **Dental** | | |
| **Category** | **Expansion** | **Non-expansion** |
| ALL | 15 | 22 |
| UNINSURED | 31 | 39 |
| INSURED: Medicaid | 15 | 20 |
| INSURED: Private health insurance | 10 | 10 |
| **Mental Health** | | |
| **Category** | **Expansion** | **Non-expansion** |
| ALL | 4 | 6 |
| UNINSURED | 8 | 13 |
| INSURED: Medicaid | 4 | 3 |
| INSURED: Private health insurance | 1 | 2 |
| **Eyeglasses** | | |
| **Category** | **Expansion** | **Non-expansion** |
| ALL | 10 | 14 |
| UNINSURED | 20 | 21 |
| INSURED: Medicaid | 10 | 16 |
| INSURED: Private health insurance | 5 | 8 |

## Accessible Data for Figure 6: Percentage of Low-Income Adults in Expansion and Non-Expansion States and by Insurance Status Who Reported Having a Usual Place of Care, 2016

| Had a Usual Place of Care | | |
|---|---|---|
| **Category** | **Expansion** | **Non-expansion** |
| ALL | 82 | 68 |
| UNINSURED | 45 | 46 |
| INSURED: Medicaid | 88 | 83 |
| INSURED: Private health insurance | 86 | 78 |

## Accessible Data for Figure 7: Percentage of Low-Income Adults in Expansion and Non-Expansion States and by Insurance Status Who Reported Using Selected Health Care Services, 2016

| **Blood Cholesterol Check** | | |
|---|---|---|
| **Category** | **Expansion** | **Non-expansion** |
| ALL | 49 | 42 |
| UNINSURED | 23 | 28 |
| INSURED: Medicaid | 56 | 61 |
| INSURED: Private health insurance | 48 | 43 |
| **Blood Pressure Check** | | |
| **Category** | **Expansion** | **Non-expansion** |
| ALL | 78 | 72 |
| UNINSURED | 51 | 54 |
| INSURED: Medicaid | 82 | 88 |
| INSURED: Private health insurance | 80 | 78 |
| **Blood Sugar Check** | | |
| **Category** | **Expansion** | **Non-expansion** |
| ALL | 34 | 32 |
| UNINSURED | 15 | 24 |
| INSURED: Medicaid | 39 | 53 |
| INSURED: Private health insurance | 34 | 28 |
| **FLU Vaccine**[a] | | |
| **Category** | **Expansion** | **Non-expansion** |
| ALL | 31 | 24 |
| UNINSURED | 12 | 14 |
| INSURED: Medicaid | 34 | 35 |
| INSURED: Private health insurance | 34 | 26 |
| **Hospital Emergency Department Visit** | | |
| **Category** | **Expansion** | **Non-expansion** |
| ALL | 27 | 28 |
| UNINSURED | 21 | 28 |
| INSURED: Medicaid | 35 | 43 |
| INSURED: Private health insurance | 18 | 20 |

In: Medicaid
Editor: Alice Holt

ISBN: 978-1-53614-829-9


*Chapter 2*

# MEDICAID: ACTIONS NEEDED TO MITIGATE BILLIONS IN IMPROPER PAYMENTS AND PROGRAM INTEGRITY RISKS*

*Gene L. Dodaro*

## WHY GAO DID THIS STUDY

Medicaid, a joint federal-state health care program overseen by CMS, is a significant component of federal and state budgets, with total estimated expenditures of $596 billion in fiscal year 2017.

Medicaid allows significant flexibility for states to design and implement program innovations based on their unique needs. The resulting diversity of the program and its size, make the program particularly challenging to oversee at the federal level and also vulnerable to improper payments. In fiscal year 2017, estimated improper payments were $36.7 billion in Medicaid, up from $29.1 billion in fiscal year 2015. Further, the

* This is an edited, reformatted and augmented version of United States Government Accountability Office; Testimony Before the Committee on Homeland Security and Governmental Affairs, U.S. Senate Publication No. GAO-18-598T, dated June 27, 2018.

Medicaid program accounted for about 26 percent of the fiscal year 2017 government-wide improper payment estimate.

This testimony focuses on the (1) major risks to the integrity of the Medicaid program, and (2) actions needed to manage these risks. This testimony draws on GAO's reports issued between November 2012 and May 2018 on the Medicaid program.

## What GAO Recommends

As a part of this body of work, GAO has made 83 recommendations to address shortcomings in Medicaid oversight and suggested four matters for congressional consideration. The Department of Health and Human Services and CMS have generally agreed with these recommendations and have implemented 25 of them. GAO will continue to monitor implementation of the remaining recommendations.

## What GAO Found

GAO's work has identified three broad areas of risk in Medicaid that also contribute to overall growth in program spending, projected to exceed $900 billion in fiscal year 2025.

1) **Improper payments**, including payments made for services not actually provided. Regarding managed care payments, which were nearly half (or $280 billion) of Medicaid spending in fiscal year 2017, GAO has found that the full extent of program risk due to overpayments and unallowable costs is unknown.
2) **Supplemental payments**, which are payments made to providers—such as local government hospitals—that are in addition to regular, claims-based payments made to providers for specific services. These payments totaled more than $48 billion in fiscal year 2016

and in some cases have shifted expenditures from the states to the federal government.

3) **Demonstrations**, which allow states to test new approaches to coverage. Comprising about one-third of total Medicaid expenditures in fiscal year 2015, GAO has found that demonstrations have increased federal costs without providing results that can be used to inform policy decisions.

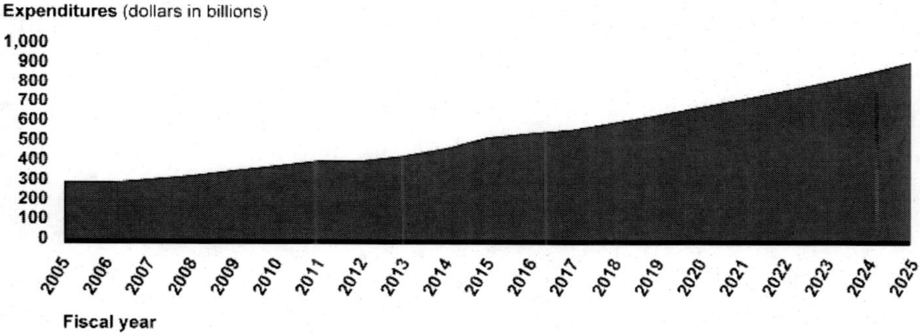


Source: 2016 Actuarial Report on the Financial Outlook for Medicaid. | GAO-18-598T.

Actual and Projected Growth Trends in Total Medicaid Spending.

GAO's work has recommended numerous actions to strengthen oversight and manage program risks.

- **Improve data.** The Centers for Medicare & Medicaid Services (CMS), which oversees Medicaid, needs to make sustained efforts to ensure Medicaid data are timely, complete, and comparable from all states, and useful for program oversight. Data are also needed for oversight of supplemental payments and ensuring that demonstrations are meeting their stated goals.
- **Target fraud.** CMS needs to conduct a fraud risk assessment for Medicaid, and design and implement a risk-based antifraud strategy for the program.
- **Collaborate.** There is a need for a collaborative approach to Medicaid oversight. State auditors have conducted evaluations that

identified significant improper payments and outlined deficiencies in Medicaid processes that require resolution.

Chairman Johnson, Ranking Member McCaskill, and Members of the Committee:

I appreciate the opportunity to be here today to discuss areas of risk to the Medicaid program and oversight efforts that can help prevent improper payments and ensure the program's fiscal integrity.[58] The federal-state Medicaid program is one of the nation's largest sources of funding for medical and health-related services. In fiscal year 2017, the program covered acute health care, long-term care, and other services for over 73 million low income and medically needy individuals. In that same year, estimated federal and state Medicaid expenditures were $596 billion.

Medicaid has been on our high-risk list since 2003, in part, because of concerns about the adequacy of fiscal oversight and the program's improper payments—including payments made for people not eligible for Medicaid or services not actually provided.[59] The Medicaid program accounted for 26.1 percent of the fiscal year 2017 government-wide improper payment estimate.[60] While efforts to reduce improper payments have been made by the Centers for Medicare & Medicaid Services (CMS), the agency within the Department of Health and Human Services (HHS) that oversees Medicaid, overall improper payments continue to increase. In fiscal year 2017, improper payments accounted for $36.7 billion of Medicaid spending, up from $29.1 billion in fiscal year 2015. Of the $36.7 billion in improper

---

[58] An improper payment is any payment that should not have been made or that was made in an incorrect amount (including overpayments and underpayments) under statutory, contractual, administrative, or other legally applicable requirements. It includes any payment to an ineligible recipient, any payment for an ineligible service, any duplicate payment, payment for services not received (except where authorized by law), and any payment that does not account for credit for applicable discounts. See 31 U.S.C. § 3321 note. Office of Management and Budget guidance also instructs agencies to report as improper payments any payments for which insufficient or no documentation is found.

[59] See GAO, *High-Risk Series: Progress on Many High-Risk Areas, While Substantial Efforts Needed on Others*. GAO-17-317 (Washington, D.C.: Feb. 15, 2017).

[60] See GAO, *Improper Payments: Actions and Guidance Could Help Address Issues and Inconsistencies in Estimation Processes*. GAO-18-377 (Washington, D.C.: May 31, 2018).

payments, $36.4 billion were overpayments and $283 million were underpayments.

The size, complexity, and diversity of Medicaid make the program particularly challenging to oversee at the federal level. Medicaid allows significant flexibility for states to design and implement program innovations based on their unique needs; however, our prior work has found that these innovations have grown considerably over time, lack complete and accurate reporting, and do not always ensure the efficient use of federal dollars. It is critical that CMS and states take appropriate measures to reduce improper payments and ensure the fiscal integrity of Medicaid; as dollars wasted detract from the program's ability to ensure that the individuals who rely on Medicaid—including low-income children and individuals who are elderly or disabled—are provided adequate care.

My testimony today will focus on

1) major risks to the integrity of the Medicaid program, and
2) actions needed to manage these risks.

My remarks are based on our large body of work examining the Medicaid program, particularly reports issued and recommendations made from November 2012 to May 2018; these reports provide further details on our scope and methodology. (A list of related reports is included at the end of this statement). For further context, my remarks also reference information reported by state auditors and the HHS Office of Inspector General (HHS-OIG), including information from two meetings with state auditors and Inspectors General we hosted in March and May 2018. We conducted all of the work on which this statement is based in accordance with generally accepted government auditing standards. Those standards require that we plan and perform the audit to obtain sufficient, appropriate evidence to provide a reasonable basis for our findings and conclusions based on our audit objectives. We believe that the evidence obtained provides a reasonable basis for our findings and conclusions based on our audit objectives.

## BACKGROUND

Among health care programs, Medicaid is the largest as measured by enrollment (over 73 million in fiscal year 2017) and the second largest as measured by expenditures ($596 billion in fiscal year 2017), second only to Medicare. The CMS Office of the Actuary projected that Medicaid spending would grow at an average rate of 5.7 percent per year, from fiscal years 2016 to 2025, with projected Medicaid expenditures reaching $958 billion by fiscal year 2025.[61] This projected growth in expenditures reflects both expected increases in expenditures per enrollee and in levels of Medicaid enrollment. Beneficiaries with disabilities and those who are elderly constitute the highest per enrollee expenditures, which are projected to increase by almost 50 percent from fiscal year 2016 to 2025. Medicaid enrollment is also expected to grow by as many as 13.2 million newly eligible adults by 2025—as additional states may expand their Medicaid programs to cover certain low-income adults under the Patient Protection and Affordable Care Act (PPACA).[62] (See Figure 1).

The partnership between the federal government and states is a central tenet of the Medicaid program. CMS provides oversight and technical assistance for the program, and states are responsible for administering their respective Medicaid programs' day-to-day operations—including determining eligibility, enrolling individuals and providers, and adjudicating claims—within broad federal requirements. Federal oversight includes ensuring that the design and operation of state programs meet federal requirements and that Medicaid payments are made appropriately. (See Figure 2 for a diagram of the federal-state Medicaid partnership framework).

---

[61] Data are from the most recently issued CMS actuarial report. See Centers for Medicare & Medicaid Services, Office of the Actuary, *2016 Actuarial Report on the Financial Outlook for Medicaid* (Washington, D.C.: 2016).

[62] The Patient Protection and Affordable Care Act, enacted on March 23, 2010, permits states to expand their Medicaid programs to cover nonelderly, nonpregnant adults who are not eligible for Medicare, and whose income does not exceed 133 percent of the federal poverty level. Because of the way the limit is calculated, using what is known as an "income disregard," the level is effectively 138 percent of the federal poverty level. Pub. L. No. 111-148, 124 Stat. 119 (2010), as amended by the Health Care and Education Reconciliation Act of 2010 (HCERA), Pub. L. No. 111-152, 124 Stat. 1029 (2010).

Joint financing of Medicaid is also a fixture of the federal-state partnership, with the federal government matching most state Medicaid expenditures using a statutory formula based, in part, on each state's per capita income in relation to the national average per capita income.

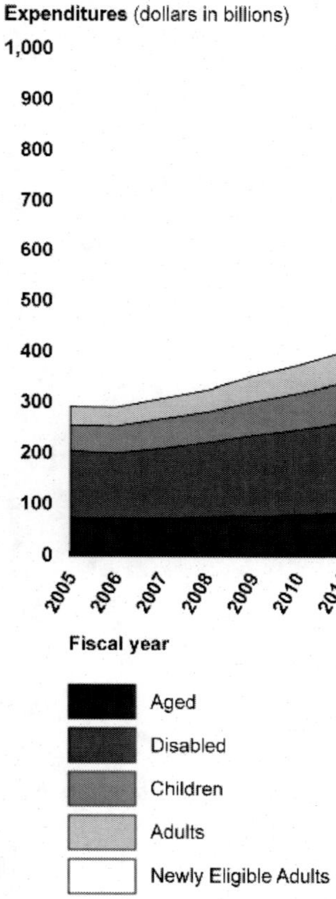


Source: GAO analysis of 2016 Actuarial Report on the Financial Outlook for Medicaid. | GAO-18-598T.

Note: Data after fiscal year 2012 are projected expenditures.

Figure 1. Growth Trends in Total Medicaid Spending by Eligibility Group.

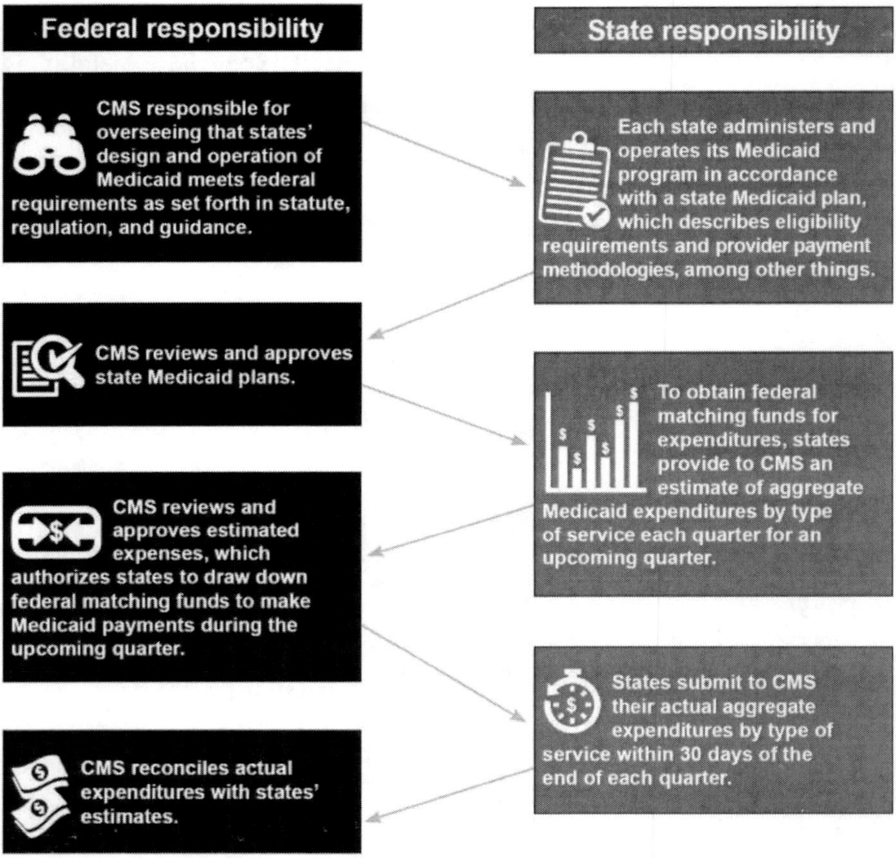


Source: GAO. | GAO-18-598T.

Note: If a state wishes to make amendments to its state Medicaid plan, it must seek approval from the Centers for Medicare & Medicaid Services (CMS). Similarly, a state that desires to change its Medicaid program in ways that deviate from certain federal requirements may seek to do so through a Medicaid demonstration waiver approved under section 1115 of the Social Security Act, which is outside of its state Medicaid plan. States must submit an application describing the proposed section 1115 demonstration to CMS for review. CMS will specify the special terms and conditions that encompass the requirements for an approved demonstration.

Figure 2. Federal-State Medicaid Partnership Framework.

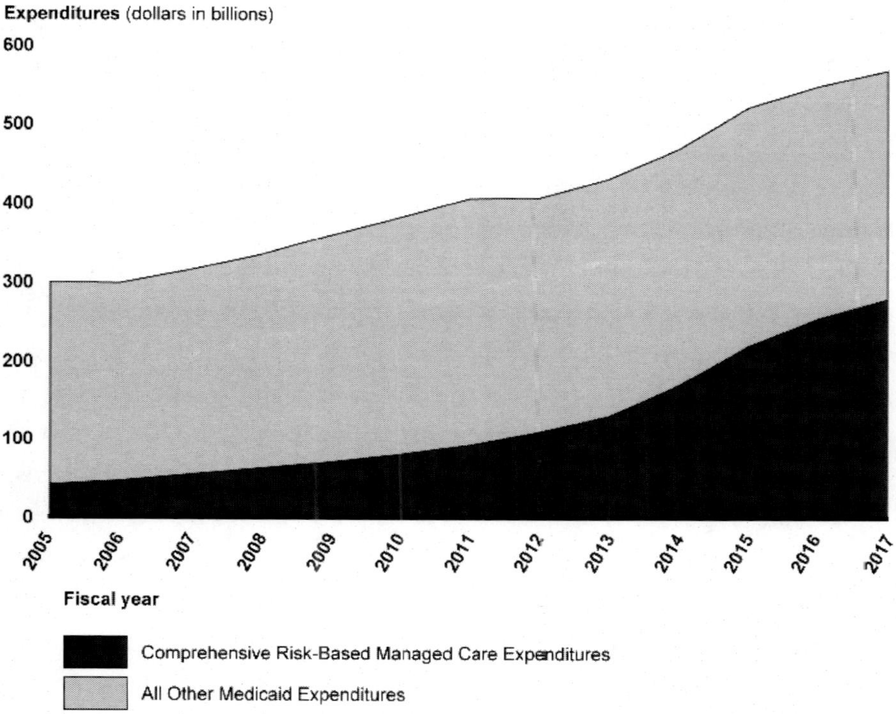


Source: GAO analysis of Centers for Medicare & Medicaid Services expenditures data. | GAO-18-598T.

Note: States may have different types of managed care arrangements in Medicaid; managed care expenditures in this figure include expenditures for comprehensive, risk-based managed care—the most common type of managed care arrangement

Figure 3. Growth in Comprehensive Risk-Based Managed Care as a Share of Total Medicaid Expenditures, Fiscal Years 2005 through 2017.

States have flexibility in determining how their Medicaid benefits are delivered. For example, states may (1) contract with managed care organizations to provide a specific set of Medicaid-covered services to beneficiaries and pay the organizations a set amount, generally on a per beneficiary per month basis; (2) pay health care providers for each service they provide on a fee-for-service basis; or (3) rely on a combination of both delivery systems.[63] Managed care continues to be a growing component of

[63] CMS has also been developing and testing a variety of value-based payment models, under which physicians and other providers are paid and responsible for the care of a beneficiary for a long

the Medicaid program. In fiscal year 2017, expenditures for managed care were $280 billion, representing almost half of total program expenditures, compared with 42 percent in fiscal year 2015. (See Figure 3).

States also have the flexibility to innovate outside of many of Medicaid's otherwise applicable requirements through Medicaid demonstrations approved under section 1115 of the Social Security Act.[64] These demonstrations allow states to test new approaches to coverage and to improve quality and access, or generate savings or efficiencies. For example, under demonstrations, states have

- extended coverage to certain populations,
- provided services not otherwise eligible for federal matching funds, and
- made incentive payments to providers for delivery system improvements.

As of November 2016, nearly three-quarters of states have CMS-approved demonstrations. In fiscal year 2015, total spending under demonstrations represented a third of all Medicaid spending nationwide. (See Figure 4).

---

period and accountable for the quality and efficiency of the care provided. Examples of these models include accountable care organizations—groups of physicians and other health care providers who voluntarily work together to provide coordinated care—and bundled payment models, which provide a "bundled" payment intended to cover the multiple services beneficiaries receive during an episode of care for certain health conditions, such as hip replacements, congestive heart failure, and pregnancy.

[64] Under section 1115 of the Social Security Act, the Secretary of Health and Human Services may waive certain Medicaid requirements and approve new types of expenditures that would not otherwise be eligible for federal Medicaid matching funds for experimental, pilot, or demonstration projects that, in the Secretary's judgment, are likely to promote Medicaid objectives. See 42 U.S.C. § 1315(a). The Secretary has delegated the approval and administration of Medicaid section 1115 demonstrations to CMS, which requires that such demonstrations be budget neutral to the federal government; that is, the federal government should spend no more for Medicaid under a state's demonstration than it would have spent without the demonstration. There are other types of waivers that states can apply for and use, including those approved under section 1915(c) of the Social Security Act, which authorizes the Secretary of Health and Human Services to waive requirements that states providing home and community based services would otherwise need to meet in the absence of the waiver.

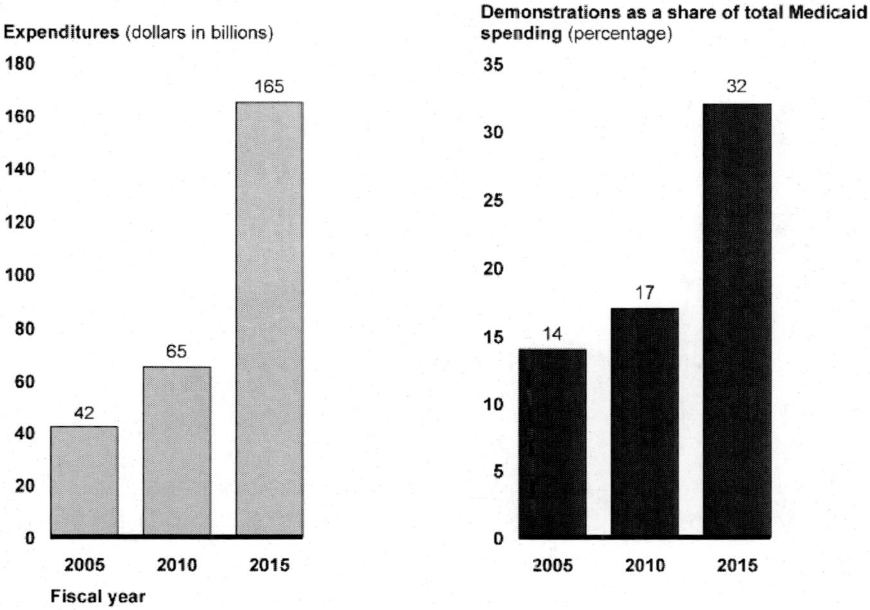


Source: GAO analysis of Centers for Medicare & Medicaid Services demonstration expenditures data. | GAO-18-598T.

Figure 4. Total Expenditures under Medicaid Section 1115 Demonstrations, Fiscal Years 2005, 2010, and 2015.

In addition to other types of improper payments, Medicaid presents opportunities for fraud, because of the size, expenditures, and complexities of the program—including the variation in states' design and implementation. Medicaid Fraud Control Units (MFCU)—state entities responsible for investigating and prosecuting Medicaid fraud—have reported on Medicaid fraud convictions and recovered monies, in their annual reports.[65] For example, over the past 5 years, MFCUs have reported an average of 1,072 yearly Medicaid fraud convictions. They also reported

[65] Nearly all states have MFCUs responsible for investigating and prosecuting Medicaid fraud. MFCUs are funded jointly by the federal government and the states, and HHS-OIG provides oversight.

about $680 million in recoveries related to fraud in fiscal year 2017—almost double the recoveries from fiscal year 2016.[66]

## THREE BROAD AREAS OF RISK THREATEN THE FISCAL INTEGRITY OF MEDICAID

Our prior work has identified three broad areas of risk to the fiscal integrity of Medicaid: improper payment rates, state use of supplemental payments, and oversight of demonstration programs.

### Estimated Improper Payments Exceed 10 Percent, and Do Not Fully Account for All Program Risks

CMS annually computes the national Medicaid improper payment estimate as a weighted average of states' improper payment estimates for three component parts—fee-for-service, beneficiary eligibility determinations, and managed care. The improper payment estimate for each component is developed under its own methodology.[67] The national rate in fiscal year 2017 was 10.1 percent, or $36.7 billion. Since 2016, Medicaid has exceeded the 10 percent criterion set in statute. As such, the program was not fully compliant with the Improper Payments Elimination and Recovery Act of 2010.[68]

In May 2018, we reported that the Medicaid managed care component of the improper payment estimate does not fully account for all program

---

[66] See Department of Health and Human Services, Office of Inspector General, *Medicaid Fraud Control Units Fiscal Year 2017 Annual Report*, OEI-09-18-00180 (Washington, D.C.: March 2018).

[67] CMS has not calculated the beneficiary eligibility determinations component estimate since 2014 and has held constant this component of the national rate at 3.1 percent. Beginning in the 2019 reporting year, the agency plans to resume improper payment estimates for eligibility determinations.

[68] When an agency is determined to not be in compliance with one or more of the Improper Payments Elimination and Recovery Act criteria by its Inspector General, it must submit a plan to Congress describing the actions it will take to come into compliance.

risks in managed care.[69] We identified 10 federal and state audits and investigations (out of 27 focused on Medicaid managed care) that cited about $68 million in overpayments and unallowable managed care organization costs that were not accounted for by the managed care improper payment estimate. Another of these investigations resulted in a $137.5 million settlement to resolve allegations of false claims.[70] We further noted that the full extent of overpayments and unallowable costs is unknown, because the 27 audits and investigations we reviewed were conducted over more than 5 years and involved a small fraction of the more than 270 managed care organizations operating nationwide as of September 2017.

Some examples of the state audits that identified overpayments and unallowable costs include the following:

- The Washington State Auditor's Office found that two managed care organizations made $17.5 million in overpayments to providers in 2010, which may have increased the state's 2013 capitation rates.[71]
- The Texas State Auditor's Office found that one managed care organization reported $3.8 million in unallowable costs for advertising, company events, gifts, and stock options, along with $34 million in other questionable costs in 2015.[72]
- The New York State Comptroller found that two managed care organizations paid over $6.6 million to excluded and deceased providers from 2011 through 2014.[73]

---

[69] States may have different types of managed care arrangements in Medicaid; our findings apply to comprehensive, risk-based managed care, the most common type of managed care arrangement. See GAO, *Medicaid: CMS Should Take Steps to Mitigate Program Risks in Managed Care*, GAO-18-291 (Washington, D.C.: May 7, 2018).

[70] See GAO-18-291.

[71] Washington State Auditor, *Performance Audit: Health Care Authority's Oversight of the Medicaid Managed Care Program*, Audit No. 1011450 (April 14, 2014).

[72] Texas State Auditor, *An Audit Report on HealthSpring Life and Health Insurance Company, Inc., a Medicaid STAR+PLUS Managed Care Organization*, Report No. 17-025 (Austin, Tex.: February 2017).

[73] New York State Office of the State Comptroller, *Medicaid Managed Care Organization Fraud and Abuse Detection*, Report 2014-S-51 (Albany, N.Y.: July 15, 2016). HHS-OIG has the authority to exclude providers from federal health care programs, and maintains a list of all currently excluded providers called the List of Excluded Individuals/Entities. No payment

To the extent that such overpayments and unallowable costs are unidentified and not removed from the cost data used to set managed care payment rates, they may allow inflated future payments and minimize the appearance of program risks in Medicaid managed care. This potential understatement of the program risks in managed care also may curtail investigations into the appropriateness of managed care spending. The continued growth of Medicaid managed care makes ensuring the accuracy of managed care improper payment estimates increasingly important.

In May 2018, we acknowledged that although CMS has increased its focus on and worked with states to improve oversight of Medicaid managed care; its efforts—for example, updated regulations and audits of managed care providers—did not ensure the identification and reporting of overpayments and unallowable costs.[74] In May 2016, CMS updated its regulations for managed care programs, including that states arrange an independent audit of the data submitted by MCOs, at least once every 3 years. We found that although this requirement has the potential to enhance state oversight of managed care; CMS was reviewing the rule for possible revision of its requirements.[75] We also noted that another effort to address program risks in managed care—the use of CMS program integrity contractors to audit providers that are paid by managed care organizations—has been limited. To address the program risks that are not measured as a part of CMS's methodology to estimate improper payments, in May 2018 we recommended that CMS take steps to mitigate such risks, which could include revising its methodology or ocusing additional audit resources on managed care. HHS concurred with this recommendation.[76]

may be made from any federal health care program for any items or services furnished, ordered, or prescribed by an excluded provider.

[74] GAO-18-291.

[75] CMS indicated it will issue a Notice of Proposed Rulemaking in 2018 to streamline Medicaid managed care regulations and reduce burden. See Department of Health and Human Services, Medicaid and CHIP Managed Care, *Spring 2018 Unified Agenda of Federal Regulatory and Deregulatory Actions*, (CMS-2480-P), RIN 0938-AT40, accessed in May 14, 2018, http://www.reginfo.gov.

[76] GAO-18-291.

**Table 1. Examples of GAO Recommendations to Address Medicaid Program Risks Associated with Managed Care, Provider Enrollment, and Beneficiary Eligibility Determinations**

| Program risks | GAO recommendations | Recommendation status |
|---|---|---|
| Addressing key risks, such as the extent of overpayments and unallowable costs, that are not measured in the managed care component of the Centers for Medicare & Medicaid Services' (CMS) improper payment estimate | One recommendation aimed at mitigating identified risks, such as revising the methodology to calculate the managed care component or focusing additional audit resources on managed care.[a] | CMS concurred with our recommendation, and indicated that it will review regulatory authority and audit resources to determine the best way to account for Medicaid program risks that are not accounted for in the managed care component. |
| Ensuring that only eligible providers are enrolled in Medicaid | Four recommendations aimed at assessing the databases used to screen providers, improve collaboration and coordination with other federal agencies on sharing databases and establishing a common identifier across databases, and providing guidance to state Medicaid agencies.[b] | CMS has addressed two of the four recommendations. To implement one remaining recommendation, CMS will need to determine whether the remaining databases (used by states and health plans to screen providers) that it has studied should be added to the agency's list of the databases used for screening purposes. For the other remaining recommendation, CMS needs to explore the use of a common identifier for screening providers across databases. |
| Ensuring that only eligible beneficiaries are enrolled in Medicaid | Two recommendations that CMS review federal determinations of Medicaid eligibility for accuracy, and take steps to increase assurance that expenditures for the different eligibility groups are correctly reported and appropriately matched.[c] | CMS established a more rigorous approach for verifying financial and nonfinancial information needed to determine Medicaid beneficiaries' eligibility. The agency stated that it would include reviews of federal eligibility determinations in states that have delegated that authority as a part of its review of states' eligibility determinations. The results of this effort will be reported in 2019. |

Source: GAO | GAO-18-598T.

[a]See GAO, *Medicaid: CMS Should Take Steps to Mitigate Program Risks in Managed Care*, GAO-18-291 (Washington, D.C.: May 7, 2018).

[b]See GAO, *Medicaid Program Integrity: Improved Guidance Needed to Better Support Efforts to Screen Managed Care Providers*, GAO-16-402 (Washington, D.C.: April 22, 2016).

[c]See GAO, *Medicaid: Additional Efforts Needed to Ensure that State Spending is Appropriately Matched with Federal Funds*, GAO-16-53 (Washington, D.C.: Oct. 16, 2015). Under the Patient Protection and Affordable Care Act, state Medicaid expenditures for certain Medicaid enrollees are subject to higher federal matching percentages.

Our prior work on Medicaid has also identified other program risks associated with provider enrollment and beneficiary eligibility that may contribute to improper payments. In Table 1 above, we identify some examples of the previous recommendations we have made to address these types of program risks, and what, if any, steps CMS has taken in response to our recommendations.

## Lack of Transparency and Federal Oversight of States' Use of Supplemental Payments Increase Program Risk

Supplemental payments are payments made to providers—such as local government hospitals and other providers—that are in addition to the regular, claims-based payments made to providers for services they provided.[77] Like all Medicaid payments, supplemental payments are required to be economical and efficient.[78]

Supplemental payments have been growing and totaled more than $48 billion in 2016. Our prior work has identified several concerns related to supplemental payments, including the need for more complete and accurate reporting, criteria for economical and efficient payments, and written guidance on the distribution of payments.[79]

---

[77] Two types of supplemental payments exist in Medicaid: (1) disproportionate share hospital (DSH) payments, which states are required to make to hospitals serving low-income and Medicaid patients to offset those providers' uncompensated care costs; and (2) non-DSH supplemental payments that states may, but are not required, to make to hospitals and other providers that, for example, serve high-cost Medicaid beneficiaries. Unless otherwise noted, our findings apply to both types of supplemental payments.

[78] Payments must also be sufficient to assure quality of care and to enlist enough providers so that care and services are available to Medicaid beneficiaries at least to the extent available to the general population in the geographic area. 42 U.S.C. § 1396a(a)(30)(A).

[79] See, for example, GAO, *Medicaid: Federal Guidance Needed to Address Concerns About Distribution of Supplemental Payments*, GAO-16-108 (Washington, D.C.: Feb. 5, 2016); and *Medicaid: CMS Oversight of Provider Payments Is Hampered by Limited Data and Unclear Policy*, GAO-15-322 (Washington, D.C.: April 10, 2015).

### *Complete and Accurate Reporting*

Our prior work has identified increased use of provider taxes and transfers from local government providers to finance the states' share of supplemental payments, which, although allowed under federal law, effectively shift Medicaid costs from the states to the federal government.

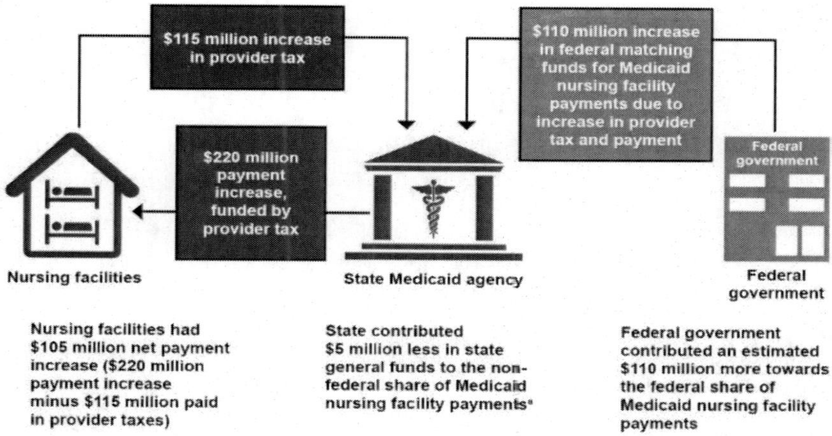


Source: GAO. | GAO-18-598T.

Figure 5. Example of How One State's Use of Non-State Sources to Fund Medicaid Payments to Nursing Facilities Shifted Medicaid Costs to the Federal Government in State Fiscal Year 2015.

In particular, we previously reported in July 2014 that states' share of Medicaid supplemental payments financed with funds from providers and local governments increased the federal share from 57 percent in state fiscal year 2008 to 70 percent in state fiscal year 2012.[80] The full extent of this shift in states' financing structure was unknown, because CMS had not ensured that states report complete and accurate data on the sources of funds they use to finance their share of Medicaid payments, and CMS's efforts had fallen short of obtaining complete data.[81] (See Table 2 below for our

---

[80] See GAO, *Medicaid Financing: States' Increased Reliance on Funds from Health Care Providers and Local Governments Warrants Improved CMS Data Collection [Reissued on March 13, 2015]*, GAO-14-627 (Washington, D.C.: July 29, 2014).

[81] Federal law requires that no less than 40 percent of the state's share of Medicaid payments be state funds—which can include state general funds, health care provider taxes imposed by the state, and intra-agency funds from non-Medicaid state agencies— but up to 60 percent may

recommendation and actions CMS has taken). For example, in July 2014, we reported that in one state, a $220 million payment increase for nursing facilities resulted in an estimated $110 million increase in federal matching funds to the state, and a net payment increase to the facilities of $105 million.[82] (See Figure 5).

### *Criteria for Economical and Efficient Payments*

Our prior work has demonstrated that CMS lacks the criteria, data, and review processes to ensure that one type of supplemental payments—non-DSH supplemental payments—are economical and efficient.[83] For example, in April 2015, we identified public hospitals in one state that received such supplemental and regular Medicaid payments that, when combined, were hundreds of millions in excess of the hospitals' total Medicaid costs and tens of millions in excess of their total operating costs—unbeknownst to CMS.[84] Accordingly, we concluded that CMS's criteria and review processes did not ensure that it can identify excessive payments and determine if supplemental payments are economical and efficient. (See Table 2 below for our recommendations and actions CMS has taken).

### *Written Guidance on the Distribution of Payments*

According to CMS policy, Medicaid payments, including supplemental payments, should be linked to the provision of Medicaid services and not contingent on the provision of local funds. However, in February 2016 we reported that CMS did not have written guidance that clarifies this policy. In February 2016, we found examples of hospitals with large uncompensated costs associated with serving the low-income and Medicaid population that received relatively little in supplemental payments, while other hospitals with relatively low uncompensated care costs—but that were able to

---

be financed by local governments and local government providers. We have reported that, absent complete and accurate data, CMS cannot ensure that states' use of local funding sources does not exceed the 60 percent. See GAO-14-627.

[82] See GAO-14-627.

[83] Non-DSH supplemental payments that states may, but are not required to, make to hospitals and other providers that, for example, serve high-cost Medicaid beneficiaries.

[84] See GAO-15-322.

contribute a large amount of funds for the state's Medicaid share— received large supplemental payments relative to those costs, raising questions as to whether CMS policies are being followed.[85]

## Table 2. Examples of GAO Recommendations to Address Medicaid Program Risks Associated with Supplemental Payments

| Program risks | GAO recommendations | Recommendation status |
|---|---|---|
| Complete and accurate reporting | One recommendation aimed at the Centers for Medicare & Medicaid Services (CMS) taking steps to ensure states report accurate and complete information on all sources of funds they use to finance their share of Medicaid spending.[a] | CMS did not concur with GAO's recommendation, although the agency stated that it will examine efforts to improve data collection for oversight. |
| Criteria for economical and efficient payments | Two recommendations called for CMS to (1) develop a policy that establishes criteria for defining when payments made to individual providers are economical and efficient, and (2) subsequently develop a process for identifying and reviewing payments to individual providers in order to determine whether they meet the criteria.[b] | CMS told us in April 2018 that it is developing a proposed rule on supplemental payment financing and oversight that may address these recommendations, although it does not have a time frame for its release. |
| Written guidance on the distribution of payments | One recommendation aimed at CMS issuing written guidance for states clarifying its policy of the distribution of supplemental payments.[c] | CMS told us in April 2018 that it is developing a proposed rule on supplemental payment financing and oversight that may address this recommendation, although it does not have a time frame for its release. |

Source: GAO | GAO-18-598T.

[a]See GAO, *Medicaid Financing: States' Increased Reliance on Funds from Health Care Providers and Local Governments Warrants Improved CMS Data Collection*, [Reissued on March 13, 2015], GAO-14-627 (Washington, D.C.: July 29, 2014).

[b]See GAO, *Medicaid: CMS Oversight of Provider Payments Is Hampered by Limited Data and Unclear Policy*, GAO-15-322 (Washington, D.C.: April 10, 2015).

[c]See GAO, *Medicaid: Federal Guidance Needed to Address Concerns About Distribution of Supplemental Payments*, GAO-16-108 (Washington, D.C.: Feb. 5, 2016).

[85] See GAO-16-108.

(See Table 2 for our recommendation and actions CMS has taken). Recognizing that Congress could help address some of the program risks associated with supplemental payments, in November 2012, we suggested that Congress consider requiring CMS to

- improve state reporting of supplemental payments, including requiring annual reporting of facility-specific payment amounts;
- clarify permissible methods for calculating these supplemental payments; and
- implement annual independent certified audits to verify state compliance with methods for calculating supplemental payments.[86]

Subsequent to our work highlighting the need for complete and accurate reporting, in January 2017 a bill was introduced in the House of Representatives that, if enacted, would require annual state reporting of non-DSH supplemental payments made to individual facilities, require CMS to issue guidance to states that identifies permissible methods for calculating non-DSH supplemental payments to providers, and establish requirements for such annual independent audits.[87] Another bill was introduced in October 2017 that would require states to submit annual reports that identify the sources and amount of funds used to finance the state share of Medicaid payments.[88] As of May 2018, no action had been taken on either proposed bill.

[86] See GAO, *Medicaid: More Transparency of and Accountability for Supplemental Payments are Needed*, GAO-13-48 (Washington, D.C.: Nov. 26, 2012).

[87] The Improving Oversight and Accountability in Medicaid Non-DSH Supplemental Payments Act was introduced on January 13, 2017 and referred to the House Committee on Energy and Commerce. See H.R. 541, 115th Cong. § 2 (2017).

[88] The Medicaid Requiring Expenditures for Public Objectives to be Reflective of Total Spending Act (Medicaid REPORTS Act) was introduced on October 12, 2017 and referred to in the House Energy and Commerce Committee Subcommittee on Health. See H.R. 4054, 115th Cong. § 2 (2017).

## Absent Better Oversight, Demonstrations May Increase Federal Fiscal Liability

Demonstration programs, comprising about one-third of total Medicaid expenditures in fiscal year 2015, can be a powerful tool for states and CMS to test new approaches to providing coverage and delivering services that could reduce costs and improve outcomes. However, our prior work has identified several concerns related to demonstrations, including the need for ensuring that (1) demonstrations meet the policy requirements of budget neutrality—that is, they must not increase federal costs—and (2) evaluations are used to determine whether demonstrations are having their intended effects.[89]

### *Budget Neutrality of Medicaid Demonstrations*

Demonstration spending limits, by HHS policy, should not exceed spending that would have occurred in the absence of a demonstration. In multiple reports examining more than a dozen demonstrations between 2002 and 2017, we have identified a number of questionable methods and assumptions that HHS has permitted states to use when estimating costs. We found that federal spending on Medicaid demonstrations could be reduced by billions of dollars if HHS were required to improve the process for reviewing, approving, and making transparent the basis for spending limits approved for Medicaid demonstrations.[90] The following are some examples of what we have previously found:

---

[89] See, for example, GAO, *Medicaid Demonstrations: Evaluations Yielded Limited Results, Underscoring Need for Changes to Federal Policies and Procedures*, GAO-18-220 (Washington, D.C.: Jan 19, 2018); and *Medicaid Demonstrations: Federal Action Needed to Improve Oversight of Spending*, GAO-17-312 (Washington, D.C.: April 3, 2017).

[90] See, for example, GAO-17-312 and GAO, *Medicaid Demonstrations: HHS's Approval Process for Arkansas's Medicaid Expansion Waiver Raises Cost Concerns*, GAO-14-689R (Washington, D.C.: Aug. 8, 2014); *Medicaid Demonstration Waivers: Approval Process Raises Cost Concerns and Lacks Transparency*, GAO-13-384 (Washington, D.C.: June 25, 2013); *Medicaid Demonstration Waivers: Recent HHS Approvals Continue to Raise Cost and Oversight Concerns*, GAO-08-87 (Washington, D.C.: Jan. 31, 2008); and *Medicaid and SCHIP: Recent HHS Approvals of Demonstration Waiver Projects Raise Concerns*, GAO-02-817 (Washington, D.C.: July 12, 2002).

- In August 2014, we reported that HHS had approved a spending limit for Arkansas's demonstration—to test whether providing premium assistance to purchase private coverage through the health insurance exchange would improve access for newly eligible Medicaid beneficiaries—that was based, in part, on hypothetical, not actual, costs. Specifically, the spending limit was based on significantly higher payment amounts the state assumed it would have to make to providers if it expanded coverage under the traditional Medicaid program, and HHS did not request any data to support the state's assumptions. We estimated that by allowing the state to use hypothetical costs, HHS approved a demonstration spending limit that was over $775 million more than what it would have been if the limit was based on the state's actual payment rates for services under the traditional Medicaid program.[91]
- We also reported in August 2014 that HHS officials told us it granted Arkansas and 11 other states additional flexibility in their demonstrations in order to increase spending limits if costs proved higher than expected.[92] We concluded that granting this flexibility to the states to adjust the spending limit increased the fiscal risk to the federal government.
- More recently, in April 2017, we reported that two states used unspent federal funds from their previous demonstrations to expand the scope of subsequent demonstrations by $8 billion and $600 million, respectively. We concluded that inflating the spending limits in this way inappropriately increased the federal government's fiscal liability for Medicaid.[93]

---

[91] See GAO-14-689R.

[92] In September 2014, the Chairman of the House Committee on Energy & Commerce and the Ranking Member of the Senate Committee on Finance sent a letter to CMS asking, among other things, how the agency planned to ensure that spending for those newly eligible under Arkansas's demonstration would not cost the federal government more than it would have cost under traditional Medicaid.

[93] See GAO-17-312.

We have previously made recommendations to improve oversight of spending on demonstrations, and HHS recently took action that partially responds to one of these recommendations. (See Table 3 for examples of the recommendations and actions HHS has taken). Specifically, under a policy implemented in 2016, HHS restricted the amount of unspent funds states can accrue for each year of a demonstration, and has also reduced the amount of unspent funds that states can carry forward to new demonstrations. For 10 demonstrations it has recently approved, HHS estimated that the new policy has reduced total demonstration spending limits by $109 billion for 2016 through 2018, the federal share of which is $62.9 billion. These limits reduce the effect, but do not specifically address all of the questionable methods and assumptions that we have identified regarding how HHS sets demonstration spending limits.

**Table 3. Examples of GAO Recommendations to Address Medicaid Program Risks Associated with Spending on Medicaid Demonstrations**

| Program risks | GAO recommendations | Recommendation status |
|---|---|---|
| Methods for determining budget neutrality | One recommendation that the Department of Health and Human Services (HHS) better ensure that valid methods are used to demonstrate budget neutrality.[a] | HHS has taken some steps in recent years to improve allowable methods for ensuring budget neutrality, but still needs written guidance on methodologies for demonstrating budget neutrality. |
| Lack of criteria for determining spending limits | One recommendation that HHS update its written budget neutrality policy to reflect the actual criteria and processes used to develop and approve demonstration spending limits.[b] | HHS announced and began implementing policy changes in 2016 that address some, but not all of our concerns, which it formalized in 2017. The agency expects to release additional guidance later in 2018. Once HHS provides additional written guidance on its criteria and processes, we will be in a position to consider closing this recommendation. |

Source: GAO | GAO-18-598T.

[a]See GAO, *Medicaid and SCHIP: Recent HHS Approvals of Demonstration Waiver Projects Raise Concerns*, GAO-02-817 (Washington, D.C.: July 12, 2002)

[b]See *GAO, Medicaid Demonstration Waivers: Approval Process Raises Cost Concerns and Lacks Transparency*, GAO-13-384 (Washington, D.C.: June 25, 2013).

***Evaluation of Medicaid Demonstrations***

In a January 2018 report, we questioned the usefulness of both state-led and federal evaluations of section 1115 demonstrations, particularly with regard to how these evaluation results may inform policy decisions.[94]

- State-led evaluations. We identified significant limitations among selected state-led demonstration evaluations, including gaps in reported evaluation results for important parts of the demonstrations. (See Table 4). These gaps resulted, in part, from CMS requiring final, comprehensive evaluation reports after the expiration of the demonstrations rather than at the end of each 3- to 5-year demonstration cycle. In October 2017, CMS officials stated that the agency planned to require final reports at the end of each demonstration cycle for all demonstrations, although it had not established written procedures for implementing this new policy. We concluded in January 2018 that without written procedures for implementing such requirements, gaps in oversight could continue.[95]
- Federal evaluations. Evaluations of federal demonstrations led by CMS have also been limited due to data challenges and a lack of transparent reporting. For example, delays obtaining data directly from states, among other things, led CMS to considerably reduce the scope of a large, multi-state evaluation, which was initiated in 2014 to examine the impact of state demonstrations in four policy areas deemed to be federal priorities.[96] In our January 2018 report, we found that although CMS had made progress in obtaining needed

---

[94] See GAO-18-220.

[95] CMS also planned to allow states to conduct less rigorous evaluations for certain types of demonstrations, but had not established criteria defining under what conditions these limited evaluations would be allowed, when we issued our January 2018 report.

[96] The policy areas are (1) delivery system reform incentive payment programs, which provide incentive payments to providers that engage in various improvement projects that align with state delivery system reform objectives; (2) premium assistance to purchase insurance coverage in the exchange under PPACA; (3) beneficiary engagement policies, such as requiring monthly contributions; and (4) use of managed care to deliver Medicaid long-term supports and services.

data, CMS had no policy for making the results public. By not making these results public in a timely manner, we concluded that CMS was missing an opportunity to inform important federal and state policy discussions.

**Table 4. Examples of Gaps in States' Evaluations of Medicaid Section 1115 Demonstrations GAO Identified**

| State | Example of gaps in evaluations |
|---|---|
| Arizona | The state was required to evaluate whether providing long-term services and supports under a managed care delivery model improved access and quality of care. The evaluation report lacked information on important measures of access and quality. |
| Arkansas | The state was required to evaluate the effects of using Medicaid funds to purchase private insurance for more than 200,000 beneficiaries. The evaluation did not address a key hypothesis that using private insurance would improve continuity of coverage for these beneficiaries, who were expected to have frequent changes in income that could lead to coverage gaps. |
| Massachusetts | The state was required to evaluate the effectiveness of its approach of providing up to $690 million in incentive payments to seven hospitals to improve quality of care and reduce per capita costs. Evaluation reports submitted after 5 years provided no conclusions on the impact of the payments in these areas. |

Source: GAO. | GAO-18-598T.

In light of our concerns about state-led and federal demonstration evaluations, in January 2018, we recommended that CMS (1) establish written procedures for requiring final evaluation reports at the end of each demonstration cycle, (2) issue criteria for when it will allow limited evaluations of demonstrations, and (3) establish a policy for publicly releasing findings from federal evaluations of demonstrations. HHS concurred with these recommendations.[97]

[97] See GAO-18-220.

## Fundamental Actions Needed to Strengthen Oversight and Manage Program Risks

Across our body of work, we have made 83 recommendations to CMS and HHS and suggested 4 matters for congressional consideration to address a variety of concerns about the Medicaid program. The agencies generally agreed with our recommendations and have implemented 25 of these recommendations to date, and CMS still needs to take fundamental actions in three areas—having more timely, complete, and reliable data; conducting fraud risk assessments; and strengthening federal-state collaboration—to strengthen Medicaid oversight and better manage program risks.

### More Complete, Timely, Reliable Data for Oversight

An overarching challenge for CMS oversight of the Medicaid program is the lack of accurate, complete, and timely data. Our work has demonstrated how insufficient data have affected CMS's ability to ensure proper payments, assess beneficiaries' access to services, and oversee states' financing strategies.

As part of its efforts to address longstanding data concerns, CMS has taken some steps toward developing a reliable national repository for Medicaid data, most notably the Transformed Medicaid Statistical Information System (T-MSIS). Through T-MSIS, CMS will collect detailed information on Medicaid beneficiaries—such as their citizenship, immigration, and disability status—as well as any expanded diagnosis and procedure codes associated with their treatments. States are to report data more frequently—and in a timelier manner—than they have previously, and T-MSIS includes approximately 2,800 automated quality checks.[98] The T-MSIS initiative has the potential to improve CMS's ability to identify

[98] In particular, we found that the usefulness of CMS data on Medicaid is limited because of issues with completeness, accuracy, and timeliness. With regard to timeliness, we found that available data were reported up to 3 years late and were previously submitted on a quarterly basis. Under T-MSIS, data are to be reported monthly.

improper payments, help ensure beneficiaries' access to services, and improve program transparency, among other benefits.

As we reported in December 2017, implementing the T-MSIS initiative has been—and will continue to be—a multi-year effort. CMS has worked closely with states and has reached a point where nearly all states are reporting T-MSIS data. While recognizing the progress made, we noted that more work needs to be done before CMS or states can use these data for program oversight:

- All states need to report complete T-MSIS data. For our December 2017 report, we reviewed a sample of six states and found that none were reporting complete data.[99]
- T-MSIS data should be formatted in a manner that allows for state data to be compared nationally. In December 2017, we reported that state officials had expressed concerns that states did not convert their data to the T-MSIS format in the same ways, which could limit cross-state comparisons.[100]

In our December 2017 report, we recommended that CMS take steps to expedite the use of T-MSIS data, including efforts to (1) obtain complete information from all states; (2) identify and share information across states to improve data comparability; and (3) implement mechanisms by which states can collaborate on an ongoing basis to improve the completeness, comparability, and utility of T-MSIS data. We also recommended that CMS articulate a specific plan and associated time frames for using T-MSIS data for oversight.[101] The agency concurred with our recommendations, but has not yet implemented them.

Our prior work has also noted areas where other data improvements are critical to program oversight:

---

[99] The six selected states were not reporting complete data as of August 2017. See GAO, *Medicaid: Further Action* Needed *to Expedite Use of National Data for Program Oversight*, GAO-18-70 (Washington, D.C.: Dec. 8, 2017).

[100] See GAO-18-70.

[101] We concluded that absent a specific plan and time frames, CMS's ability to use these data to oversee the program, including ensuring proper payments, was limited. See GAO-18-70.

- In July 2014, we found that there was a need for data on supplemental payments that states make to individual hospitals and other providers. In particular, our findings and related recommendation from July 2014 indicate that CMS should develop a data collection strategy that ensures that states report accurate and complete data on all sources of funds used to finance the states' share of Medicaid payments.[102]
- In January 2017, we found limitations in the data CMS collects to monitor the provision of, and spending on, personal care services—services that are at a high risk for improper payments, including fraud.[103] In particular, data on the provision of personal care services were often not timely, complete, or consistent. Data on states' spending on these services were also not accurate or complete. In January 2017, we recommended that CMS improve personal care services data by (1) establishing standard reporting guidance for key data, (2) ensuring linkage between data on the provision of services and reported expenditures, (3) ensuring state compliance with reporting requirements, and (4) developing plans to use data for oversight.[104] The agency concurred with two recommendations and neither agreed nor disagreed with the other two recommendations, and has not yet implemented any.

## More Complete Fraud Risk Assessment and Better Fraud Targeting

In December 2017, we examined CMS's efforts managing fraud risks in Medicaid and compared it with our Fraud Risk Framework, which provides

---

[102] Better data on supplemental payments could also help ensure that states comply with federal requirements regarding how much local governments may contribute to the state's share of Medicaid payments. See GAO-14-627.

[103] Personal care services are key components of long-term, in-home care, providing assistance with basic activities, such as bathing, dressing, and toileting, to millions of individuals seeking to retain their independence and to age in place.

[104] See GAO, *Medicaid: CMS Needs Better Data to Monitor the Provision of and Spending on Personal Care Services,* GAO-17-169 (Washington, D.C.: Jan. 12, 2017).

a comprehensive set of key components and leading practices that serve as a guide for agency managers to use when developing efforts to combat fraud in a strategic, risk-based way.[105] This framework describes leading practices in four components: commit, assess, design and implement, and evaluate and adapt. (See Figure 6). The Fraud Reduction and Data Analytics Act of 2015, enacted in June 2016, requires the Office of Management and Budget (OMB) to establish guidelines incorporating the leading practices from our Fraud Risk Framework for federal agencies to create controls to identify and assess fraud risks, and design and implement antifraud control activities.[106] In July 2016, OMB published guidance, and among other things, this guidance affirms that managers should adhere to the leading practices identified in our Fraud Risk Framework.[107]

In a December 2017 report, we found that CMS's efforts partially aligned with our fraud risk framework. In particular, CMS had

- shown a commitment to combating fraud, in part, by establishing a dedicated entity—the Center for Program Integrity—to lead antifraud efforts, and offering and requiring antifraud training for stakeholder groups, such as providers, beneficiaries, and health-insurance plans; and
- taken steps to identify fraud risks, such as by designating specific provider types as high risk and developing associated control activities.

However, CMS had not conducted a fraud risk assessment for Medicaid, and had not designed and implemented a risk-based antifraud strategy.[108] A fraud risk assessment allows managers to fully consider fraud risks to their programs, analyze their likelihood and impact, and prioritize risks.

---

[105] See GAO, *A Framework for Managing Fraud Risks in Federal Programs*, GAO-15-593SP (Washington, D.C.: July 28, 2015).

[106] Pub. L. No. 114-186, § 3, 130 Stat. 546 (2016).

[107] Office of Management and Budget, *Management's Responsibility for Enterprise Risk Management and Internal Control*, Circular No. A-123 (Washington, D.C.: July 15, 2016).

[108] See GAO, *Medicare and Medicaid: CMS Needs* to *Fully Align Its Antifraud Efforts with the Fraud Risk Framework*, GAO-18-88 (Washington, D.C.: Dec. 5, 2017).

Managers can then design and implement a strategy with specific control activities to mitigate these fraud risks, as well as design and implement an appropriate evaluation. We concluded that through these actions, CMS could better ensure that it is addressing the full portfolio of risks and strategically targeting the most-significant fraud risks facing Medicaid. As a result, in December 2017 we made three recommendations to CMS, two of which were to conduct fraud risk assessments, and create an antifraud strategy for Medicaid, including an approach for evaluation.[109] HHS concurred with our recommendations, but has not yet implemented them.

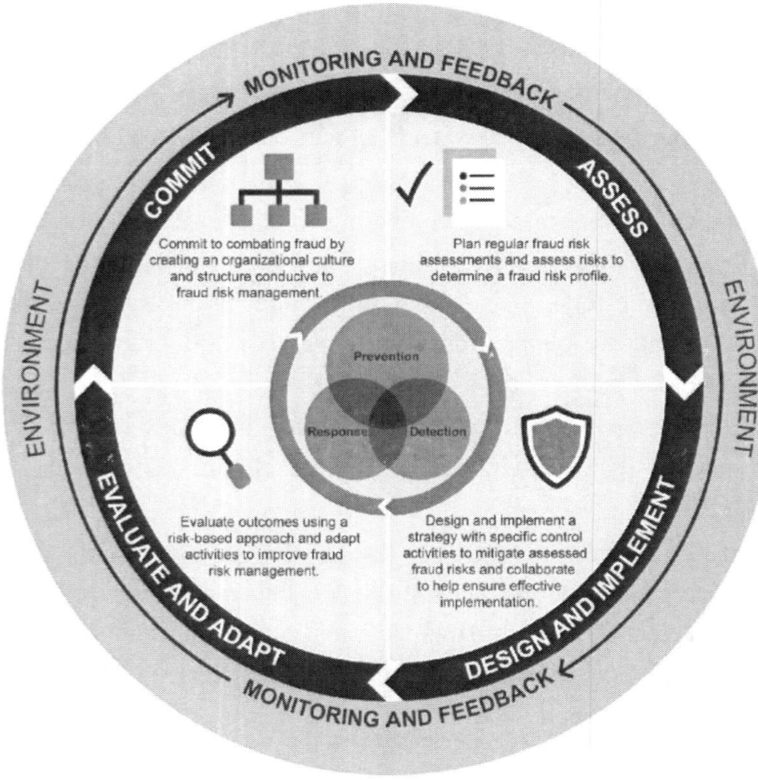


Source: GAO. | GAO-18-598T.

Figure 6. The Fraud Risk Management Framework.

[109] See GAO-18-88.

## Greater Federal-State Collaboration to Strengthen Program Oversight

The federal government and the states play important roles in reducing improper payments and overseeing the Medicaid program, including overseeing spending on Medicaid supplemental payments and demonstrations. Our prior work shows that oversight of the Medicaid program could be further improved through leveraging and coordinating program integrity efforts with state agencies, state auditors, and other partners.

### *Collaborative Audits with State Agencies*

As we have previously reported, CMS has made changes to its Medicaid program integrity efforts, including a shift to collaborative audits—in which CMS's contractors and states work in partnership to audit Medicaid providers. In March 2017, we reported that collaborative audits had identified substantial potential overpayments to providers, but barriers—such as staff burden or problems communicating with contractors—had limited their use and prevented states from seeking audits or hindered the success of audits.[110] We recommended that CMS address the barriers that limit state participation in collaborative audits, including their use in managed care delivery systems. CMS concurred with this recommendation and has taken steps to address them for a number of states, but has not yet made such changes accessible to a majority of states.

### *State Auditors and Federal Partners*

We have found that state auditors and the HHS-OIG offer additional oversight and information that can help identify program risks. To that end, we routinely coordinate our audit efforts with the state auditors and the HHS-OIG. For example, we have convened and facilitated meetings between CMS and state audit officials to discuss specific areas of concern

---

[110] See GAO, *Medicaid Program Integrity: CMS Should Build on Current Oversight Efforts by Further Enhancing Collaboration with States*, GAO-17-277 (Washington, D.C.: March 15, 2017).

in Medicaid and future opportunities for collaboration. The state auditors and CMS officials commented on the benefits of such coordination, with the state auditors noting that they can assist CMS's state program integrity reviews by identifying program risks.

State auditors also have conducted program integrity reviews to identify improper payments and deficiencies in the processes used to identify them. We believe that these reviews could provide insights into program weaknesses that CMS could learn from and potentially address nationally. Coordination also provides an opportunity for state auditors to learn methods for conducting program integrity reviews. The following are recent examples of reviews conducted:

- In 2017, the Oregon Secretary of State Audits Division found approximately 31,300 questionable payments to Coordinated Care Organizations (which receive capitated monthly payments for beneficiaries, similar to managed care organizations), based on a review of 15 months of data. In addition, the state auditor found that approximately 47,600 individuals enrolled in Oregon's Medicaid program were ineligible, equating to $88 million in avoidable expenditures.[111]
- Massachusetts' Medicaid Audit Unit's recent annual report (covering the time period from March 15, 2017, through March 14, 2018) reported that the state auditor identified more than $211 million in unallowable, questionable, duplicative, unauthorized, or potentially fraudulent billing in the program.[112]
- A 2017 report released by the Louisiana Legislative Auditor's Office stated that the office reviewed Medicaid eligibility files and

[111] State of Oregon, Secretary of State, Dennis Richardson and Oregon Audits Division Director, Kip Memmott, *Oregon Health Authority Should Improve Efforts to Detect and Prevent Improper Medicaid Payments* Report 2017- 25 (Salem, Ore.: November 2017).

[112] Commonwealth of Massachusetts, Office of the State Auditor Suzanne M. Bump, *Office of the State Auditor—Annual Report Medicaid Audit Unit, March 15, 2017-March 14, 2018* (Boston, Mass.: March 15, 2018).

claims data covering January 2011 through October 2016, and found $1.4 million in questionable duplicate payments.[113]

- In fiscal year 2017, the Mississippi Division of Medicaid reported that they recovered more than $8.6 million through various audits of medical claims paid to health care providers. The division also referred seven cases to the state's attorney general's office, in which the division had identified $3.1 million in improper billing.[114]

At a May 2018 federal and state auditor coordination meeting that we participated in, the HHS-OIG provided examples of the financial impact of its work related to improper payments, including

- one review of managed care long term services and supports that identified $717 million potential federal savings,
- three reviews of managed care payments made after beneficiaries' death that identified $18.2 million in federal funds to be recovered, and
- two reviews of managed care payments made for beneficiaries with multiple Medicaid IDs that identified $4.3 million in federal funds to be recovered.

### *Healthcare Fraud Prevention Partnership*

The Healthcare Fraud Prevention Partnership (HFPP) is an important tool to help combat Medicaid fraud. In 2012, CMS created the HFPP to share information with public and private stakeholders, and to conduct studies related to health care fraud, waste, and abuse. According to CMS, as of October 2017, the HFPP included 89 public and private partners—including Medicare—and Medicaid-related federal and state agencies, law enforcement agencies, private health insurance plans, and antifraud and other health care organizations. The HFPP has conducted studies that pool

---

[113] Louisiana Legislative Auditor, State of Louisiana, *Duplicate Payments for Medicaid Recipients with Multiple Identification Numbers* (Baton Rouge, La.: March 29, 2017).

[114] Mississippi Division of Medicaid, *Medicaid Recovers $8.6 Million in Fiscal Year 2017* (Jackson, Miss.), accessed May 29, 2018, https://medicaid.ms.gov/medicaid-recovers-8-6-million-in-fiscal-year-2017/.

and analyze multiple payers' claims data to identify providers with patterns of suspect billing across private health insurance plans. In August 2017, we reported that the partnership participants separately told us the HFPP's studies helped them identify and take action against potentially fraudulent providers and payment vulnerabilities of which they might not otherwise have been aware, and fostered both formal and informal information sharing.[115]

Chairman Johnson, Ranking Member McCaskill, and Members of the Committee, this concludes my prepared statement. I would be pleased to respond to any questions you may have.

## GAO Staff Acknowledgments

Other individuals, in addition to Carolyn L. Yocom, who made key contributions to this testimony include Leslie V. Gordon (Assistant Director), Deirdre Gleeson Brown (Analyst-in-Charge), Muriel Brown, Helen Desaulniers, Melissa Duong, Julianne Flowers, Sandra George, Giselle C. Hicks, Drew Long, Perry Parsons, Russell Voth, and Jennifer Whitworth.

[115] See GAO, *Medicare: CMS Fraud Prevention System Uses Claims Analysis to Address Fraud*, GAO-17-710 (Washington, D.C.: Aug. 30, 2017).

In: Medicaid
Editor: Alice Holt

ISBN: 978-1-53614-829-9


*Chapter 3*

# MEDICAID: CMS HAS TAKEN STEPS TO ADDRESS PROGRAM RISKS BUT FURTHER ACTIONS NEEDED TO STRENGTHEN PROGRAM INTEGRITY*

*Gene L. Dodaro*

## WHY GAO DID THIS STUDY

Medicaid, a joint federal-state health care program overseen by CMS, is a significant component of federal and state budgets, with total estimated expenditures of $596 billion in fiscal year 2017. Medicaid allows significant flexibility for states to design and implement program innovations based on their unique needs. The resulting diversity of the program and its size make the program particularly challenging to oversee at the federal level. For

* This is an edited, reformatted and augmented version of United States Government Accountability Office Testimony Before the Committee on Homeland Security and Governmental Affairs, U.S. Senate, Accessible Version, Publication No. GAO-18-687T, dated Tuesday, August 21, 2018.

example, in fiscal year 2017 estimated improper payments were $36.7 billion. Further, the Medicaid program accounted for about 26 percent of the fiscal year 2017 government-wide improper payment estimate.

This testimony focuses on the (1) major risks to the integrity of the Medicaid program, and examples of actions CMS has taken to address these risks; and (2) other actions needed to strengthen oversight of the program. This testimony draws on GAO's reports issued between November 2012 and July 2018 on the Medicaid program, and information on a program integrity strategy CMS announced in June 2018.

## What GAO Recommends

As a part of its body of work on Medicaid, GAO has made 86 recommendations to address shortcomings in oversight and suggested four matters for congressional consideration. CMS has generally agreed with these recommendations and has implemented 30 of them. GAO will continue to monitor implementation of the remaining recommendations.

## What GAO Found

GAO's work has identified three broad areas of risk to Medicaid program integrity as it reported in its June 2018 testimony before this Committee. For today's testimony, GAO provides examples of actions taken and plans by the Centers for Medicare & Medicaid Services (CMS) to address these areas of risk, and highlights additional efforts needed to strengthen program oversight.

1. *Improper payments***.** To reduce improper payments and ensure only eligible individuals enroll, CMS plans to resume audits of beneficiary eligibility determinations and conduct new types of audits starting in three states. However, given the growth in

Medicaid managed care, which was nearly half of Medicaid spending in fiscal year 2017, additional actions are needed to ensure that managed care payments are appropriate. For example, CMS still needs to establish processes to ensure that overpayments to providers are identified and accounted for by states when setting future payment rates.

2. *Supplemental payments.* Supplemental payments—which totaled $48 billion in fiscal year 2016—are payments made to providers in addition to regular, claims-based payments for specific services. Partially in response to GAO recommendations, CMS plans to issue a proposed rule in spring 2019 to establish new reporting requirements for supplemental payments. To address GAO's recommendations, the rule would need to clearly establish approval criteria and review processes to ensure these payments are economical and efficient, as well as arrange for more accurate reporting of how states are financing their share of these payments, among other things.
3. *Demonstrations.* Demonstrations—which made up one-third of Medicaid spending in fiscal year 2015—allow states and CMS to test new coverage and service delivery approaches. CMS recently limited states' ability to accrue unspent demonstration funds, resulting in an estimated $63 billion in federal savings from 2016 through 2018. Additional actions by CMS, such as ensuring demonstration budget neutrality—that demonstrations do not increase federal costs—and state evaluations of demonstrations are properly conducted, could result in significant savings and better informed policy decisions.

As reported in GAO's June 2018 testimony, GAO's prior work has also identified the following fundamental actions needed to strengthen oversight.

- Improve data. CMS's Transformed Medicaid Statistical Information System initiative has the potential to improve program oversight, but more needs to be done to collect complete and comparable data from all states.

- Implement a fraud-risk strategy. CMS established the Center for Program Integrity to lead antifraud efforts and has required antifraud training for stakeholders. However, CMS still needs to conduct a fraud risk assessment and implement a risk-based antifraud strategy for Medicaid.
- Collaborate. Increased collaboration between the federal government and the states can help reduce improper payments. State auditors are uniquely qualified to partner with CMS in its oversight of Medicaid. CMS could help improve program integrity by providing state auditors with a substantive and ongoing role in auditing state Medicaid programs.

* * *

Chairman Johnson, Ranking Member McCaskill, and Members of the Committee:

I appreciate the opportunity to be here today along with the Administrator of the Centers for Medicare & Medicaid Services (CMS) to discuss areas of risk to the Medicaid program and efforts that can help ensure the program's fiscal integrity.[116] The Administrator and I have met on two occasions to discuss the risks facing the Medicaid program, and the senior leadership teams from our agencies meet quarterly to discuss these risks, CMS's actions to address these risks, and GAO's open recommendations. I appreciate the constructive dialogue that our agencies have established on oversight of the Medicaid program.

The federal-state Medicaid program is one of the nation's largest sources of funding for medical and health-related services. In fiscal year 2017, Medicaid covered acute health care, long-term care, and other services for over 73 million low-income and medically needy individuals. In that same

[116] CMS, within the Department of Health and Human Services (HHS), oversees the Medicaid program at the federal level.

year, estimated federal and state Medicaid expenditures were $596 billion. Medicaid has been on our high-risk list since 2003, in part, because of concerns about the adequacy of fiscal oversight and the program's improper payments—including payments made for people not eligible for Medicaid and services not actually provided.[117] The Medicaid program accounted for 26.1 percent of the fiscal year 2017 government-wide improper payments estimate, or $36.7 billion.[118] Of the $36.7 billion in improper payments, $36.4 billion were overpayments and $283 million were underpayments.

The partnership between the federal government and states is a central tenet of the Medicaid program. Within broad federal requirements, states have significant flexibility to design and implement their programs based on their unique needs, resulting in 56 distinct state Medicaid programs.[119] These programs are administered at the state level and overseen at the federal level by CMS. The resulting variability of state Medicaid programs complicates federal efforts to oversee program payments and beneficiaries' access to services, making collaborative activities a necessary strategy to improving Medicaid oversight. It is critical that CMS and states leverage available federal and state resources, as dollars wasted detract from the program's ability to ensure that the individuals who rely on Medicaid—including low-income children and individuals who are elderly or disabled—are provided adequate care.

In my June 2018 testimony before this Committee, I laid out major risks to the integrity of the Medicaid program and actions needed to manage these

---

[117] See GAO, *High-Risk Series: Progress on Many High-Risk Areas, While Substantial Efforts Needed on Others*, GAO-17-317 (Washington, D.C.: Feb. 15, 2017).

[118] See GAO, Improper Payments: Actions and Guidance Could Help Address Issues and Inconsistencies in Estimation Processes, GAO-18-377 (Washington, D.C.: May 31, 2018). An improper payment is any payment that should not have been made or that was made in an incorrect amount (including overpayments and underpayments) under statutory, contractual, administrative, or other legally applicable requirements. It includes any payment to an ineligible recipient, any payment for an ineligible service, any duplicate payment, payment for services not received (except where authorized by law), and any payment that does not account for credit for applicable discounts. See 31 U.S.C. § 3321 note. Office of Management and Budget guidance also instructs agencies to report as improper payments any payments for which insufficient or no documentation is found.

[119] Medicaid programs are administered by the 50 states, the District of Columbia, American Samoa, Guam, the Commonwealth of the Northern Mariana Islands, Puerto Rico, and the U.S. Virgin Islands.

risks.[120] Today, I will provide examples of actions CMS has taken to address these major risks, and identify where additional actions are needed. Specifically, my testimony will focus on

1. major risks to the integrity of the Medicaid program, and examples of actions CMS has taken to address these risks; and
2. other actions needed to strengthen oversight of the program.

My statement is based on our large body of work examining the Medicaid program, particularly reports issued and recommendations made from November 2012 to July 2018; these reports provide further details on our scope and methodology. (A list of related reports is included at the end of this statement.) It is also based on information from CMS's June 2018 planned program integrity strategy, as well as interviews with and documents from CMS officials. We conducted all of the work on which this statement is based in accordance with generally accepted government auditing standards. Those standards require that we plan and perform the audit to obtain sufficient, appropriate evidence to provide a reasonable basis for our findings and conclusions based on our audit objectives. We believe that the evidence obtained provides a reasonable basis for our findings and conclusions based on our audit objectives. We obtained agency views on the information in this statement and have incorporated comments as appropriate.

## BACKGROUND

Among health care programs, Medicaid is the largest as measured by enrollment and the second largest as measured by expenditures, second only to Medicare. The CMS Office of the Actuary projected that Medicaid spending would grow at an average rate of 5.7 percent per year, from fiscal

---

[120] See GAO, *Medicaid: Actions Needed to Mitigate Billions in Improper Payments and Program Integrity Risks*, GAO-18-598T (Washington, D.C.: June 27, 2018).

years 2016 to 2025, with projected Medicaid expenditures reaching $958 billion by fiscal year 2025.[121] This projected growth in expenditures reflects both expected increases in expenditures per enrollee and in levels of Medicaid enrollment. Beneficiaries with disabilities and those who are elderly constitute the highest per enrollee expenditures, which are projected to increase by almost 50 percent from fiscal year 2016 to 2025. Medicaid enrollment is also expected to grow by as many as 13.2 million newly eligible adults by 2025—as additional states may expand their Medicaid programs to cover certain low-income adults under the Patient Protection and Affordable Care Act (PPACA).[122] (See figure 1.)

Under the federal-state partnership, CMS provides oversight and technical assistance for the Medicaid program, and states are responsible for administering their respective programs' day-to-day operations— including determining eligibility, enrolling individuals and providers, and adjudicating claims—within broad federal requirements. Federal oversight includes ensuring that the design and operation of state programs meet federal requirements and that Medicaid payments are made appropriately. Joint financing of Medicaid is also a fixture of the federal-state partnership, with the federal government matching most state Medicaid expenditures using a statutory formula known as the federal medical assistance percentage, that is based, in part, on each state's per capita income in relation to the national average per capita income.

[121] Data are from the most recently issued CMS actuarial report. See Centers for Medicare & Medicaid Services, Office of the Actuary, *2016 Actuarial Report on the Financial Outlook for Medicaid* (Washington, D.C.: 2016).

[122] The Patient Protection and Affordable Care Act, enacted on March 23, 2010, permits states to expand their Medicaid programs to cover nonelderly, nonpregnant adults who are not eligible for Medicare, and whose income does not exceed 133 percent of the federal poverty level. Because of the way the limit is calculated, using what is known as an "income disregard," the level is effectively 138 percent of the federal poverty level. Pub. L. No. 111-148, 124 Stat. 119 (2010), as amended by the Health Care and Education Reconciliation Act of 2010 (HCERA), Pub. L. No. 111-152, 124 Stat. 1029 (2010).

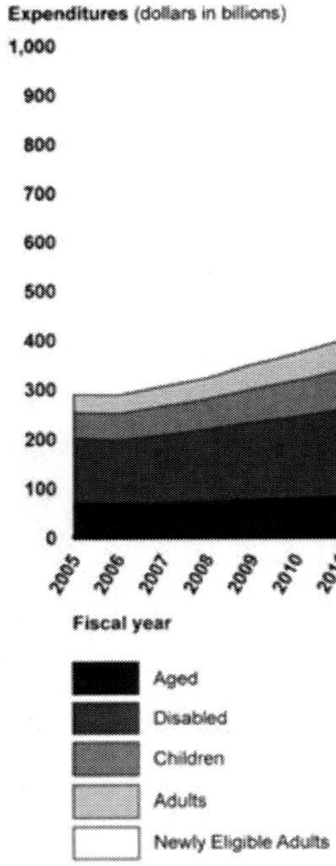


Source: GAO analysis of 2016 Actuarial Report on the Financial Outlook for Medicaid. | GAO-18-687T.

Note: Data after fiscal year 2012 are projected expenditures.

Figure 1. Growth Trends in Total Medicaid Spending by Eligibility Group.

States have flexibility in determining how their Medicaid benefits are delivered. For example, states may (1) contract with managed care organizations (MCO) to provide a specific set of Medicaid-covered services to beneficiaries and pay the organizations a set amount, generally on a per beneficiary per month basis; (2) pay health care providers for each service they provide on a fee-for-service (FFS) basis; or (3) rely on a combination of both delivery systems.[123] Managed care continues to be a growing

[123] CMS has also been developing and testing a variety of value-based payment models, under which physicians and other providers are paid and responsible for the care of a beneficiary for a long period of time and accountable for the quality and efficiency of the care provided. Examples of these models include accountable care organizations—groups of physicians and other health care providers who voluntarily work together to provide coordinated care—and bundled payment models, which provide a "bundled" payment intended to cover the multiple services beneficiaries receive during an episode of care for certain health conditions, such as hip replacements, congestive heart failure, and pregnancy.

component of the Medicaid program. In fiscal year 2017, expenditures for managed care were $280 billion, representing almost half of total program expenditures, compared with 42 percent in fiscal year 2015. Another growing component of Medicaid spending is supplemental payments to providers—such as local government hospitals and other providers—that are in addition to the regular, claims-based payments to providers for specific services. Supplemental payments have increased over the last decade and totaled more than $48 billion in 2016.

**Data Table for Figure 1: Growth Trends in Total Medicaid Spending by Eligibility Group**

| Fiscal year | Aged | Blind/Disabled Children | | Adults | Newly Eligible Adults |
|---|---|---|---|---|---|
| 2005 | 70 | 131 | 51 | 36 | 0 |
| 2006 | 68 | 129 | 53 | 37 | 0 |
| 2007 | 68 | 138 | 58 | 40 | 0 |
| 2008 | 72 | 146 | 60 | 43 | 0 |
| 2009 | 74 | 158 | 66 | 50 | 0 |
| 2010 | 76 | 167 | 72 | 55 | 0 |
| 2011 | 80 | 177 | 78 | 62 | 0 |
| 2012 | 81 | 178 | 77 | 62 | 0 |
| 2013 | 82 | 192 | 83 | 67 | 0 |
| 2014 | 80 | 194 | 88 | 71 | 24 |
| 2015 | 80 | 205 | 95 | 76 | 58 |
| 2016 | 82 | 213 | 97 | 80 | 66 |
| 2017 | 87 | 222 | 101 | 85 | 67 |
| 2018 | 94 | 234 | 107 | 91 | 67 |
| 2019 | 101 | 250 | 114 | 97 | 71 |
| 2020 | 109 | 264 | 122 | 103 | 76 |
| 2021 | 116 | 280 | 129 | 110 | 81 |
| 2022 | 126 | 297 | 138 | 116 | 87 |
| 2023 | 135 | 315 | 146 | 123 | 91 |
| 2024 | 145 | 334 | 154 | 131 | 97 |
| 2025 | 156 | 355 | 163 | 138 | 103 |

States also have the flexibility to innovate outside of many of Medicaid's otherwise applicable requirements through Medicaid demonstrations approved under section 1115 of the Social Security Act.[124] These demonstrations allow states to test new approaches to coverage and to improve quality and access, or generate savings or efficiencies. For example, under demonstrations, states have

- extended coverage to certain populations,
- provided services not otherwise eligible for federal matching funds, and
- made incentive payments to providers for delivery system improvements.

As of November 2016, nearly three-quarters of states had CMS-approved demonstrations. In fiscal year 2015, total spending under demonstrations represented a third of all Medicaid spending nationwide. (See figure 2.)

**Data Table a Figure 2. Total Expenditures under Medicaid Section 1115 Demonstrations, Fiscal Years 2005, 2010, and 2015**

| Fiscal year | Expenditures (dollars in billions) |
|---|---|
| 2005 | 42 |
| 2010 | 65 |
| 2015 | 165 |

[124] Under section 1115 of the Social Security Act, the Secretary of Health and Human Services may waive certain Medicaid requirements and approve new types of expenditures that would not otherwise be eligible for federal Medicaid matching funds for experimental, pilot, or demonstration projects that, in the Secretary's judgment, are likely to promote Medicaid objectives. See 42 U.S.C. § 1315(a). The Secretary has delegated the approval and administration of Medicaid section 1115 demonstrations to CMS, which requires that such demonstrations be budget neutral to the federal government; that is, the federal government should spend no more for Medicaid under a state's demonstration than it would have spent without the demonstration. There are other types of waivers that states can apply for and use, including those approved under section 1915(c) of the Social Security Act, which authorizes the Secretary of Health and Human Services to waive requirements that states provide home and community based services that they would otherwise need to meet in the absence of the waiver.

**Data Table b Figure 2. Total Expenditures under Medicaid Section 1115 Demonstrations, Fiscal Years 2005, 2010, and 2015**

| Fiscal year | Demonstrations as a share of total Medicaid spending (percentage) |
|---|---|
| 2005 | 14 |
| 2010 | 17 |
| 2015 | 32 |

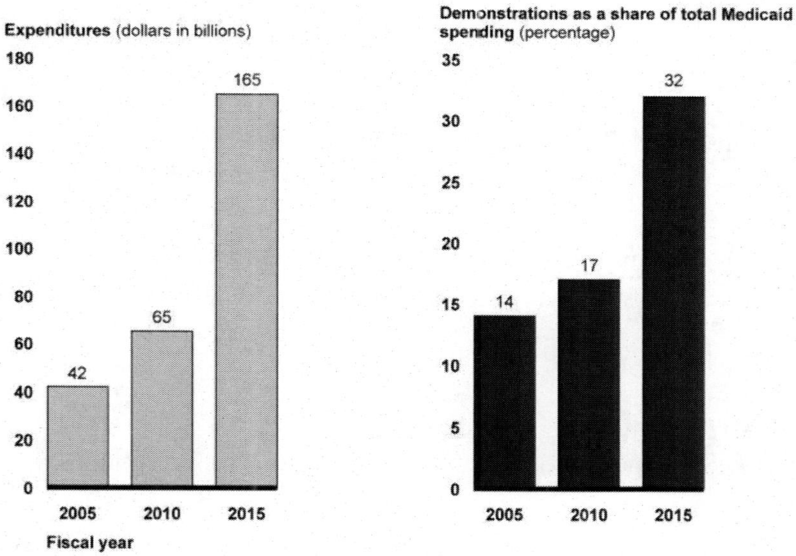


Source: GAO analysis of Centers for Medicare and Medicaid Services demonstration expenditures data. | GAO-18-687T.

Figure 2. Total Expenditures under Medicaid Section 1115 Demonstrations, Fiscal Years 2005, 2010, and 2015.

# Additional Actions Could Enhance CMS's Efforts to Address Major Risks to the Medicaid Program

In our June 2018 testimony before this Committee, we identified three broad areas of risk to Medicaid program integrity. These risk areas are improper payments, supplemental payments, and demonstrations. CMS has taken or plans to take specific steps to address these risks, but additional actions are still needed to manage these risks and strengthen oversight of the Medicaid program, as we have recommended previously.

## Improper Payments

In fiscal year 2017, the estimate of improper payments was 10.1 percent of Medicaid spending, or $36.7 billion.[125] CMS annually computes the Medicaid improper payment estimate as a weighted average of states' improper payment estimates for three component parts—fee-for-service, managed care, and beneficiary eligibility determinations. The improper payment estimate for each component is developed under its own methodology within CMS's Payment Error Rate Measurement (PERM) program, with each having different improper payment estimates and oversight concerns.

### *Fee-for-Service*

The FFS component of improper payments measures errors in a sample of FFS claims, which are records of services provided and the amount the Medicaid program paid for these services. For the majority of sampled FFS claims, the PERM review contractor performs a medical review, which includes a review of the medical documentation to determine errors that do not meet federal and state policies, such as medically unnecessary services, diagnosis coding errors, and policy violations.[126]

In fiscal year 2017, CMS reported a FFS improper payment estimate of 12.9 percent, or $25 billion. CMS's analysis of improper payments in FFS notes that many claims deemed improper lacked adequate provider

---

[125] Since 2016, Medicaid has exceeded the 10 percent criterion set in statute by the Improper Payments Elimination and Recovery Act of 2010. When an agency is determined to not be in compliance with one or more of the Improper Payments Elimination and Recovery Act criteria by its Inspector General, it must submit a plan to Congress describing the actions it will take to come into compliance.

[126] All FFS claims are also subject to a data processing review, which includes a verification of provider eligibility, beneficiary information, and that the payment for a covered service was accurately calculated and paid.

documentation, such as not having national provider identification numbers on claims.[127] Our work has also detailed concerns related to the accuracy of provider enrollment, as well as broader concerns regarding the data available to CMS to ensure proper oversight of providers.[128] According to information provided by CMS about its June 2018 program integrity strategy, the agency plans to assist states with screening Medicaid providers, as well as conduct Medicaid provider education to reduce erroneous billing.

However, we have previously noted that without better data, CMS may not be able to identify patterns that indicate inappropriate provider billing. Our prior recommendations in this area have focused on data improvements; CMS has agreed with these recommendations and we are tracking their implementation. Our concerns about provider oversight, however, are longstanding and will require significant and consistent efforts on the part of CMS and the states. Addressing our concerns would require efforts to develop systems that can accurately track and screen providers, as well as ensure that any ineligible providers are appropriately excluded and that such exclusions are communicated across states.

### *Managed Care*

The managed care component measures errors that occur in the payments that state Medicaid agencies make to MCOs on behalf of enrollees. The PERM assesses whether any payments made to the MCOs were in amounts different than those the state Medicaid agency is contractually required to pay, which are approved by CMS. In contrast to the FFS component, the managed care component of the PERM includes

---

[127] [12]Specifically, 46.6 percent of estimated Medicaid improper payments in fiscal year 2017 were caused by non-compliance with provider screening and national provider identification requirements.

[128] See GAO, *Medicaid: CMS Needs Better Data to Monitor the Provision of and Spending on Personal Care Services*, GAO-17-169 (Washington, D.C.: Jan. 12, 2017) and *Medicaid: Program Oversight Hampered by Data Challenges, Underscoring Need for Continued Improvement*, GAO-17-173 (Washington, D.C.: Jan. 6, 2017). Personal care services provide assistance to beneficiaries of all ages who have limited ability to care for themselves because of physical, developmental, or intellectual disabilities. Personal care services assist beneficiaries with activities of daily living such as bathing, dressing, and toileting.

neither a medical review of services delivered to enrollees, nor reviews of MCO records or data.

In fiscal year 2017, CMS reported a managed care improper payment estimate of 0.3 percent or $500 million, an estimate that does not determine whether MCO payments to providers were for services that were medically necessary, actually provided, accurately billed and delivered by eligible providers, or whether the MCO costs were allowable and appropriate. We have previously recommended that CMS take steps to mitigate the program risks that are not measured in the PERM, which could include actions such as revising the PERM methodology or focusing additional audit resources on managed care. CMS agreed with our recommendation and information on its June 2018 program integrity strategy mentions plans to check whether MCOs' reported financial statements accurately reflect the services provided. CMS plans to compare encounter claims to the services provided by MCOs. It also noted plans to implement reviews of high-risk vulnerabilities that we and the Department of Health and Human Services' (HHS) Office of the Inspector General (HHS-OIG) have identified. We will review the particulars of how CMS plans to implement these actions when they become available.

In July 2018, we reported on key payment risks in Medicaid managed care and found that, while CMS has taken some steps to improve program integrity in managed care—including strengthening regulations, and beginning to include managed care in the monitoring and auditing process—these efforts remain incomplete. For example, CMS had not developed a process to help ensure that overpayments to providers are identified by the states. We made three recommendations including that CMS ensure states account for overpayments in setting future MCO payment rates. CMS agreed with our recommendations.

### *Beneficiary Eligibility*

The beneficiary eligibility component of improper payments measures errors in state determinations of whether enrollees meet categorical and financial criteria for receipt of benefits under the Medicaid program. The eligibility component assesses determinations for both FFS and managed care enrollees. Prior to 2014, to assess improper payments attributable to erroneous eligibility determinations, the PERM relied on state-conducted eligibility reviews that are reported to CMS. Since 2014, the beneficiary eligibility component estimate has been set at 3.1 percent. This represents $11.3 billion of improper payments estimated for 2017.

Beginning in the 2019 reporting year, CMS plans to resume improper payment estimates for eligibility determinations, but these reviews will be performed by CMS contractors, not states. Our prior work has identified gaps in CMS's efforts to ensure that only eligible individuals are enrolled in Medicaid, and that Medicaid expenditures for enrollees—particularly those eligible as a result of the PPACA expansion—are matched appropriately by the federal government.[129] CMS concurred with these recommendations and has taken action to establish a more rigorous approach for verifying financial and nonfinancial information needed to determine Medicaid beneficiaries' eligibility.

Information on CMS's June 2018 program integrity strategy mentions plans to initiate audits of state beneficiary eligibility determinations in three states previously reviewed by the HHS-OIG (California, Kentucky and New York). These audits will include an assessment of the impact of changes to state eligibility policy as a result of Medicaid expansion; for example, CMS plans to review whether beneficiaries were found eligible for the correct Medicaid eligibility category. However, our recommendations from October 2015 remain unimplemented and—without knowing the results of the 2019 beneficiary eligibility estimates and details of CMS's actions—it remains unclear whether CMS policies and actions will improve oversight of states' eligibility determinations.

---

[129] See, for example, GAO, Medicaid: Additional Efforts Needed to Ensure that State Spending is Appropriately Matched with Federal Funds GAO-16-53 (Washington, D.C.: Oct 16, 2015); and Medicaid: Additional Actions Needed to Help Improve Provider and Beneficiary Fraud Controls GAO-15-313 (Washington, D.C.: May 14, 2015).

## Supplemental Payments

In our June 2018 testimony before this Committee, we described several concerns related to supplemental payments, which are payments made to providers—such as local government hospitals and other providers—that are in addition to the regular, claims-based payments made to providers.[130] Supplemental payments have been growing and totaled more than $48 billion in 2016. According to CMS officials, CMS plans to take steps to address program risks associated with supplemental payments. For example, CMS officials indicated that it anticipates issuing a proposed rule in early 2019 that would establish new reporting requirements for supplemental payments.[131] We will examine the rule, once finalized to determine the extent to which it addresses the program risks we have identified including, for example, the need for

- more complete and accurate reporting on the sources of funds states use to finance their share of Medicaid payments;
- criteria, data, and a review process to ensure that certain supplemental payments are economical and efficient; and
- written guidance clarifying CMS's policy that requires a link between the distribution of supplemental payments and the provision of Medicaid-covered services.

## Demonstration Programs

Demonstration programs, which comprised about one-third of total Medicaid expenditures in 2015, can be a powerful tool for states and CMS

---

[130] See, for example, GAO, Medicaid: Federal Guidance Needed to Address Concerns about Distribution of Supplemental Payments, GAO-16-108 (Washington, D.C.: Feb. 5, 2016); and Medicaid: CMS Oversight of Provider Payments Is Hampered by Limited Data and Unclear Policy, GAO-15-322 (Washington, D.C.: April 10, 2015). Also, see GAO-18-598T.

[131] See also, Office of Management and Budget, Medicaid Supplemental Payment and Accountability, Spring 2018 Unified Agenda of Regulatory and Deregulatory Actions, (CMS-2392-P), RIN 0938-AT50, see https://www.reginfo.gov/public/do/eAgendaViewRule?pubId=201804&RIN=0938-AT50 (accessed July 27, 2018).

to test new approaches to providing coverage and delivering services that could reduce costs and improve outcomes. However, our prior work has identified several concerns related to demonstrations, including the need to ensure that (1) demonstrations meet the policy requirements of budget neutrality—that is, they must not increase federal costs—and (2) evaluations are used to assess whether demonstrations are having their intended effects.[132]

We have also identified a number of questionable methods used to establish spending limits for demonstration programs, and CMS has taken important steps to improve oversight of spending on demonstrations and address some of the concerns we have raised. CMS policy limits demonstration spending to the costs estimated to have occurred without the demonstration. In our prior work, we identified a number of questionable methods and assumptions that CMS permitted states to use when estimating these costs.[133] Under a policy implemented in 2016, CMS restricted states' ability to accrue unspent funds—the difference between estimated costs and demonstration spending—for each year a demonstration operates, and reduced the amount of unspent funds that states can carry forward to new demonstrations. CMS estimated that this policy reduced total demonstration spending limits by $109 billion for 2016 through 2018, the federal share of which was $62.9 billion. This policy change reduces the effect, but does not specifically address all, of the questionable methods that we have identified regarding how CMS sets demonstration spending limits.[134] Additional actions that address states' methods of estimating costs could result in

[132] See, for example, GAO, Medicaid Demonstrations: Evaluations Yielded Limited Results, Underscoring Need for Changes to Federal Policies and Procedures, GAO-18-220 (Washington, D.C.: Jan 19, 2018); and Medicaid Demonstrations: Federal Action Needed to Improve Oversight of Spending, GAO-17-312 (Washington, D.C.: April 3, 2017). Also, see GAO-18-598T.

[133] See, for example, GAO, Medicaid Demonstration Waivers: Recent HHS Approvals Continue to Raise Cost and Oversight Concerns, GAO-08-87 (Washington, D.C.: Jan. 31, 2008).

[134] For example, CMS did not ensure budget neutrality in its approval of a demonstration that involved using premium assistance to purchase private coverage. The CMS-approved spending limit was based, in part, on hypothetical costs that were significantly higher than they would have been under the traditional Medicaid program, and CMS did not request any data to support these assumptions. See GAO, *Medicaid Demonstrations: HHS's Approval Process for Arkansas's Medicaid Expansion Waiver Raises Cost Concerns*, GAO-14-689R (Washington, D.C.: Aug. 8, 2014).

significant savings. For example, as we have previously reported, CMS continues to need written guidance on the methodologies for demonstrating budget neutrality and updates to policies to reflect the actual criteria and processes CMS uses to develop and approve demonstration spending limits.[135]

In a January 2018 report, we also raised concerns about state-led and federal evaluations of demonstration programs, particularly with regard to how results from these evaluations may inform policy decisions. We identified gaps in reported results from state-led evaluations that were due, in part, to CMS requiring final, comprehensive evaluation reports after the expiration of the demonstrations rather than at the end of each 3- to 5-year demonstration cycle. We also found that evaluations of federal demonstrations led by CMS have been limited due to data challenges and a lack of transparent reporting. We recommended that CMS (1) establish written procedures for requiring final evaluation reports at the end of each demonstration cycle, (2) issue criteria for when it will allow limited evaluations of demonstrations, and (3) establish a policy for publicly releasing findings from federal evaluations of demonstrations. In April 2018, HHS reported that CMS had begun developing and piloting procedures and criteria related to these recommendations, and we will continue to monitor CMS's progress in this area.

## Improving Data, Implementing a Fraud-Risk Strategy, and Increasing Collaboration Would Further Strengthen Medicaid Oversight

Across our body of work, we have made 86 recommendations to CMS and suggested 4 matters for congressional consideration to strengthen oversight of the Medicaid program, particularly from reports issued from November 2012 through July 2018. CMS has generally agreed with these

---

[135] See, GAO-18-598T.

recommendations and has implemented 30 of them to date. Among the open recommendations, opportunities exist for CMS to fundamentally strengthen program oversight by improving data about Medicaid's performance, implementing a strategy to address the risk of fraud, and strengthening federal-state collaboration.

## Improving Data

CMS's oversight of the Medicaid program relies heavily on state-reported data on multiple aspects of the program, including expenditures and service utilization. However, our work has demonstrated how the lack of timely, accurate, and comparable data has affected CMS's ability to ensure proper payments, assess beneficiaries' access to services, and oversee states' financing strategies. As part of its efforts to address longstanding data concerns, CMS has taken steps toward developing a reliable national repository for Medicaid data, most notably the Transformed Medicaid Statistical Information System (T-MSIS). Through T-MSIS, CMS has said that

- it will collect detailed information on Medicaid beneficiaries—such as their citizenship, immigration, and disability status—as well as any expanded diagnosis and procedure codes associated with their treatments; and
- states are to report data more frequently—and in a timelier manner— than they have previously.[136]

---

[136] In particular, we found that the usefulness of CMS data on Medicaid is limited because of issues with completeness, accuracy, and timeliness. With regard to timeliness, we found that available data were reported up to 3 years late and were previously submitted on a quarterly basis. Under T-MSIS, data are to be electronically transmitted to CMS on a monthly basis.

Implementing the T-MSIS initiative has been a significant, multi-year effort. CMS has worked closely with states and has reached a point where all states, the District of Columbia, and Puerto Rico are reporting T-MSIS data. The T-MSIS initiative has the potential to improve CMS's ability to identify improper payments, help ensure beneficiaries' access to services, and improve program transparency, among other benefits. In addition, CMS noted as part of its June 2018 program integrity strategy that one of its priorities is to ensure that Medicaid data are accurate and complete. CMS also noted that the agency has an ongoing goal to use advanced analytics to improve Medicaid eligibility and payment data in TMSIS and use these data for program integrity purposes.

As we reported in December 2017, CMS has made progress toward implementing T-MSIS, but more work needs to be done before the agency or states can use these data for program oversight.[137] For example, we recommended in our December 2017 report that CMS take steps to expedite the use of T-MSIS data, including efforts to obtain complete and comparable data from all states. We also recommended that CMS articulate a specific plan and associated time frames for using T-MSIS data for oversight. The agency concurred with our recommendations, and has taken some steps but has not fully implemented them. For example, the agency reported in March 2018 that it has developed a database on data quality findings, which could be used to identify solutions for common problems across states. HHS stated that it has begun to develop a data quality scorecard for T-MSIS users, which aggregates data quality findings in a user-friendly tool. HHS stated that it will (1) continue to work to obtain complete T-MSIS information from all states; (2) take additional steps to share information across states on TMSIS data limitations; and (3) implement ways for states to collaborate regarding T-MSIS. We will continue to monitor CMS's efforts to improve its data systems and their use for oversight.

---

[137] See GAO, *Medicaid: Further Action Needed to Expedite Use of National Data for Program Oversight*, GAO-18-70 (Washington, D.C.: Dec. 8, 2017).

## Implementing a Fraud-Risk Strategy

As we reported in December 2017, CMS had taken steps to manage fraud risks facing Medicaid.[138] In that report we determined that CMS had shown commitment to combating fraud, in part, by establishing a dedicated entity—the Center for Program Integrity—to lead antifraud efforts, and offering and requiring antifraud training for stakeholder groups, such as providers, beneficiaries, and health insurance plans.[139] We identified training as a way to help CMS further create a culture of integrity and compliance, and recommended that CMS provide and require fraud-awareness training to its employees. In response to this recommendation, CMS officials stated in August 2018 that the agency has developed a training video related to fraud, and is developing annual training for all CMS employees on fraud, waste, and abuse. We will continue to monitor the implementation of this recommendation.

Additionally, in our December 2017 report, we determined that CMS had taken steps to identify some fraud risks through several control activities that target areas the agency has designated as higher risk within Medicaid. However, we found that CMS had not conducted a fraud risk assessment or designed and implemented a risk-based antifraud strategy for Medicaid. A fraud risk assessment allows managers to fully consider fraud risks to their programs, analyze their likelihood and impact, and prioritize risks. Managers can then design and implement a strategy with specific control activities to mitigate these fraud risks, as well as design and implement an appropriate evaluation. We identified a significant opportunity for CMS to organize and focus its antifraud and program integrity activities and related resources. We recommended that CMS conduct a fraud risk assessment and create an antifraud strategy for Medicaid, including an approach for evaluation. CMS concurred with our recommendations. CMS officials stated they are exploring how to apply the fraud risk framework to the Medicaid

---

[138] GAO, *Medicare and Medicaid: CMS Needs to Fully Align Its Antifraud Efforts with the Fraud Risk Framework*, GAO-18-88 (Washington, D.C.: Dec. 5, 2017).

[139] Fraud involves obtaining something of value through willful misrepresentation.

program more broadly; however, the agency has not yet implemented these recommendations.

## Strengthening Federal-State Collaboration

The federal government and the states, together, play important roles in reducing improper payments and overseeing the Medicaid program. Our prior work has shown that oversight of the Medicaid program could be further improved through leveraging and coordinating program integrity efforts with state agencies, state auditors, and other partners. Given their roles and responsibilities—which can include carrying out or overseeing their state's single audits—state auditors are uniquely positioned to help CMS in its oversight of state Medicaid programs.[140] Through their program integrity reviews, state auditors have identified improper payments in the Medicaid program and deficiencies in the processes used to identify them. Some examples of the state auditors' work include the following:

- In 2017, the Oregon Secretary of State Audits Division found approximately 31,300 questionable payments to Coordinated Care Organizations (which receive capitated monthly payments for beneficiaries, similar to MCOs), based on a review of 15 months of data. In addition, the state auditor found that approximately 47,600

[140] Organizations based in the United States with expenditures of federal funding of $500,000 or more ($750,000 or more for fiscal years beginning on or after December 26, 2014) within the organization's fiscal year are required to send an audit report to the Office of Management and Budget (OMB), in accordance with the Single Audit Act, as amended, and OMB implementing guidance. See 31 U.S.C. §§ 7501-7507; 2 C.F.R., pt. 200, subpt. F. (2017) (as added by 78 Fed. Reg. 78590, 78608 (Dec. 26, 2013)). A single audit consists of (1) an audit and opinions on the fair presentation of the financial statements and the schedule of expenditures of Federal awards; (2) gaining an understanding of and testing internal control over financial reporting, and the entity's compliance with laws, regulations, and contract or grant provisions that have a direct and material effect on certain federal programs (i.e., the program requirements); and (3) an audit and an opinion on compliance with applicable program requirements for certain federal programs.

individuals enrolled in Oregon's Medicaid program were ineligible, equating to $88 million in avoidable expenditures.[141]

- Massachusetts' Medicaid Audit Unit's recent annual report (covering the time period from March 15, 2017 through March 14, 2018) reported that the state auditor identified more than $211 million in unallowable, questionable, duplicative, unauthorized, or potentially fraudulent billing in the program.[142]
- A 2017 report released by the Louisiana Legislative Auditor's Office stated that the office reviewed Medicaid eligibility files and claims data covering January 2011 through October 2016, and found $1.4 million in questionable duplicate payments.[143]
- In fiscal year 2017, the Mississippi Division of Medicaid reported that it recovered more than $8.6 million through various audits of medical claims paid to health care providers. The division also referred seven cases to the state's attorney general's office, in which the division had identified $3.1 million in improper billing.[144]

Many state auditors are uniquely positioned to help CMS and state Medicaid agencies identify program risks and provide additional oversight of the program. These auditors have detailed knowledge of and experience with auditing their state Medicaid programs, including managed care organizations, as well as Medicaid financial and data systems. We have made recommendations to CMS regarding improving its capacity to audit Medicaid providers and MCOs. As such, CMS could help improve program

---

[141] State of Oregon, Secretary of State, Dennis Richardson and Oregon Audits Division Director, Kip Memmott, *Oregon Health Authority Should Improve Efforts to Detect and Prevent Improper Medicaid Payments,* Report 2017- 25 (Salem, Ore.: November 2017).

[142] Commonwealth of Massachusetts, Office of the State Auditor Suzanne M. Bump, *Office of the State Auditor—Annual Report Medicaid Audit Unit, March 15, 2017-March 14, 2018* (Boston, Mass.: March 15, 2018).

[143] Louisiana Legislative Auditor, State of Louisiana, *Duplicate Payments for Medicaid Recipients with Multiple Identification Numbers Louisiana Department of Health* (Baton Rouge, La.: March 29, 2017).

[144] Mississippi Division of Medicaid, *Medicaid Recovers $8.6 Million in Fiscal Year 2017* (Jackson, Miss.), accessed May 29, 2018, https://medicaid.ms.gov/medicaid-recovers-8-6-million-in-fiscal-year-2017/.

integrity by providing state auditors with a substantive and ongoing role in auditing their state Medicaid programs.

We will continue to monitor CMS's efforts to strengthen its oversight of Medicaid and its progress in addressing our open recommendations.

Chairman Johnson, Ranking Member McCaskill, and Members of the Committee, this concludes my prepared statement. I would be pleased to respond to any questions you may have.

## GAO Staff Acknowledgments

Other individuals, in addition to Carolyn L. Yocom, who made key contributions to this testimony include William Black (Assistant Director), Deirdre Brown, Kristin Ekelund, Mary Giffin, Leslie V. Gordon, Drew Long, Vikki Porter, Russell Voth, and Jennifer Whitworth.

In: Medicaid
Editor: Alice Holt
ISBN: 978-1-53614-829-9


*Chapter 4*

# MEDICAID: CMS NEEDS TO BETTER TARGET RISKS TO IMPROVE OVERSIGHT OF EXPENDITURES*

*United States Government Accountability Office*

## ABBREVIATIONS

| | |
|---|---|
| CMS | Centers for Medicare & Medicaid Services |
| FMAP | Federal Medical Assistance Percentage |
| FMR | Financial Management Review |
| HHS | Department of Health and Human Services |
| IHS | Indian Health Service |
| PPACA | Patient Protection and Affordable Care Act |

* This is an edited, reformatted and augmented Accessible Version of United States Government Accountability Office Report to Congressional Requesters, Publication No. GAO-18-564, dated August 2018.

## WHY GAO DID THIS STUDY

Medicaid has grown by over 50 percent over the last decade, with about $370 billion in federal spending in fiscal year 2017. CMS is responsible for assuring that expenditures— reported quarterly by states—are consistent with Medicaid requirements and matched with the correct amount of federal funds. CMS's review of reported expenditures has become increasingly complex due to variation in states' Medicaid programs and an increasing number of different matching rates.

GAO was asked to examine CMS's oversight of state-reported Medicaid expenditures. In this chapter, GAO examined how CMS assures that (1) expenditures are supported and consistent with requirements; and (2) the correct federal matching rates were applied to expenditures subject to a higher match. GAO also examined the financial impact of resolved errors. GAO reviewed documentation for the most recently completed quarterly reviews by 3 of CMS's 10 regional offices for six states that varied by Medicaid program expenditures and design. GAO also reviewed policies, procedures, and data on resolved errors; and interviewed CMS and state officials. GAO assessed CMS's oversight processes against federal standards for internal control.

## WHAT GAO RECOMMENDS

GAO is making three recommendations, including that CMS improve its risk-based targeting of oversight efforts and resources, and clarify related internal guidance. The Department of Health and Human Services concurred with these recommendations.

## WHAT GAO FOUND

The Centers for Medicare & Medicaid Services (CMS), which oversees Medicaid, has various review processes in place to assure that expenditures reported by states are supported and consistent with Medicaid requirements. The agency also has processes to review that the correct federal matching rates were applied to expenditures receiving a higher than standard federal matching rate, which can include certain types of services and populations. These processes collectively have had a considerable federal financial benefit, with CMS resolving errors that reduced federal spending by over $5.1 billion in fiscal years 2014 through 2017.

However, GAO identified weaknesses in how CMS targets its resources to address risks when reviewing whether expenditures are supported and consistent with requirements.

- CMS devotes similar levels of staff resources to review expenditures despite differing levels of risk across states. For example, the number of staff reviewing California's expenditures—which represent 15 percent of federal Medicaid spending—is similar to the number reviewing Arkansas' expenditures, which represents 1 percent of federal Medicaid spending.
- CMS cancelled in-depth financial management reviews in 17 out of 51 instances over the last 5 years. These reviews target expenditures considered by CMS to be at risk of not meeting program requirements.

CMS told GAO that resource constraints contributed to both weaknesses. However, the agency has not completed a comprehensive assessment of risk to (1) determine whether oversight resources are adequate and (2) focus on the most significant areas of risk. Absent such an assessment, CMS is missing an opportunity to identify errors in reported expenditures that could result in substantial savings to the Medicaid program.

GAO also found limitations in CMS's processes for reviewing expenditures that receive a higher federal matching rate.

- Internal guidance for examining variances in these expenditures was unclear, and not all reviewers in the three CMS regional offices

GAO reviewed were investigating significant variances in quarter-to-quarter expenditures.

- Review procedures for expenditures for individuals newly eligible for Medicaid under the Patient Protection and Affordable Care Act were not tailored to different risk levels among states. For example, in its reviews of a sample of claims for this population, CMS reviewed claims for the same number of enrollees—30—in California as for Arkansas, even though California had 10 times the number of newly eligible enrollees as Arkansas.

Without clear internal guidance and better targeting of risks in its review procedures for expenditures receiving higher matching rates, CMS may overpay states.

* * *

August 6, 2018

The Honorable Orrin G. Hatch
Chairman
Committee on Finance United States Senate

The Honorable Greg Walden
Chairman
Committee on Energy and Commerce House of Representatives

The Honorable Michael C. Burgess
Chairman
Subcommittee on Health
Committee on Energy and Commerce
House of Representatives

The Honorable Fred Upton
House of Representatives

Over the last decade, Medicaid—a joint, federal-state program that finances health care coverage for low-income and medically needy populations—has increased by over 50 percent, both in terms of enrollment and cost. In fiscal year 2017, Medicaid covered an estimated 73.5 million individuals at an estimated cost of $596 billion, including about $369 billion in federal spending.[145] Federal projections indicate that those costs will continue to grow.[146]

The Centers for Medicare & Medicaid Services (CMS), the agency within the Department of Health and Human Services (HHS) that oversees Medicaid, is responsible for providing federal funds on the basis of state estimates of expenditures. CMS subsequently reconciles states' actual expenditures against those estimates. Thus, a key part of CMS's oversight responsibility is to review state-reported expenditures to assure that they are supported and consistent with Medicaid requirements.[147] Each quarter, states report their expenditures to CMS through its CMS-64 form. CMS regional offices are responsible for reviewing these reported expenditures and working with states to resolve any questionable expenditures. If CMS identifies errors—which can include (1) errors in the amounts reported or (2) reported expenditures that are not allowable—the agency can require states to reduce reported expenditures or return federal funds. Because Medicaid requirements include higher than standard federal matching rates for certain types of services and for certain populations of enrollees, part of CMS's review process is to assure that expenditures are being matched at the correct rate.[148] For example, states receive higher matching rates for services provided in Indian Health Service (IHS) facilities and for family

---

[145] Department of Health and Human Services, Centers for Medicare & Medicaid Services, Office of the Actuary, *2016 Actuarial Report on the Financial Outlook for Medicaid* (Washington, D.C.: 2017).

[146] See, CMS, *2016 Actuarial Report on the Financial Outlook for Medicaid.*

[147] This includes assessing whether expenditures are consistent with regulatory requirements, agency guidance, and program provisions established in state Medicaid plans (which describe how the state will administer its Medicaid program and are subject to CMS approval), and other agreements between the state and CMS, among other things.

[148] In general, the amount of federal funds that states receive for Medicaid services is determined by a standard formula—the Federal Medical Assistance Percentage (FMAP), which results in a specific federal matching rate for each state. However, there are a number of exceptions and different federal matching rates can apply for certain types of beneficiaries, services, or administrative costs.

planning services. They also receive higher matching rates for individuals newly eligible under the Patient Protection and Affordable Care Act (PPACA), referred to in this chapter as Medicaid expansion enrollees.[149]

While there is a common reporting form, state expenditure reporting varies depending upon the populations and services states cover and how they deliver and finance care. These variations reflect the diversity of the design of states' Medicaid programs; however, the task of reviewing reported expenditures has grown increasingly complex due to this variation, and is further complicated by the growing number of different federal matching rates for expenditures. When reporting errors or inappropriate expenditures go undetected, it can result in overpayment by the federal government.

Given the significance of federal Medicaid expenditures and past concerns about the challenges CMS has faced in ensuring that expenditures are being matched at the correct rate, you asked us to examine CMS oversight of state-reported expenditures. This chapter examines the following:

1. CMS's policies and procedures for assuring that state-reported Medicaid expenditures are supported and consistent with Medicaid requirements.
2. How CMS assures that correct federal matching rates are applied to expenditures subject to a higher than standard matching rate.
3. The financial impact of CMS's efforts to resolve errors in reported expenditures.

---

[149] Under PPACA, states may opt to expand their Medicaid programs by covering nearly all adults with incomes at or below 133 percent of the federal poverty level beginning January 1, 2014. See Pub. L. No. 111-148, 124 Stat. 119 (2010), as amended by the Health Care and Education Reconciliation Act of 2010 (HCERA), Pub. L. No. 111-152, 124 Stat. 1029 (2010). For purposes of this report, references to PPACA include the amendments made by HCERA. PPACA also provides for a 5 percent disregard when calculating income for determining Medicaid eligibility, which effectively increases this income level to 138 percent of the federal poverty level. See 42 U.S.C. § 1396a(a)(10)(A)(i)(VIII), (e)(14)(I). In 2016, states received a 100 percent federal match for their medical expenditures for the enrollees included in our study. See 42 U.S.C. § 1396d(y).

To examine CMS's policies and procedures for assuring that state-reported Medicaid expenditures are supported and consistent with Medicaid requirements, we reviewed CMS's internal guidance to regional offices on conducting quarterly reviews of reported expenditures. We also reviewed CMS's guidance to states on reporting expenditures, including the reporting forms. To examine how CMS's regional offices implemented this guidance, we selected 3 of 10 regional offices to achieve geographic variation. We selected regional offices 3, 6, and 9, which cover states in the East, South, and West of the United States. Within our three regional offices, we selected six states to review CMS's oversight: Arkansas, California, Maryland, Nevada, Pennsylvania, and Texas. We selected these states to achieve variation in program expenditures, enrollment, and program features, including whether they expanded Medicaid eligibility under PPACA. Together these six states account for approximately 30 percent of total federal Medicaid expenditures in fiscal year 2015. We visited our selected regional offices to conduct a walkthrough of their review of expenditures for our selected states for the most recently completed quarter at the time we planned our site visits, generally the first quarter of fiscal year 2017.[150]

We obtained and examined copies of reviewers' documentation of the steps taken to complete their quarterly reviews in the six selected states, including the completed review guides, summary memos, and correspondence with state officials. We also reviewed CMS's internal guidance for conducting financial management reviews, and obtained and examined documentation of reviews conducted from 2014 through 2017 (the first 4 years of expansion under PPACA), and resources assigned to review functions. In reviewing documentation of the quarterly reviews and the financial management reviews, we determined whether current procedures were resulting in reviewers identifying errors, but did not assess the magnitude of the errors identified. We interviewed officials from CMS's central office and our three selected regional offices about their review policies, processes, and resources. We also interviewed Medicaid officials

[150] We selected first quarter fiscal year 2017 because it was the most recently completed quarterly review at the time we selected our states. For California, the most recently completed quarterly review was for the fourth quarter of fiscal year 2015.

from our six selected states about their experiences submitting data and undergoing CMS's review processes. In evaluating this information, we compared policies and procedures against the Standards for Internal Control in the Federal Government.[151]

To examine how CMS assures that correct matching rates are applied to expenditures, we reviewed CMS policies and procedures for reviewing expenditures subject to a higher than standard federal matching rate, including the quarterly review guide. In addition, we examined the extent to which these were consistently applied by reviewing the quarterly review documentation for our three selected regional offices. Specifically, we examined how they reviewed expenditure reporting for four types of expenditures for which states receive a higher federal matching rate: IHS, services for certain women with breast or cervical cancer, family planning, and Medicaid expansion.[152] We selected these four expenditure types because they cover a variety of services and populations, and under CMS's quarterly review guidance, they are subject to specific review procedures. We also tested CMS's reviews by completing our own reviews of reported expenditures in the six states. Specifically, we calculated the variance in expenditures from the quarter under review to the previous quarter, which is in line with CMS's review guidance. We also interviewed CMS officials, including officials in our selected regional offices about their review process. In evaluating the measures CMS has taken to assure that correct matching rates are applied to different expenditures, we compared policies and procedures against the Standards for Internal Control in the Federal Government.[153]

To examine the financial impact of errors resolved by CMS, we reviewed data on errors resolved in fiscal years 2014 through 2017, the four most recent

---

[151] GAO, *Standards for Internal Control in the Federal Government*, GAO-14-704G (Washington, D.C.: Sept. 10, 2014). Internal control is a process effected by an entity's oversight body, management, and other personnel that provides reasonable assurance that the objectives of an entity will be achieved.

[152] The Centers for Disease Control and Prevention provide breast and cervical cancer screening and diagnostic services to certain low-income and uninsured women. States can use Medicaid funds to cover treatment for women who are diagnosed with breast or cervical cancer through this program, and they receive a higher than standard federal match for these expenditures.

[153] See GAO-14-704G.

years of available data.[154] Specifically, we reviewed data on the magnitude of errors resolved through states reducing reported expenditures and on errors resolved by CMS issuing a disallowance, which requires a state to return federal funds. We also reviewed data on deferrals of federal funds (i.e., CMS defers payment until issues are resolved) as of the end of fiscal year 2017. We asked CMS officials responsible for overseeing data on errors to describe the reliability of the data, including any limitations. For the data on disallowances, deferrals, and errors resolved by states reducing reported expenditures, we reviewed relevant documentation; examined the data for obvious errors, such as missing values; and compared the results to other supporting documentation to ensure accuracy, when possible. We determined that all data were sufficiently reliable for the purposes of our reporting objectives. We also reviewed the documentation from the three selected regional offices' quarterly expenditure reviews for examples of errors resolved in our six selected states. Using the data on disallowances, and documentation from the quarterly expenditure reviews, we analyzed the range in types of errors and the range in the financial impact of errors resolved by CMS. We also interviewed CMS officials from the regional offices and CMS's central office about the errors resolved and their procedures for issuing deferrals and disallowances.

We conducted this performance audit from April 2017 to August 2018 in accordance with generally accepted government auditing standards. Those standards require that we plan and perform the audit to obtain sufficient, appropriate evidence to provide a reasonable basis for our findings and conclusions based on our audit objectives. We believe that the evidence obtained provides a reasonable basis for our findings and conclusions based on our audit objectives.

---

[154] Errors resolved by CMS included expenditures that were identified through the quarterly review and though other types of review, such as financial management reviews. Examples of errors include expenditures that were unallowable, expenditures not supported by state documentation, and expenditures claimed under the incorrect federal match.

# BACKGROUND

## State Expenditure Reporting

In order to receive federal matching funds, states report expenditures quarterly to CMS on the CMS-64.[155] States are required to report their expenditures to CMS within 30 days of the end of each quarter, but may adjust their past reporting for up to 2 years after the expenditure was made, referred to as the 2-year filing limit. Adjustments can reflect resolved disputes or reclassifications of expenditures. Expenditures reported after the 2-year filing limit are generally not eligible for a federal match, with certain exceptions.[156]

The CMS-64 is a series of forms that capture expenditure data for different aspects of states' Medicaid programs, such as different types of services, populations, and different federal matching rates.[157] (See table 1 for examples of the expenditure types captured by the CMS-64.) States report their expenditures quarterly on the CMS-64 at an aggregate level— such as a state's total expenditures for such categories of services as inpatient hospital services—and these reported expenditures are not linked to individual enrollees or services. States' reporting may vary depending on the features of their Medicaid program. Some examples of this variation include the following:

- States that expanded eligibility under PPACA would need to report expenditures not only by the type of services (e.g., inpatient hospital

---

[155] Reported expenditures must represent actual expenditures for which all supporting documentation, in readily reviewable form, has been compiled and is available immediately at the time the claim is filed.

[156] The 2-year limit does not apply to any claim for any adjustment to prior year costs if they stem from HHS's Office of Inspector General or GAO audit findings, court-ordered retroactive payments, or where the state had good cause—as determined by HHS—to file late due to circumstances beyond the state's control.

[157] CMS has a specified list of 49 categories of service, many of which are broken out into further subcategories including specific provider types, services, and programs, such as Medicare.

services), but also by populations receiving different federal matching rates, such as expansion enrollees.

- States with waivers—that is, where the state received approval from HHS to waive certain Medicaid requirements in order to test and evaluate new approaches for delivering and financing care under a demonstration—would need to report those expenditures associated with these waivers on additional forms.[158]

## CMS Oversight of State Expenditure Reporting

CMS is responsible for assuring that expenditures reported by states are supported and allowable, meaning that the state actually made and recorded the expenditure and that the expenditure is consistent with Medicaid requirements. CMS regional offices perform the ongoing oversight, with enhanced oversight procedures in the 20 states with the highest federal Medicaid expenditures.[159] (See figure 1)

CMS is required to review the expenditures reported by states each quarter. (See figure 2.) Regional office reviewers have 50 days to review the expenditures and compute the federal share of states' Medicaid expenditures.

As part of the quarterly review, regional office reviewers also check that expenditures receive the correct matching rate. In general, the amount of federal funds that states receive for Medicaid services is determined annually by a statutory formula—the Federal Medical Assistance Percentage (FMAP), which results in a specific federal matching rate for each state.

---

[158] States can apply for a variety of Medicaid waivers including waivers referred to as 1115 demonstrations. Under section 1115 of the Social Security Act, the Secretary of Health and Human Services may waive certain federal Medicaid requirements and approve new types of expenditures that would not otherwise be eligible for federal Medicaid matching funds for experimental, pilot, or demonstration projects that, in the Secretary's judgment, are likely to promote Medicaid objectives. States must apply to HHS for approval for their Medicaid waivers, each requiring a separate approval process.

[159] In fiscal year 2016, the top 20 states represented over 75 percent of federal Medicaid expenditures, with federal expenditures ranging from approximately $6 billion to over $53 billion per state.

However, there are a number of exceptions where higher federal matching rates can apply for certain types of beneficiaries, services, or administrative costs. See table 2 for examples of higher matching rates that apply for expenditures for certain types of enrollees, services, or administrative costs.

Source: GAO analysis of Centers for Medicare and Medicaid Services (CMS) documentation and expenditure data; Map Resources (map). | GAO-18-564.

Notes: Regional office 2 also oversees Puerto Rico and the U.S. Virgin Islands, and regional office 9 oversees American Samoa, Guam, and the Northern Mariana Islands. Expenditures represented are for medical services and exclude administrative expenditures.

Figure 1. Jurisdiction of CMS Regions, Including States with Highest Expenditures, Fiscal Year 2017.

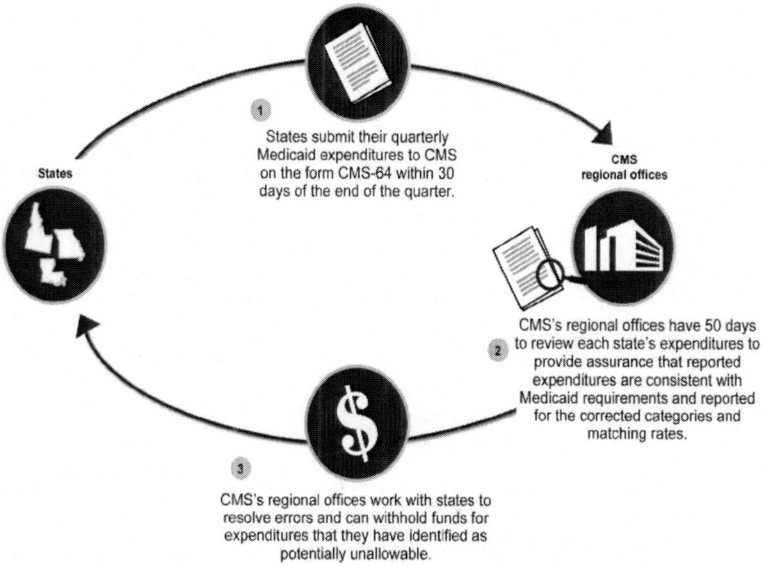


Source: GAO analysis of Centers for Medicare and Medicaid Services (CMS) regulations and guidance. | GAO-18-564.

Figure 2. CMS Quarterly Review Process.

## Table 1. Examples of Expenditure Types Reported by States on the CMS-64 Form

| Expenditure Type | Description |
|---|---|
| Inpatient hospital services | Payments to hospitals for inpatient services. |
| Supplemental payments to hospital | Payments made in addition to the payment for services on behalf of individual enrollees. |
| Managed care | Payments to managed care organizations, which are responsible for providing services to enrollees in return for a predetermined per person per month payment. |
| Waiver expenditures | Payments made for services delivered through and populations covered by Medicaid waivers; reporting requirements are specific to the terms and conditions of the waiver agreement. |
| Prior period adjustments | Adjustments made to previously reported expenditures; each adjustment must reflect the category of service being adjusted and the matching rate at the time the expenditure was originally incurred. |
| Medicaid expansion | Payments for services on behalf of Medicaid expansion enrollees by general categories of service. |

Source: GAO review of documentation from the Centers for Medicare & Medicaid Services (CMS).| GAO-18-564.

**Table 2. Examples of Higher Federal Matching Rates and Corresponding Federal Expenditures, Fiscal Year 2016**

| Type of expenditure | Federal Medical Assistance Percentage (FMAP) (percent) | Federal expenditures (dollars in millions) | Share of total federal Medicaid spending (percent) |
|---|---|---|---|
| Medicaid expansion population[a] | 100[b] | 65,160 | 17.9 |
| Indian Health Service | 100 | 1,854 | 0.5 |
| Family planning | 90 | 1,550 | 0.4 |
| Design and development of eligibility and enrollment systems | 90 | 1,382 | 0.4 |
| Breast or cervical cancer treatment | Enhanced FMAP[c] | 459 | 0.1 |

Source: GAO analysis of Centers for Medicare & Medicaid Services data. | GAO-18-564.

[a] This includes expenditures for medical services provided to individuals who are newly eligible for Medicaid under the Patient Protection and Affordable Care Act (PPACA).See 42 U.S.C..§ 1396d(y). Under PPACA, states also received an increased FMAP determined by formula for individuals who were not otherwise eligible for Medicaid but were covered by Medicaid under a demonstration or a program funded only by the state prior to the enactment of PPACA, ranging from 85 to 95 percent in 2016.

[b] This FMAP is scheduled to gradually diminish to 90 percent by 2020.

[c] States receive an increased match equivalent to their enhanced FMAP—the match for their Children's Health Insurance Program—for their expenditures for treatment provided to certain women with breast or cervical cancer. Like the Medicaid FMAP, the enhanced FMAP varies by state.

When CMS identifies questionable expenditures or errors through its reviews, there are several ways that they can be resolved, as summarized below.

- Deferral of federal funds. CMS can defer federal matching funds if, during the quarterly review, the regional office reviewer needs additional information to determine whether a particular expenditure is allowable. The reviewer may recommend that CMS defer the expenditure until the state provides additional support or corrects the reporting.[160]

- State reducing reported expenditures. If the state agrees that the questionable expenditure is an error, the state can submit an adjusted report during the quarterly review or make an adjustment in a subsequent quarter.[161] These adjustments prevent federal payments for those expenditures.
- Disallowance of expenditure. If CMS determines an expenditure is not allowable, CMS can issue a disallowance, and the state returns federal funds through reductions in future federal allocations. States may appeal disallowances.

## CMS HAS PROCESSES IN PLACE TO ASSURE THAT STATE-REPORTED MEDICAID EXPENDITURES ARE SUPPORTED AND ALLOWABLE, BUT WEAKNESSES LIMIT ITS ABILITY TO EFFECTIVELY TARGET RISK

CMS uses a variety of processes to assure that state-reported expenditures are supported during quarterly reviews and performs focused financial management reviews on expenditures considered at risk of not complying with Medicaid requirements. Although we found that CMS was identifying errors and compliance issues using both review methods, we also found weaknesses in how CMS targets its oversight resources to address risks.

[160] According to CMS guidance, deferrals are taken as temporary actions and, if states do not provide additional supporting documentation or correct reporting, the deferral may result in CMS taking a disallowance.

[161] CMS refers to the savings from these reductions as averted funds at risk. In order to qualify as averted funds at risk, the funds must be federal expenditures, which had been claimed by the state and were credited back to CMS as a result of intervention by regional office officials. Specifically, the state must have agreed to make an adjustment for the entire amount in question, retracted the claim prior to the submission of the CMS-64, or made a prior period adjustment that was verified.

## CMS Uses Quarterly Reviews, Supplemented with More Focused Reviews, to Assure that Reported Expenditures Are Supported and Allowable and Has Detected Errors in the Process

CMS uses quarterly reviews to assess whether expenditures are supported by the state's accounting systems; are in accordance with CMS approved methodologies, plans, and spending caps; and whether there are significant unexplained variances—changes in expenditures—from one quarter to the next (referred to as a variance analysis).[162] CMS review procedures include validation measures that check to ensure that expenditures were reported within the 2-year limit, which is a check done on all types of expenditures. Another validation measure compares expenditures to various approval documents.[163] For example, when a state has a waiver in place, expenditures are reviewed against waiver agreements that authorize payment for specified services or populations. Other examples include comparing supplemental payment expenditures to caps set for those expenditures. (See table 3.)

Our examination of the quarterly reviews indicated that the reviews involved significant coordination with other CMS staff and the state. In addition to reviewing state documentation, officials from two regional offices told us that they consult other regional office staff who oversee the approval of new expenditures to ensure that expenditures reflect approved program features. For example, officials in region 9 told us that in reviewing managed care expenditures, they consult with their colleagues who review the state's payment methodologies for capitated payments.[164]

---

[162] According to state Medicaid officials, states enter the expenditures manually into the CMS-64. Manual entry increases the risk of entry errors such as mistyped amounts, and the quarterly review compares the information states have entered into the CMS-64 with their accounting records to verify amounts, among other things.

[163] CMS has a guide for reviewers conducting the quarterly reviews. It serves as a template for the review itself and contains instructions and procedures for conducting and documenting each step of the review.

[164] Capitated payments to Medicaid managed care organizations are typically made on a predetermined, per person per month basis. CMS is responsible for reviewing state payment

## Table 3. Examples of CMS Validation Procedures for Selected Types of Expenditures

| Expenditure type | Validation measure used in quarterly review |
|---|---|
| Category of service | The reviewer must verify that the amounts reported by service are supported by the state's accounting records.<br>The reviewer conducts a variance analysis, which compares current expenditures to previous quarter expenditures and investigates significant differences. The reviewer develops a threshold for significance based on professional judgment. |
| Waiver expenditures | The reviewer must verify that the state is reporting the expenditures as required under the terms of the waiver agreement. If there have been changes to the waiver agreement, the reviewer must verify that reported expenditures are consistent with those changes. |
| Prior period adjustments | States may adjust claims filed in earlier quarters to reflect, for example, expenditures that were not claimed earlier or claimed on the wrong service line. The reviewer must determine whether<br>• adjustments were filed within the 2-year window,<br>• reported at the correct matching rate, and<br>• meet the requirements for an exception (if not submitted within 2 years of the quarter in which the expenditure was incurred). |
| Supplemental payments | Supplemental payments are payments to providers that are in addition to the payment for service on behalf of individual enrollees. The reviewer must check that the payments do not exceed the annual cap under the CMS approved state Medicaid plan or waiver. Based on professional judgment the reviewer may test a sample of reported payments to ensure that they were claimed in accordance with approved methodologies. |

Source: GAO analysis of Centers for Medicare & Medicaid Services (CMS) guidance. | GAO-18-564.

[a] States may seek permission from CMS to provide services under waivers of traditional Medicaid requirements; for example, in order to provide services to a targeted population or to a limited number of beneficiaries. Waivers are developed and proposed by states and must be approved by CMS in order for states to receive federal matching funds for medical expenditures.

In reviewing information technology development expenditures—which are subject to a higher federal matching rate— reviewers for all six selected states examined advanced planning documents, which requires coordination with staff who approve those documents to ensure that the state was receiving the correct matching rates and staying within the approved

---

rates for managed care organizations to ensure that they are reasonable and appropriate for the populations and services covered.

amounts.[165] With regard to coordination with states, we found that regional reviewers for all six reviews contacted states to follow-up on issues identified during the review. Officials also described being in regular contact with states to stay abreast of program, system, and staffing changes to inform their reviews. For example, according to regional officials, Arkansas experienced some significant and unexpected staffing challenges in 2016 that resulted in delays in the state reporting expenditures and returning federal overpayments, and the reviewer worked closely with state staff to track the state's progress.

We found evidence that reviewers identified errors during their quarterly reviews. In the six quarterly reviews we examined, regional offices identified errors in three of the six states.[166] For example, region 3 reviewers found errors in Maryland's expenditure reporting—including claims for the wrong matching rate for two enrollees who were not eligible for PPACA's Medicaid expansion and reporting provider incentive payments on the wrong line—and worked with the state to correct those errors. Additionally, region 9 reviewers found errors in California's reporting of expenditures. For example, they found that the state reported waiver expenditures for the incorrect time period, which has implications for CMS's ability to monitor and enforce spending limits for the waiver. Reviewers worked with the state to correct those errors.

To supplement the quarterly reviews, CMS generally directs regional offices to conduct a focused financial management review (FMR) each year on an area of high risk within the region, typically within one state.[167] According to regional officials, CMS uses these reviews to investigate expenditures in greater depth and detail than is reasonable within the timeframes of a quarterly review. For example, reviewers can examine individual claims for services from providers or the methodologies

---

165 Advanced planning documents specify, among other things, CMS approval for the planned information technology activities, allocated funding, and timeframes.

166 We examined the documentation of the quarterly reviews conducted for the first quarter of fiscal year 2017 for Arkansas, Maryland, Nevada, Pennsylvania, and Texas, and the fourth quarter of fiscal year 2015 for California, which was the most recent quarter reviewed at the time of our work.

167 Risks can include new expenditure types or areas where the state has historically experienced challenges in reporting.

developed for certain payment types. Regional reviewers also use these reviews to investigate errors that could not have been detected by the quarterly review. For example, regional office 6 officials told us that they uncovered inappropriate financing arrangements when they used an FMR to examine how Texas financed the state share of its supplemental payments to hospitals in one of its counties. To do so, the regional office reviewed payments from the state to the provider, project plans, and interviewed providers—steps that are not part of the quarterly review process. Rather, in the quarterly review, the reviewer only checks that state-reported payments are supported by state accounting records and are within applicable caps; thus, inappropriate financing of the state share would not have been detected through the quarterly review.

**Table 4. Areas of Focus of Planned Financial Management Reviews (FMR) and Associated Federal Funds at Risk, Fiscal Years 2014-2017**

| FMR areas | Number of proposed FMRs | Federal funds at risk (dollars in millions) |
|---|---|---|
| Medicaid expansion | 6 | 6,578 |
| Supplemental payments | 2 | 2,500 |
| Mental health | 4 | 413 |
| Information technology[a] | 4 | 150 |
| School-based administrative | 2 | 14 |
| Managed care | 2 | 3b |
| Other[c] | 11 | 2,747 |

Source: GAO review of Centers for Medicare & Medicaid Services documentation | GAO-18-564.

Note: Planned FMRs included 10 planned for fiscal year 2014, 10 for fiscal year 2016, and 11 in fiscal year 2017. CMS did not plan for any FMRs in 2015.

[a] These expenditures include payments for eligibility and enrollment systems, state Medicaid management information systems, and incentive payments to providers for health information technology.

[b] One region did not identify the federal funds at risk in its FMR focused on managed care.

[c] Other topics included state financing, prescription drugs, and home health services, among others.

In fiscal years 2014 through 2017, CMS used FMRs to review various expenditures considered to be at risk for not complying with Medicaid requirements. Specifically, as outlined in annual work plans, regional offices planned to conduct 31 FMRs and estimated that the total amount of federal funds at risk in expenditure areas covered by their planned reviews was $12 billion.[168] (See app. I.) Planned FMRs targeted a wide range of topics, with the reviews most frequently targeting expenditures for the Medicaid expansion population. (See table 4.)

We found that CMS frequently identified compliance issues through FMRs. As of March 2018, CMS reported that reviewers had identified compliance issues with financial impact in 11 of the 31 planned FMRs, though most of those findings were still under review. More findings from the planned FMRs are likely as some of the reviews were still ongoing. We reviewed the draft results for 5 FMRs.[169] Among these, CMS found that four states were reporting expenditures that were not allowable. For example, as noted earlier, a 2014 FMR on supplemental payments in Texas revealed inappropriate funding arrangements, and CMS issued a disallowance for approximately $27 million. In some cases, FMRs did not have apparent financial findings, but identified significant internal control weaknesses in the state and recommended specific corrective actions— such as better aligning eligibility and expenditures systems to better detect and correct irregularities—that would provide greater assurances that federal funds are appropriately spent.

Both the quarterly reviews and the FMRs occur in conjunction with other ongoing CMS financial oversight activities. For example in addition to reviewing expenditures, regional office reviewers assess how states estimate their costs, set payment rates for managed care and home and community based services, and allocate costs among different Medicaid administrative activities under their cost allocation plans. CMS officials told us that issues relating to state compliance with Medicaid requirements for expenditures could be identified during these other oversight activities and could inform follow-up during the quarterly reviews or be the subject of a

[168] Within these areas, regional offices identified approximately $4.9 billion, $4.2 billion, and $3.4 billion in federal funds at risk each year in 2014, 2016, and 2017, respectively. Regional offices did not conduct FMRs in 2015.

[169] We reviewed FMRs conducted in California in 2014; Texas in 2014; Maryland in 2016; Arkansas in 2017; and Indiana in 2017.

FMR.[170] Officials also told us that since FMRs were instituted, the agency has built in more front-end procedures for preventing problems with the accuracy and allow-ability of reported expenditures. As examples, they cited their work on managed care rate reviews, among other things.

## Weaknesses Limit CMS's Ability to Effectively Target Risk in Its Oversight of Expenditures

We identified two weaknesses in how CMS is allocating resources for overseeing state-reported expenditures that limited the agency's ability to target risk in its efforts to assure that these expenditures are supported and consistent with Medicaid requirements. First, we found that CMS has allocated similar staff resources to states with differing levels of risk. For example, the staff resources dedicated to reviewing California's expenditures—ranking first nationally in expenditures and constituting 15 percent of all federal Medicaid expenditures—are comparable to significantly smaller states in other regions, despite California's history of reporting challenges and its inability to provide electronic records, which requires on-site review.[171] (See figure 3.) CMS has allocated 2.2 staff to review California's expenditures in contrast to one person to review Arkansas' expenditures, which constitute 1 percent of federal Medicaid expenditures, and Arkansas does not have a similar history of complex reporting challenges. We also found that California's reviewers have set a higher threshold for investigating variances in reported expenditures than in the five other selected states. Specifically, reviewers investigated variances in California of plus or minus 10 percent if the variances represented more

[170] In addition, officials in one regional office told us they coordinate with HHS's Office of Inspector General, which also conducts audits and reviews of Medicaid expenditures. These audits can involve testing state-reported Medicaid expenditures for compliance with Medicaid requirements.

[171] As we previously reported, California's reporting of the state's Medicaid waiver expenditures had not aligned with the requirements of the waiver agreement from 2010- 2015, leaving CMS unable to assess whether the state was in compliance with the spending limits for the waiver during this period. See GAO, *Medicaid Demonstrations: Federal Action Needed to Improve Oversight of Spending*, GAO-17-312 (Washington, D.C.: April 3, 2017).

than 2 percent of medical expenditures, or $450 million in the quarter we reviewed. The state experienced an approximately 24 percent increase in its prescription drug expenditures—roughly $200 million—during that quarter, but the variance was deemed not significant.[172] In contrast, for two of our five other selected states, we found that reviewers generally investigated variances of plus or minus 10 percent regardless of the dollar amount of the variance and in the remaining three states they had significantly lower dollar thresholds than used for California.

As of May 2018, California was not submitting supporting documents for reported expenditures electronically. Reviewers for the Centers for Medicare & Medicaid Services (CMS) reviewed piles of summary level supporting documents each quarter (as seen below) and had to be on-site at state offices in Sacramento in a room full of hard copy documents when further investigation was required. These challenges are in addition to reporting delays, which CMS officials told us resulted from a fragmented program that processes expenditures through four different information systems, and a high volume of prior period adjustments each quarter (over 3,000 pages of them in the quarter we reviewed).

Summary level supporting documentation examined by region 9 officials in reviewing California's expenditures for the fourth quarter, fiscal year 2015.

Source: GAO.| GAO-18-564.

Figure 3. Challenges in Reviewing California's Reported Medicaid Expenditures.

[172] According to CMS, this variance was not investigated because the regional office was aware of delays in the state's reporting of prescription drug expenditures that accounted for some of the variance.

Second, CMS reported cancelling the FMR requirement for regional offices in 17 out of 51 instances in the last 5 years when faced with resource constraints. In some cases, CMS excused individual regional offices from conducting planned FMRs due to staff shortage as the agency did for regions 3 and 7 in 2014; region 8 in 2016; and regions 3, 7, 8, and 9 in 2018. In 2015, according to CMS officials, all 10 regions were excused from conducting an FMR, because the regional offices needed their staff to focus on implementing new procedures for validating expenditures for the Medicaid expansion population. In addition to cancelling FMRs, CMS was delayed in finalizing FMRs. Among the eight FMRs that were conducted in fiscal year 2014,

- three have been issued as final reports,
- CMS decided no report was needed on a fourth, and
- the four remaining FMRs from 2014 were still under review as of March 2018, delaying important feedback to states on their vulnerabilities.[173]

According to CMS officials, resource constraints have contributed to both of these weaknesses. Our analysis of staffing data indicated that, from fiscal years 2014 to 2018, the number of full time equivalent staff dedicated to financial oversight activities declined by approximately 19 percent across all 10 regions.[174] These staff are responsible not only for completing the quarterly reviews and FMRs, but also other financial oversight activities, including resolving audit findings and other on-going oversight activities noted previously.[175] During this period, federal Medicaid expenditures are

[173] In 2006, we reported that the value of the FMRs lay in not just identifying disallowances but also in providing feedback on policy issues and programmatic vulnerabilities and in elevating these to the attention of both state and federal staff. GAO, *Medicaid Financial Management: Steps Taken to Improve Federal Oversight but Other Actions Needed to Sustain Efforts,* GAO-06-705 (Washington, D.C.: June 22, 2006).

[174] In fiscal year 2014, CMS allocated 154.5 full time equivalent staff to financial management oversight. This allocation declined to 125 staff in fiscal year 2018.

[175] According to CMS officials, regional office financial management oversight staff are responsible for follow-up work associated with audits conducted by HHS's Office of Inspector General.

estimated to have increased by approximately 31 percent, and the reporting of expenditures has grown more complex.[176] In addition to the decline in dedicated staff, officials told us they faced challenges in filling vacancies either because of hiring restrictions or challenges in recruiting qualified candidates[177] Officials described instances where regional offices shared resources with other offices to address critical gaps in resources. For example region 9 was able to obtain part-time assistance from a region 6 reviewer to help review California's expenditures. However, CMS officials told us that they had not permanently reallocated resources between regional offices, because all regional offices are under-resourced given their various oversight responsibilities as of May 2018. With regard to cancelling FMRs, CMS officials noted that other oversight responsibilities, including the quarterly reviews, are required under statute or regulation and thus have a higher priority than FMRs.

Compounding its resource allocation challenges, CMS has not conducted a comprehensive, national assessment of risk to determine whether resources for financial oversight activities are (1) adequate and (2) allocated—both across regional offices and oversight tools—to focus on the greatest areas of risk. Agency officials told us that they have not conducted a formal risk assessment, because they are assessing risk on an on-going basis, allocating resources within each region accordingly and sharing resources across regions to the extent possible. However, this approach does not make clear whether the level of resources dedicated to financial oversight nationally is adequate given the risk.

Federal internal control standards for risk assessment require agencies to identify and analyze risks related to achieving the defined objectives (i.e., assuring that state-reported expenditures are in accordance with Medicaid rules), and respond to risks based on the significance of the risk. Without

---

[176] Both state and regional office officials told us that the length of states' quarterly reports has grown over the last 5 years, increasing from several hundred pages to over a 1,000 pages. Officials said that this included new lines of reporting that require additional time to complete and review. A number of factors drove this change, including additional reporting on the Medicaid expansion and increased implementation of Medicaid waivers.

[177] According to CMS officials, the regional offices have been under a partial hiring freeze since 2014.

completing a comprehensive, national assessment of risk and determining whether staff resources dedicated to financial oversight are adequate and allocated commensurate with risk, CMS is missing an opportunity to improve its ability to identify errors in reported expenditures that could result in hundreds of millions of dollars in potential savings to the Medicaid program.

## Vulnerabilities Exist in CMS's Review of Expenditures for Which States Receive Higher Federal Matching Rates

CMS reviewers in the selected regional offices we reviewed did not consistently perform variance analyses—which compare changes in expenditures from the quarter under review to the previous quarter—of higher matched expenditures during quarterly reviews. Further, the sampling procedures used to examine Medicaid expansion expenditures did not account for varying risks across states.

### CMS Did Not Consistently Conduct Variance Analyses When Reviewing Certain Types of Expenditures that Receive Higher Federal Matching Rates

CMS has multiple procedures in place to review expenditures that receive a higher federal matching rate. As with other expenditures, reviewers are required to complete a variance analysis, comparing reported expenditures in the quarter under review to those reported in the prior quarter and investigating variances above a certain threshold. However, we found that our three selected regional offices were not consistently conducting these analyses across several different types of expenditures with higher matching rates.

While CMS's internal guidance required that regional offices conduct variance analyses on expenditures with higher matching rates, we found that for the quarter we investigated (generally the 1st quarter of fiscal year 2017), our selected regional offices did not consistently do so for three types of expenditures that we reviewed: IHS, family planning, and certain women with breast or cervical cancer. Two of the three regional offices (regions 3 and 9) did not conduct or did not document these required variance analyses, and the remaining regional office (region 6) conducted the analyses but deviated from standard procedures outlined in CMS guidance, as summarized below.

- *CMS region 3.* Reviewers did not conduct variance analyses for either Maryland or Pennsylvania. Regional office staff with whom we spoke said that as part of the quarterly review they conduct the standard variance analysis on category of service lines of the CMS-64. Expenditures for IHS, family planning and services for certain women with breast or cervical cancer are not separately identified at that level. Although CMS reviewers said they thought the standard analysis was sufficient, net changes within a broad service category may obscure major changes within these higher matched expenditures. For example, examining changes in total inpatient hospital expenditures would not necessarily reveal a significant variance limited to inpatient expenditures in IHS facilities that receive a higher federal match.
- *CMS region 9.* Reviewers told us that they examined higher matched expenditures for California; however, no variance analyses of IHS, family planning, or breast or cervical cancer services were included in the work papers provided to us. In addition, they told us that they do not conduct a variance analysis on IHS, family planning, and services for certain women with breast or cervical cancer for Nevada, noting that expenditures in these areas tend to be quite small.
- *CMS region 6.* Reviewers conducted a variance analysis of these higher matched expenditures for Arkansas and Texas and provided us documentation; however, the documentation showed some deviation from the required steps specified in CMS's guidance. For

example, for Texas, spending on two of the three categories was beyond the threshold for significance, but the reviewer did not document any follow-up with the state.

Although expenditures for IHS, family planning, and certain women with breast or cervical cancer constituted a small share of total federal spending on Medicaid services—roughly 1 percent—combined spending on these categories was approximately $1 billion in the first quarter of fiscal year 2017. Our analysis indicated that variances in spending for these three services ranged widely across our six states, and in four of the states, some of their expenditures were above the thresholds for significance. (See figure 4.)

**Table 5. Variances for Certain Higher-Match Expenditure Types in Selected States that Were Not Investigated by CMS, First Quarter, Fiscal Year 2017**

| Regional office | State | Threshold of significance[a] | Expenditure type | Per-centage | Amount (dollars) | Significant but not investigated |
|---|---|---|---|---|---|---|
| 3 | Maryland | 10 percent variance and over $200,000 | Indian Health Services | 0 | 0 | |
| | | | Family planning | 7,708 | 8,277,623 | yes |
| | | | Breast or cervical cancer treatment[b] | 17 | 137,110 | |
| | Pennsyl-vania | 10 percent variance and over $250,000 | Indian Health Services | 0 | 0 | |
| | | | Family planning | -0.1 | -17,276 | |
| | | | Breast or cervical cancer treatment[b] | -11 | -665,469 | yes |
| 6 | Arkansas | 10 percent variance | Indian Health Services | 288 | 223,816 | yes |
| | | | Family planning | 6 | 111,133 | |
| | | | Breast or cervical cancer treatment[b] | 0 | 0 | |
| | Texas | 10 percent variance | Indian Health Services | -45 | -6,650 | yes |
| | | | Family planning | -14 | -1,991,944 | yes |
| | | | Breast or cervical cancer treatment[b] | -1 | -261,243 | |

**Table 5. (Continued)**

| Regional office | State | Threshold of significance[a] | Expenditure type | Per-centage | Amount (dollars) | Significant but not investigated |
|---|---|---|---|---|---|---|
| 9 | California | 10 percent variance and 2 percent of Medicaid payments | Indian Health Services | -21 | -3,264,514 | |
| | | | Family planning | -3 | -3,690,457 | |
| | | | Breast or cervical cancer treatment[b] | 38 | 5,587,226 | |
| | Nevada | 5 percent variance and 5 percent of Medicaid payments | Indian Health Services | -27 | -1,472,367 | |
| | | | Family planning | 10 | 300,156 | |
| | | | Breast or cervical cancer treatment[b] | -11 | -71,178 | |

Source: GAO analysis of Centers for Medicare & Medicaid Services (CMS) data and documentation. | GAO-18-564.

Notes: Columns not checked as "significant but not investigated," reflect, in all cases, variances that were deemed not significant. Expenditures represented are for medical services and exclude administrative expenditures.

[a] Thresholds of significance were provided by CMS reviewers in each region and are based on the reviewers' professional judgement.

[b] States receive a higher than standard federal matching rate for Medicaid expenditures for treatment provided to certain low-income and uninsured women who are diagnosed with breast or cervical cancer.

For example, in regional office 3, Maryland experienced a significant variance in its family planning expenditures—an increase of approximately $8 million dollars or 7,700 percent from the previous quarter—but there was no indication in the documentation provided that the regional office identified or investigated that variance. Similar to the variance analyses for other higher matched expenditure types, we found that the selected regional offices did not consistently conduct variance analyses on expenditures reported for the Medicaid expansion population. First, although five of our six states opted to expand Medicaid under PPACA, two of the five states (Maryland and Pennsylvania) were not subjected to a variance analysis for their expansion populations, a segment that accounted for nearly $7 billion in Medicaid expenditures in fiscal year 2016.[178] Among the remaining three

[178] Texas has not expanded Medicaid under PPACA and therefore did not have any expansion expenditures.

states, CMS regional office staff conducted a variance analysis, but in two of them, the reviewers did not document whether they investigated significant variances, leaving it unclear whether this required step was taken. Specifically, for two of the three remaining states—Arkansas and Nevada—reviewers did not document which variances were deemed significant or that any such variances were discussed with state officials.

The guidance specified in CMS's quarterly review guide is not always clear or consistent. For example:

- For IHS, family planning, and certain women with breast or cervical cancer, the guidance is explicit that the analysis is required, but the automated variance report used by reviewers for the step does not include these expenditures.
- For Medicaid expansion expenditures, the review guide is not explicit about whether a variance analysis is required, but CMS has an automated variance report available for these expenditures, which suggests that such an analysis was expected.
- The guidance suggests that a variance analysis should be conducted for expansion enrollees; however, it does not specify whether the analysis should be conducted in conjunction with—or take the place of—more in-depth examinations.

According to federal internal controls standards for information and communication, agencies should communicate the information necessary for staff to achieve the agency's objectives.[179] CMS's guidance on conducting variance analyses for types of expenditures with higher federal matching rates has not been sufficiently clear to assure that such analyses are being consistently conducted. By not consistently conducting such checks, errors may be going undetected and CMS may be providing federal funds at a higher matching rate than is allowable.

[179] See GAO-14-704G.

## The Sampling Procedures Used to Examine Medicaid Expansion Expenditures Did Not Account for Varying Risks across States

CMS has additional procedures in place to review service expenditures reported for the Medicaid expansion population, a category of expenditures that received a 95 percent federal match in 2017. Specifically, in addition to a variance analysis, CMS guidance specifies that each regional office reviewer is to review claims for a sample. The guide directs the reviewer to obtain a full list of all expansion enrollees from the state and to select 30 to 40 for further review. Next, the reviewer is to obtain supporting documentation from the state listing the eligibility factors for the sampled enrollees, such as age, pregnancy status, Medicare enrollment, and income. The reviewer is to select a single claim for each enrollee and verify that the corresponding expenditures were reported under the correct federal matching rate category—i.e., that the sample claim for each individual was accounted for in the relevant section of the CMS-64. The review guide specifies that the sample review be conducted each quarter unless the state has had four consecutive quarters with three or fewer errors, in which case, the sampling must be performed only annually.[180]

We found that regional offices were identifying errors in their sampling reviews. For example, region 3 reviewers found that Pennsylvania had incorrectly categorized an individual in the sample as a Medicaid expansion enrollee, with the selected expenditures initially reported as eligible for the higher matching rate. According to CMS central office officials, the sampling methodology has helped identify systemic issues with state expenditure systems in some states and resulted in corrections, adjustments, and in one case, a disallowance. Under current procedures, among our five selected states that expanded Medicaid under PPACA, all five were determined to have had four consecutive clean quarters according to agency officials; that

[180] If a state has four to six errors, CMS is to defer an extrapolated share of Medicaid expansion expenditures and the state must develop a corrective action plan. Similarly, if a state has seven or more errors, the state must develop a corrective action plan, but CMS may defer the entire Medicaid expansion expenditure.

is, the state had three or fewer errors in each quarter.[181] Nationally, all but one of the 33 states that have implemented Medicaid expansion under PPACA had four consecutive clean quarters as of March 2018, according to CMS officials.

We found, however, that CMS's procedures for sampling reviews had a key weakness in that they did not account for varying risks across states, as illustrated in the following examples.

- We found that sample size does not account for significant differences in program size. For example, both California and Arkansas have expanded Medicaid under PPACA, and regional office staff told us they reviewed claims for 30 expansion enrollees in each of the two states, despite the fact that California has over 10 times as many expansion enrollees as Arkansas.[182] Region 9 officials told us that for California they had initially sampled 100 enrollees during the first quarter they were required to conduct this analysis, but the review was time consuming given staff resources, and they were advised by CMS's central office to limit their sample to 30 individuals. CMS officials told us that the sampling procedures are resource intensive and that the sample size they decided upon was what they thought they had the resources to complete.
- Additionally, the sample size does not account for previously identified risks in a state's program. Specifically, as we noted in a 2015 report, CMS's sampling review of expansion expenditures was not linked to or informed by reviews of eligibility determinations conducted by CMS, some of which identified high levels of

[181] A recent report on California's eligibility determination procedures by HHS's Office of Inspector General revealed that, based on a sample of 150 enrollees, an estimated 450,000 Medicaid expansion enrollees may not have been eligible for coverage. The sample consisted of new enrollees who signed up between October 1, 2014 and March 31, 2015. See Department of Health and Human Services, Office of Inspector General, *California Made Medicaid Payments on Behalf of Newly Eligible Beneficiaries Who Did Not Meet Federal and State Requirements*, A-09-16-02023 (Washington, D.C.: February 2018).

[182] In fiscal year 2016, Arkansas reported 321,000 expansion enrollees. In the same period, California reported 3,673,900 expansion enrollees.

> eligibility determination errors.[183] According to CMS officials, the expenditure review is primarily intended to ensure that states are correctly assigning expenditures for the expanded eligibility groups as initially determined, not whether the eligibility determination is correct.

Federal standards for internal control related to risk assessment require that agencies identify, analyze, and respond to risks.[184] However, because CMS's sampling methodology does not account for risk factors like program size and high levels of eligibility determination errors, the agency's review of expansion population expenditures may be missing opportunities to detect systemic issues with improperly matched expenditures.

**Financial Impact of Expenditure Reviews Compared with Program Integrity Recoveries**

The impact of CMS's expenditure review activities is greater than the impact from other program integrity efforts. For example, in fiscal year 2015, CMS resolved errors through expenditure reviews that saved over $1.4 billion in federal funds. In the same year, CMS reported that efforts by states and the federal government to identify improper payments to providers—for example, services that were billed by a provider but were not received by a beneficiary—resulted in recoveries that totaled $852.9 million, in both state and federal funds.

Source: GAO analysis | GAO-18-564.

Quarterly variance analyses and sampling of Medicaid expansion enrollees can be supplemented by financial management reviews. For fiscal year 2016, CMS recommended regional offices conduct FMRs on

---

[183] See GAO, *Medicaid: Additional Efforts Needed to Ensure that State Spending is Appropriately Matched with Federal Funds*, GAO-16-53 (Washington, D.C.: Oct. 16, 2015). We previously found that eight of the nine states we reviewed reported errors resulting in incorrect eligibility determinations. We recommended that CMS use information obtained from assessments of state eligibility determinations to inform its review of expenditures for different eligibility groups. As of April 2017, CMS reported that the agency was establishing a process to have the reviews interact with one another.

[184] GAO-14-704G.

expenditure claims for expansion enrollees. As of March 2018, however, regional offices had completed an FMR on Medicaid expansion expenditures in only one state, with no findings, and were in the process of completing FMRs for five other states. According to CMS officials, no additional reviews in this area were planned for fiscal year 2018.

## CMS Resolved over $5.1 Billion in Expenditure Errors in Fiscal Years 2014 through 2017

In fiscal years 2014 through 2017, CMS's regional offices resolved expenditure errors that reduced federal spending by over $5.1 billion, with at least $1 billion in errors resolved in each of three of those four years. Errors were resolved through states agreeing to reduce their reported expenditures, which prevented federal payments to the state for those expenditures; and through CMS issuing disallowances, under which states are required to return federal funds.[185] Although CMS resolved over $1 billion in expenditure errors in each year of fiscal years 2014 through 2016, CMS resolved less than $600 million in fiscal year 2017. CMS officials explained that this change likely reflects delays in clearance of disallowances due to the transition between presidential administrations. (See fig. 3.) In addition to these resolved errors, as of the end of 2017, CMS had $4.47 billion in outstanding deferrals of federal funds, where CMS was delaying federal funds until additional information was provided. Expenditures flagged for deferrals may or may not represent errors.

---

[185] It is likely that regional offices resolved more than $5.1 billion during this period, because regional offices do not consistently report amounts resolved through states reducing reported expenditures to CMS central office. One regional office—which oversees 2 states in the top 20 for spending—told us they track these amounts but do not report them to CMS. CMS officials also told us that from 2014 through 2017, regional offices were not always documenting the financial impact of errors that were resolved by states reducing reported expenditures due to resource and time constraints. Officials told us that they have directed the regional offices to document these expenditures and submit them to CMS central office going forward.

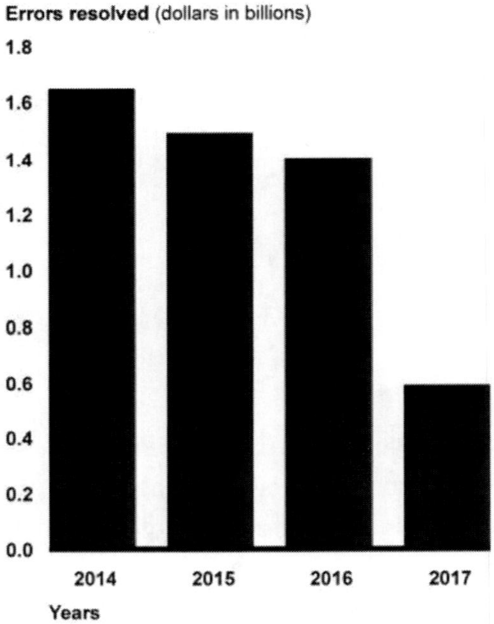


Source: GAO analysis of Centers for Medicare and Medicaid Services (CMS) data. | GAO-18-564.

Note: These numbers reflect the federal savings from errors resolved by states reducing reported expenditures and through disallowances. The amounts may understate the total amount of errors resolved, because CMS regional offices did not consistently report the amounts of errors resolved through states reducing reported expenditures to CMS central office.

Figure 4. Federal Financial Impact of Errors Resolved by CMS, Fiscal Years 2014-2017.

**CMS Methods for Resolving Errors and Addressing Questionable Expenditures**

- Reach agreement with the state to reduce its reported expenditures by the amount in error (either in the quarter under review or the next quarter).
- Issue a disallowance, which requires the state to return federal funds for expenditures that are not allowable.
- Defer federal funds if CMS needs additional information as to whether an expenditure is allowable.

Source: GAO analysis | GAO-18-564.

**Table 6. Resolved Errors from Fiscal Years 2014 through 2017 and Outstanding Deferrals as of Fiscal Year 2017, By CMS Regional Office**

| | Resolved expenditure errors, fiscal years 2014-2017 | | | |
|---|---|---|---|---|
| **Regional office** | **States within region**[a] | **Reductions in reported expenditures (dollars in millions)** | **Disallowed amounts (dollars in millions)** | **Outstanding deferred funds, as of quarter 4, fiscal year 2017 (dollars in millions)**[b] |
| 1 | CT, ME, MA, NH, RI, VT | 0.2 | 62.8 | 45.4 |
| 2 | NY, NJ | 600.0 | 1,729.7 | 321.4 |
| 3 | DE, DC, MD, PA, VA, WV | 116.2 | 328.2 | 225.1 |
| 4 | AL, FL, GA, KY, MS, NC, SC, TN | 1,205.1 | 211.1 | 5.1 |
| 5 | IL, IN, MI, MN, OH, WI | 51.9 | 144.8 | 2.0 |
| 6 | AR, LA, NM, OK, TX | Not Reported | 233.5 | 333.6 |
| 7 | IA, KS, MO, NE | 21.1 | 13.0 | 3.5 |
| 8 | CO, MT, ND, SD, UT, WY | 118.6 | 2.1 | 163.6 |
| 9 | AZ, CA, HI, NV | 263.3 | 15.8 | 3,373.1 |
| 10 | AK, ID, OR, WA | 1.7 | 0.0 | 0.6 |
| *Total* | | *2,378.1* | *2,741.1* | *4,473.5* |

Source: GAO analysis of Centers for Medicare & Medicaid Services (CMS) data. | GAO-18-564.
[a] Regional office 2 also oversees Puerto Rico and the U.S. Virgin Islands, and regional office 9 oversees American Samoa, Guam, and the Northern Mariana Islands.
[b] Active deferrals of federal funds that had not been resolved as of the fourth quarter of 2017.

All 10 CMS regional offices resolved errors from fiscal years 2014 through 2017, though the magnitude varied across regions. (See table 5.) Among the 10 regional offices, 9 reported that they had resolved errors through states agreeing to reduce reported expenditures. Additionally, 9 regional offices issued a total of 49 disallowances across 16 states, with the majority of the disallowances occurring in regional offices 2 and 3. Finally, all 10 regional offices had taken deferrals for questionable expenditures, with 22 states having outstanding "active" deferrals that had not been resolved as of the fourth quarter of fiscal year 2017, which ranged in amount from $178 to $444 million. CMS officials told us that the range of resolved errors and deferred funds across regional offices may reflect differences in the proportion of high-expenditure states. For example, regional office 4 oversees four states ranking in the top 20 in terms of Medicaid expenditures, while regional office 8 does not oversee any top-20 states. The variation may also reflect large actions taken in specific states. For example, the majority of the disallowed funds in regional office 2 from fiscal years 2014 to 2017 were due to a single disallowance of $1.26 billion in one state.

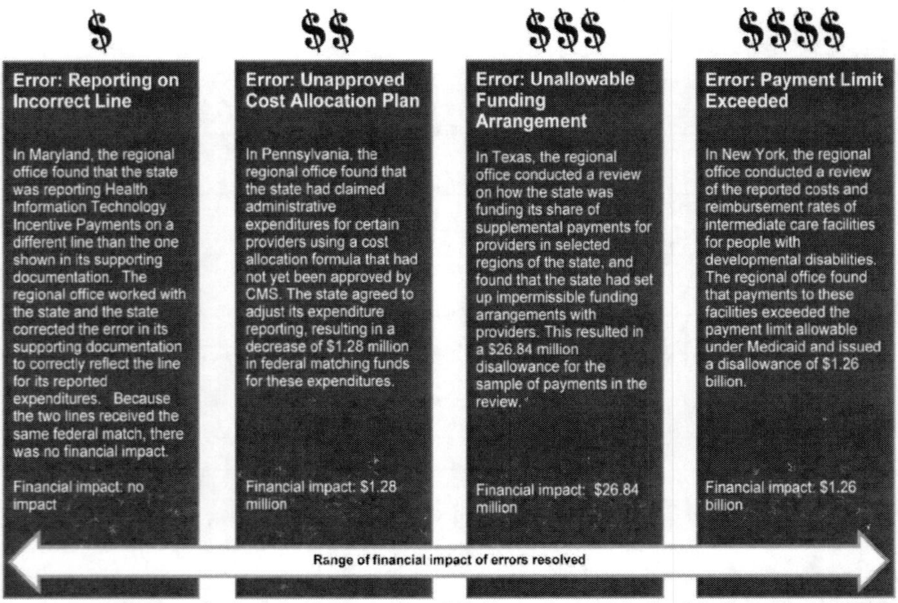


Source: GAO analysis of Centers for Medicare and Medicaid Services (CMS) documentation and data. | GAO-18-564.

Figure 5. Examples of Errors Resolved in Selected States from Fiscal Year 2014 through Fiscal Year 2016.

The financial significance of individual errors resolved by CMS's regional offices varied significantly. We found that regional offices resolved errors that ranged from reporting errors that had no federal financial impact— such as expenditures that were allowable, but were reported on the incorrect line—to hundreds of millions of dollars in expenditures that were found to be unallowable under Medicaid requirements. Over the fiscal years we reviewed, more than half of the disallowances CMS issued were less than $15 million; however, in four states CMS issued disallowances of over $100 million, including a disallowance of over $1 billion in New York. (See figure 5.) In some cases, actions taken by CMS to resolve errors were the culmination of years of work. For example, over several years the California Medicaid program reported a large volume of expenditures for which it did not yet have sufficient supporting documentation. The regional office officials told us that the state reported these expenditures in order to comply with the 2-year filing limit, and had reported these as "placeholder claims," with the intention of providing additional support at a later time. Over the course of at least 6 years, CMS deferred hundreds of millions of dollars in federal funds related to these placeholder claims. Of the active deferrals as of the end of fiscal year 2017, most of the total amount of deferred funds was taken for expenditures in California, which represented $3.4 billion of the $4.5 billion in total active deferrals. According to CMS officials, in 2015, CMS prohibited California from reporting additional placeholder claims. Region 9 officials told us that they continue to work with the state to clear the deferrals related to this issue. They were able to resolve 9 related deferrals in fiscal year 2017; however, another over 60 deferrals were still unresolved.

## CONCLUSION

The growth of federal Medicaid expenditures, estimated at about $370 billion in fiscal year 2017, makes it critically important to assure expenditures are consistent with Medicaid requirements. CMS has a variety of processes in place to review state-reported expenditures, and those reviews have resulted in CMS resolving errors that have saved the federal government a considerable amount of money; over $5 billion in the last 4 years. However, the increasing complexity of expenditure reporting is occurring as resources to review these expenditures are decreasing, hindering CMS's ability to target risk and potentially allowing for hundreds of millions of federal dollars in errors to go undetected. In the absence of a comprehensive risk assessment, which CMS has not conducted, CMS may be missing opportunities to better target resources to higher risk expenditures and increase the savings from these oversight activities.

The variety of different matching rates has contributed to the increased complexity of CMS's expenditure reviews. Although CMS has review procedures in place to assure that the correct matching rate is applied for services and populations receiving a higher federal matching rate, unclear guidance has contributed to inconsistency in the extent to which these reviews are conducted. In addition, we found weaknesses in the sampling methodology CMS requires its regional offices to use to help ensure that expenditures for Medicaid expansion enrollees—expenditures that receive a higher matching rate and that represented almost 20 percent of total federal Medicaid spending in 2016—are consistent with Medicaid requirements. In particular, the methodology does not account for risk factors like program size or vulnerabilities in state eligibility-determination processes and systems. As a result of the inconsistency in reviews and a sampling methodology that does not consider program risk, errors may be going undetected, resulting in CMS providing federal funds at higher federal matching rates than is allowable. In addition, CMS could be missing opportunities to identify any systemic issues that may contribute to such errors.

## RECOMMENDATIONS

We are making the following three recommendations to CMS:

1. The Administrator of CMS should complete a comprehensive, national risk assessment and take steps, as needed, to assure that resources to oversee expenditures reported by states are adequate and allocated based on areas of highest risk. (Recommendation 1)
2. The Administrator of CMS should clarify in internal guidance when a variance analysis on expenditures with higher match rates is required. (Recommendation 2)

3. The Administrator of CMS should revise the sampling methodology for reviewing expenditures for the Medicaid expansion population to better target reviews to areas of high risk. (Recommendation 3)

## AGENCY COMMENTS

We provided a draft of this chapter to HHS for review and comment. HHS concurred with all three recommendations, noting that it takes seriously its responsibilities to protect taxpayer funds by conducting thorough oversight of states' claims for federal Medicaid expenditures. Regarding our first recommendation—that CMS complete a comprehensive, national risk assessment and take steps to assure that resources are adequate and allocated based on risk—HHS noted that CMS will complete such an assessment, and, based on this review, will determine the appropriate allocation of resources based on expenditures, program risk, and historical financial issues. CMS will also identify opportunities to increase resources. Regarding our second recommendation—clarifying internal guidance on when a variance analysis on higher matched expenditures is required—HHS noted that CMS will issue such internal guidance. Regarding our third recommendation—that CMS revise the sampling methodology for reviewing expenditures for the Medicaid expansion population to better target reviews to areas of high risk—HHS noted CMS is considering ways to revise its methodology. HHS's comments are reproduced in appendix II.

As agreed with your offices, unless you publicly announce the contents of this chapter earlier, we plan no further distribution until 30 days from the report date. At that time, we will send copies of this chapter to the Secretary of Health and Human Services, appropriate congressional committees, and other interested parties. If you or your staff members have any questions about this chapter, please contact me. GAO staff who made key contributions to this chapter are listed in appendix III.

Carolyn L. Yocom
Director, Health Care

# APPENDIX I: CMS FINANCIAL MANAGEMENT REVIEW (FMR) TOPICS AND ESTIMATED AMOUNTS AT RISK, FISCAL YEARS 2014 THROUGH 2017

| Regional office | Fiscal year[a] | State | Topic | Estimated amount at risk[b] (dollars in millions) |
|---|---|---|---|---|
| 1 | 2014 | NH | Medicaid Management Information System transition assistance payments to providers | 14 |
| | 2016 | CT | Public psychiatric residential treatment facilities | 41 |
| | 2017 | ME | Medicare Part B premium buy-ins | 69 |
| 2 | 2014 | VI | Accuracy of federal claiming | 125 |
| | 2016 | NY | Outpatient hospital reimbursement for mental health services | 260 |
| | 2017 | NY | Review of comprehensive psychiatric emergency program rates | 64 |
| 3 | 2014[c] | VA | 1915c waiver | 302 |
| | 2016 | MD | Medicaid expansion expenditures | 450 |
| | 2017 | WV | Medicaid expansion expenditures | 628 |
| 4 | 2014 | TN | Provider taxes implemented to avoid program reductions | 869 |
| | 2016 | NC | Health homes data and expenditures reporting | 89 |
| | 2017 | KY | Medicaid expansion expenditures | 600 |
| 5 | 2014 | MN | Provider incentive payments for health information technology | 27 |
| | 2016 | OH | Medicaid expansion expenditures | 100 |
| | 2017 | IN | Medicaid expansion expenditures | 1,800 |
| 6 | 2014 | TX | 1115 demonstration provider incentive payments | 2,300 |
| | 2016 | OK | Public psychiatric residential treatment facilities | 48 |
| | 2017 | AR | Home health services | 51 |
| 7 | 2014[c] | MO | Prescription drug expenditures | 637 |
| | 2016 | MO | School district administrative claiming | 13 |
| | 2017 | KS | Managed care organizations' provider payments | Unknown |
| 8 | 2014 | UT | Provider incentive payments for health information technology | 52 |
| | 2016[d] | n/a | n/a | n/a |
| | 2017 | CO | Intermediate care facilities | 23 |
| 9 | 2014 | CA | Federally qualified health center reimbursement payments | 565 |
| | 2016 | CA | Outpatient supplemental payments | 154 |
| | 2017 | NV | Eligibility and enrollment maintenance and operations | 57 |
| 10 | 2014 | AK | Personal case services | 18 |
| | 2016 | WA | Medicaid expansion expenditures | 3,000 |

## Appendix I. (Continued)

| Regional office | Fiscal year[a] State | | Topic | Estimated amount at risk[b] (dollars in millions) |
|---|---|---|---|---|
| | 2017 | OR | School based services expenditures | 1 |
| | 2017 | WA | Managed care organizations' reporting of drug rebates | 3 |

Source: GAO summary of Centers for Medicare & Medicaid (CMS) documentation. | GAO-18-564.

[a] CMS canceled the requirement for an FMR in 2015.

[b] Amount of risk refers to a regional office's assessment of the federal funds associated with the topics that are at risk if a state's reporting is not consistent with Medicaid requirements in these areas.

[c] CMS cancelled these 2014 FMRs due to a staffing shortage.

[d] Region 8 was excused from the requirement to conduct an FMR in 2016 due to staffing constraints.

# APPENDIX II: COMMENTS FROM THE DEPARTMENT OF HEALTH AND HUMAN SERVICES

DEPARTMENT OF HEALTH & HUMAN SERVICES

OFFICE OF THE SECRETARY

Assistant Secretary for Legislation
Washington, DC 20201

Carolyn Yocom
Director, Health Care Team
U.S. Government Accountability Office
441 G Street NW
Washington, DC 20548

Dear Ms. Yocom:

Attached are comments on the U.S. Government Accountability Office's (GAO) report entitled, "*Medicaid: CMS Needs to Better Target Risks to Improve Oversight of Expenditures*" (GAO-18-564).

The Department appreciates the opportunity to review this report prior to publication.

Sincerely,

Matthew D. Bassett
Assistant Secretary for Legislation

**GENERAL COMMENTS OF THE DEPARTMENT OF HEALTH AND HUMAN SERVICES (HHS) ON THE GOVERNMENT ACCOUNTABILITY OFFICE'S DRAFT REPORT ENTITLED: MEDICAID: CMS NEEDS TO BETTER TARGET RISKS TO IMPROVE OVERSIGHT OF EXPENDITURES (GAO-18-564)**

The U.S. Department of Health and Human Services (HHS) appreciates the opportunity to review and comment on the Government Accountability Office's (GAO) draft report on Medicaid expenditures. HHS takes seriously its responsibilities to protect taxpayer funds by conducting thorough oversight of Medicaid expenditures claimed by states.

Because Medicaid is jointly funded by states and the Federal Government, and is administered by states within Federal guidelines, both HHS and states have key roles as stewards of the program, and work together closely to carry out these responsibilities. As such, HHS conducts multiple activities to oversee Medicaid expenditures and verify that Federal financial participation matches states' actual expenditures. For example, on a quarterly basis, states must submit to HHS their Medicaid expenditures and include supporting documentation such as invoices, cost reports, and eligibility records. HHS then reviews these expenditures and works with states to resolve any questionable expenditures to ensure that the appropriate amounts are spent and that higher matching rates are reported correctly. To assist states in their reporting, HHS provides guidance and training to make sure that states have mechanisms and systems to track and report expenditures accurately.

In addition, HHS regional offices perform enhanced oversight procedures in the 20 states with the highest federal Medicaid expenditures. Enhanced oversight procedures include verifying that the amounts reported are supported by the state's accounting records, and conducting variance analyses which compare current expenditures to previous quarter expenditures and investigating significant differences. HHS also verifies that states are reporting waiver expenditures as required, and that supplemental payments do not exceed the annual cap under the state's Medicaid plan or waiver. To supplement the quarterly reviews, HHS asks each regional office to conduct targeted annual financial management reviews which allow for a more intensive review of state expenditures and include an analysis of the funding source and appropriateness of a payment.

As GAO notes, HHS has multiple procedures in place to recoup Medicaid funds when necessary. HHS can defer federal matching funds during the quarterly review if additional information is needed to determine whether a particular expenditure is allowable. If a state agrees that the questionable expenditure is an error, the state can submit an adjusted report or make an adjustment in the subsequent quarter. HHS also has the authority to issue a disallowance, requiring the state to return federal funds through reductions in future federal allocations.

As a result of these oversight processes, HHS worked with states to resolve $2.1 billion and recover an additional $647 million from states, totaling $2.7 billion in questionable costs in fiscal year 2017. Furthermore, an estimated $457 million in questionable reimbursement was averted due to preventive interaction between HHS and states to promote proper state Medicaid financing[1].

GAO's recommendations and HHS' responses are below.

**GENERAL COMMENTS OF THE DEPARTMENT OF HEALTH AND HUMAN SERVICES (HHS) ON THE GOVERNMENT ACCOUNTABILITY OFFICE'S DRAFT REPORT ENTITLED: MEDICAID: CMS NEEDS TO BETTER TARGET RISKS TO IMPROVE OVERSIGHT OF EXPENDITURES (GAO-18-564)**

The Administrator of CMS should complete a comprehensive, national risk assessment and take steps as needed to assure that resources to oversee expenditures reported by states are adequate and allocated based on areas of highest risk.

**HHS Response**
HHS concurs with this recommendation. CMS will complete a comprehensive national review to assess the risk of Medicaid expenditures reported by states and allocate resources based on risk. Based on this review, CMS will identify opportunities to increase resources and review the current allocation of financial staff to determine the appropriate allocation by state based on expenditures, program risk, and historical financial issues.

**Recommendation**
The Administrator of CMS should clarify in internal guidance when a variance analysis on expenditures with higher match rates is required.

**HHS Response**
HHS concurs with this recommendation. CMS will issue internal guidance clarifying when a variance analysis on expenditures with higher match rates is required.

**Recommendation**
The Administrator of CMS should revise the sampling methodology for reviewing expenditures for the Medicaid expansion population to better target reviews to areas of high risk.

**HHS Response**
HHS concurs with this recommendation. CMS is considering ways to revise the sampling methodology for reviewing expenditures for the Medicaid expansion population.

# APPENDIX III: GAO STAFF ACKNOWLEDGMENTS

In addition to Carolyn L. Yocom, Susan Barnidge (Assistant Director), Jasleen Modi (Analyst-in-Charge), Caroline Hale, Perry Parsons, and Sierra Gaffney made key contributions to this chapter. Also contributing were Giselle Hicks, Drew Long, and Jennifer Whitworth.

# APPENDIX IV: ACCESSIBLE DATA

## Agency Comment Letter

Accessible Text for Appendix II Comments from the Department of Health and Human Services

JUL 18 2018
Carolyn Yocom
Director, Health Care Team
U.S. Government Accountability Office

Dear Ms. Yocom:

Attached are comments on the U.S. Government Accountability Office's (GAO) report entitled, *Medicaid: CMS Needs to Better Target Risks to Improve Oversight of Expenditures* (GAO-18- 564).

The Department appreciates the opportunity to review this chapter prior to publication.

Sincerely,
Matthew D. Bassett
Assistant Secretary for Legislation

Attachment

General Comments of the Department of Health and Human Services (HHS) on the Government Accountability Office's Draft Report Entitled: *Medicaid: CMS Needs to Better Target Risks to Improve Oversight of Expenditures* (Gao-18-564)

The U.S. Department of Health and Human Services (HHS) appreciates the opportunity to review and comment on the Government Accountability Office's (GAO) draft report on Medicaid expenditures. HHS takes seriously its responsibilities to protect taxpayer funds by conducting thorough oversight of Medicaid expenditures claimed by states.

Because Medicaid is jointly funded by states and the Federal Government, and is administered by states within Federal guidelines, both HHS and states have key roles as stewards of the program, and work together closely to carry out these responsibilities. As such, HHS conducts multiple activities to oversee Medicaid expenditures and verify that Federal financial participation matches states' actual expenditures. For example, on a quarterly basis, states must submit to HHS their Medicaid expenditures and include supporting documentation such as invoices, cost reports, and eligibility records. HHS then reviews these expenditures and works with states to resolve any questionable expenditures to ensure that the appropriate amounts are spent and that higher matching rates are reported correctly. To assist states in their reporting, HHS provides guidance and training to make sure that states have mechanisms and systems to track and report expenditures accurately.

In addition, HHS regional offices perform enhanced oversight procedures in the 20 states with the highest federal Medicaid expenditures. Enhanced oversight procedures include verifying that the amounts reported are supported by the state's accounting records, and conducting variance analyses which compare current expenditures to previous quarter expenditures and investigating significant differences. HHS also verifies that states are reporting waiver expenditures as required, and that supplemental payments do not exceed the annual cap under the state's Medicaid plan or waiver. To supplement the quarterly reviews, HHS asks each regional office to conduct targeted annual financial management reviews which allow for a more intensive review of state expenditures and include an analysis of the funding source and appropriateness of a payment.

As GAO notes, HHS has multiple procedures in place to recoup Medicaid funds when necessary. HHS can defer federal matching funds during the quarterly review if additional information is needed to determine whether a particular expenditure is allowable. If a state agrees that the questionable expenditure is an error, the state can submit an adjusted report or make an adjustment in the subsequent quarter. HHS also has the authority to issue a disallowance, requiring the state to return federal funds through reductions in future federal allocations.

As a result of these oversight processes, HHS worked with states to resolve $2.1 billion and recover an additional $647 million from states, totaling $2.7 billion in questionable costs in fiscal year 2017. Furthermore, an estimated $457 million in questionable reimbursement was averted due to preventive interaction between HHS and states to promote proper state Medicaid financing[1].

GAO's recommendations and HHS' responses are below.

***Recommendation***

General Comments of the Department of Health and Human Services (HHS) on the Government Accountability Office's Draft Report Entitled: *Medicaid: CMS Needs to Better Target Risks To Improve Oversight of-Expenditures* (GAO-18-564)

The Administrator of CMS should complete a comprehensive, national risk assessment and take steps as needed to assure that resources to oversee expenditures reported by states are adequate and allocated based on areas of highest risk.

***HHS Response***

HHS concurs with this recommendation. CMS will complete a comprehensive national review to assess the risk of Medicaid expenditures reported by states and allocate resources based on risk. Based on this review, CMS will identify opportunities to increase resources and review the current allocation of financial staff to determine the appropriate allocation by state based on expenditures, program risk, and historical financial issues.

***Recommendation***

The Administrator of CMS should clarify in internal guidance when a variance analysis on expenditures with higher match rates is required.

***HHS Response***

HHS concurs with this recommendation. CMS will issue internal guidance clarifying when a variance analysis on expenditures with higher match rates is required.

***Recommendation***

The Administrator of CMS should revise the sampling methodology for reviewing expenditures for the Medicaid expansion population to better target reviews to areas of high risk.

### *HHS Response*

HHS concurs with this recommendation. CMS is considering ways to revise the sampling methodology for reviewing expenditures for the Medicaid expansion population.

In: Medicaid
Editor: Alice Holt

ISBN: 978-1-53614-829-9


*Chapter 5*

# MEDICAID MANAGED CARE: IMPROVEMENTS NEEDED TO BETTER OVERSEE PAYMENT RISKS*

*United States Government Accountability Office*

## ABBREVIATIONS

| | |
|---|---|
| CMS | Centers for Medicare & Medicaid Services |
| HHS | Department of Health and Human Services |
| HHS-OIG | Department of Health and Human Services' Office of Inspector General |
| MCO | managed care organization |
| MFCU | Medicaid Fraud Control Unit |
| UPIC | Unified Program Integrity Contractor |

* This is an edited, reformatted and augmented version of United States Government Accountability Office Accessible Version of Report to Congressional Requesters, Publication No. GAO-18-528, dated July 2018.

## WHY GAO DID THIS STUDY

Federal spending on services paid for under Medicaid managed care was $171 billion in 2017, almost half of the total federal Medicaid expenditures for that year. Federal and state program integrity efforts have largely focused on Medicaid fee-for-service delivery where the state pays providers directly, rather than managed care, where it pays MCOs. As a result, less is known about the types of payment risks under managed care.

GAO was asked to examine payment risks in Medicaid managed care. In this chapter, GAO (1) identified payment risks; (2) identified any challenges to state oversight and strategies to address them; and (3) assessed CMS efforts to help states address payment risks and oversight challenges. To do this work, GAO reviewed findings on managed care payment risks and oversight challenges from federal and state audits and other sources. GAO also interviewed 49 state program integrity stakeholders in 10 states selected based on size, the percent of population in managed care, and geography. Stakeholders included the state Medicaid managed care office, state Medicaid program integrity unit, state auditor, Medicaid Fraud Control Unit, and an MCO.

## WHAT GAO RECOMMENDS

GAO recommends that CMS (1) expedite issuing planned guidance on Medicaid managed care program integrity, (2) address impediments to managed care audits, and (3) ensure states account for overpayments in setting future MCO payment rates. The Department of Health and Human Services concurred with these recommendations.

## WHAT GAO FOUND

Under Medicaid managed care, managed care organizations (MCO) receive a periodic payment per beneficiary in order to provide health care services. Managed care has the potential to help states reduce Medicaid program costs and better manage the use of health care services. However, managed care payments also have the potential to create program integrity risks. GAO identified six types of payment risks associated with managed care, including four related to payments that state Medicaid agencies make to MCOs, and two related to payments that MCOs make to providers. Of the six payment risks GAO identified, state stakeholders responsible for ensuring Medicaid program integrity more often cited the following two as having a higher level of risk:

1. incorrect fee-for-service payments from MCOs, where the MCO paid providers for improper claims, such as claims for services not provided; and
2. inaccurate state payments to MCOs resulting from using data that are not accurate or including costs that should be excluded in setting payment rates.

GAO also identified multiple challenges to program integrity oversight for managed care programs. Stakeholders most frequently cited challenges related to (1) appropriate allocation of resources, (2) quality of the data and technology used, and (3) adequacy of state policies and practices. Some stakeholders offered strategies to address these challenges, including collaborating with other entities to identify problem providers and fraud schemes, as well as having effective data systems to better manage risks.

The Centers for Medicare & Medicaid Services (CMS), which oversees Medicaid, has initiated efforts to assist states with program integrity oversight for managed care. However, some of these efforts have been delayed, and there are also gaps in oversight.

- CMS's planned Medicaid managed care guidance to states has been delayed due to the agency's internal review of the regulations; as of May 2018, no issuance date had been set for the guidance.
- CMS established a new approach for conducting managed care

audits beginning in 2016. However, only a few audits have been conducted, with none initiated in the past 2 years. In part, this is due to certain impediments identified by states, such as the lack of some provisions in MCO contracts.

- CMS has updated standards for its periodic reviews of the state capitation rates set for MCOs. However, overpayments to providers by MCOs are not consistently accounted for in determining future state payments to MCOs, which can result in states' payments to MCOs being too high.

Lack of guidance and gaps in program integrity oversight are inconsistent with federal internal control standards, as well as with CMS's goals to (1) improve states' oversight of managed care; (2) use audits to investigate fraud, waste, and abuse of providers paid by MCOs; and (3) hold MCOs financially accountable. Without taking action to address these issues, CMS is missing an opportunity to develop more robust program integrity safeguards that will help mitigate payment risks in Medicaid managed care.

* * *

July 26, 2018

The Honorable Claire McCaskill
Ranking Member
Committee on Homeland Security and Governmental Affairs
United States Senate

The Honorable Thomas R. Carper
Ranking Member
Permanent Subcommittee on Investigations
Committee on Homeland Security and Governmental Affairs
United States Senate

Federal spending on services delivered and paid for under Medicaid managed care totaled $171 billion in 2017, almost half of the total $364 billion in federal Medicaid expenditures for that year.[186] Under Medicaid managed care, states pay a set periodic amount per beneficiary to managed care organizations (MCO) for each enrolled beneficiary, and MCOs pay health care providers for the services delivered to enrollees.[187] Used effectively, managed care may help states reduce Medicaid program costs and better manage utilization of health care services.

The Centers for Medicare & Medicaid Services (CMS)—an agency within the Department of Health and Human Services (HHS)—and the states have implemented program integrity policies and processes in an effort to address payment risks in Medicaid, such as those related to fraud, waste, and abuse. However, these program integrity efforts have remained largely focused on fee-for-service arrangements, where states pay health care providers directly for services rendered. Payments for these services provided under fee-for-service arrangements are audited by multiple entities and reviewed for incorrect or fraudulent patterns at the federal and state levels. In contrast, under managed care, states do not pay providers directly, but rather pay MCOs, which are responsible for providing services through their provider networks; MCOs are responsible for overseeing the appropriateness of the payments they make to providers. Less is known about the types of Medicaid payment risks and the program integrity process and challenges under managed care. We recently reported on certain payment risks in Medicaid managed care that are not adequately accounted

[186] Medicaid is a joint federal-state program that finances health care coverage for low-income and medically needy individuals.

[187] States may have different types of managed care arrangements in Medicaid, such as primary care case management, prepaid ambulatory health plans, or comprehensive managed care, some of which have a limited benefit package or do not assume financial risk for services provided. In this report, we are referring to comprehensive, risk-based managed care provided through MCOs, which is the most common managed care arrangement. An MCO contracts with a state to provide comprehensive health care services through its network of providers, is responsible for ensuring access to Medicaid services, and is at financial risk for the cost of providing these services.

for in determining the scope of Medicaid improper payments to MCOs.[188] This lack of knowledge is of particular concern, given the recent rapid growth in enrollment in Medicaid managed care. Between 2013 and 2016 (the most recent year for which data are available), Medicaid enrollment in comprehensive, risk-based managed care increased by 56 percent, or from 35.0 million beneficiaries to 54.6 million beneficiaries.

You asked us to identify payment risks and oversight challenges associated with Medicaid managed care. In this chapter, we

1. identify any potential payment risks that exist in Medicaid managed care;
2. identify any potential oversight challenges associated with identified payment risks, and the strategies states use to address them; and
3. assess CMS's efforts to assist states in addressing these payment risks and associated oversight challenges.

To address the first two objectives, we first reviewed reports resulting from federal and state audits and investigations, regarding payment risks and improper payments in Medicaid managed care and managed care in general. Through a literature search and outreach to state auditing organizations, we identified and reviewed audit reports of Medicaid managed care programs—such as those issued by HHS's Office of Inspector General (HHS-OIG) and state audit agencies—as well as investigations involving payments to MCOs and MCO providers. We also reviewed our prior work and reports related to Medicaid program integrity. Based on this review, we identified different

---

[188] See GAO, *Medicaid: CMS Needs to Better Measure Program Risks in Managed Care*, GAO-18-291 (Washington, D.C.: May 7, 2018). In this report, we recommended that CMS measure certain program risks that are not accounted for in its current oversight of Medicaid managed care. In addition, in another report, we found that CMS has not conducted a risk assessment for Medicaid or Medicare related to fraud in these programs. See GAO, *Medicare and Medicaid: CMS Needs to Fully Align its Antifraud Efforts with the Fraud Risk Framework*, GAO-18-88 (Washington, D.C.: Dec. 5, 2017). We recommended that CMS take steps to assess risks and create strategies to address them. CMS agreed with the recommendations in both of these reports.

types of payment risks, as well as reported challenges to program integrity oversight of these risks. We next interviewed officials from a non-generalizable sample of 10 states regarding their views about the level of risk of each type of payment risk; the extent they experienced the challenges to oversight; and whether they had used any oversight strategies to address Medicaid managed care payment risks. We selected states that had a significant share of their Medicaid populations enrolled in MCOs, and to provide a mix of population sizes and geographic locations.[189] Within each state, we conducted structured interviews with a total of 49 stakeholders from the following five entities that have oversight responsibilities related to Medicaid program integrity: (1) the state Medicaid managed care office; (2) the state Medicaid program integrity unit; (3) the state auditor; (4) the state Medicaid Fraud Control Unit (MFCU); and (5) an MCO.[190]

To assess CMS's efforts to assist states in addressing these payment risks and associated oversight challenges, we reviewed CMS's managed care regulations and guidance; current program integrity plan; and documents relating to training, technical assistance, monitoring and oversight.[191] We conducted interviews with CMS officials and CMS audit contractors regarding their roles, responsibilities, and oversight activities. Additionally, we reviewed our prior work related to program integrity risks in Medicaid managed care and identified applicable federal internal control standards—specifically those related to communicating guidance and to conducting effective monitoring—that we could use to assess CMS's efforts.[192]

We conducted this performance audit from October 2016 to July 2018 in accordance with generally accepted government auditing standards.

---

[189] Selected states included California, Florida, Georgia, Hawaii, Massachusetts, Michigan, Nevada, Oregon, Tennessee, and Wisconsin. These states accounted for 34 percent of total federal and state Medicaid managed care expenditures in all states in fiscal year 2017.

[190] MCOs were identified by calculating the median enrollment of plans operating in each state in 2014 and selecting the plan with the median enrollment or next highest level of enrollment.

[191] See Department of Health and Human Services, Centers for Medicare & Medicaid Services, *Comprehensive Medicaid Integrity Plan, Fiscal Years 2014-2018.*

[192] See GAO, *Standards for Internal Control in the Federal Government*, GAO-14-704G (Washington, D.C.: Sept. 10, 2014). Internal control is a process effected by an entity's oversight body, management, and other personnel that provides reasonable assurance that the objectives of an entity will be achieved.

Those standards require that we plan and perform the audit to obtain sufficient, appropriate evidence to provide a reasonable basis for our findings and conclusions based on our audit objectives. We believe that the evidence obtained provides a reasonable basis for our findings and conclusions based on our audit objectives.

## BACKGROUND

Medicaid is jointly financed by the federal government and the states, with the federal government reimbursing states for a share of their expenditures for Medicaid covered services provided to eligible beneficiaries. The federal share of spending is based on a statutory formula that determines a federal matching rate for each state.[193]

### Medicaid Service Delivery Models

States may provide Medicaid services under either or both a fee-for-service model and a managed care model. Under a fee-for-service delivery model, states make payments directly to providers for services provided, and the federal government reimburses the state its share of spending based on these payments. Under a managed care service delivery model, states pay MCOs a capitation payment, which is a fixed periodic payment per beneficiary enrolled in an MCO—typically, per member per month. The federal government reimburses its share of spending based on the capitation payments states made to the MCO. In return for the capitated payment, each MCO is responsible for arranging for and paying providers' claims for all covered services provided to Medicaid beneficiaries. For example, MCOs

[193] The federal government matches most state Medicaid expenditures for services on the basis of the Federal Medical Assistance Percentage formula, which, using per capita income, determines each state's federal matching rate. The federal medical assistance percentage for a state can range from 50 percent to 83 percent; in fiscal year 2017, the federal share of Medicaid service expenditures was about 62 percent.

may pay providers on a fee-for-service basis or with a monthly capitation payment per beneficiary, or through some other payment approach in which the provider assumes some risk for providing covered services. In either case, MCOs are required to report to the states information on services utilized by Medicaid beneficiaries—information typically referred to as encounter data. Figure 1 illustrates these models.

## State and MCO Program Integrity Responsibilities

Program integrity refers to the proper management and function of the Medicaid program to ensure that quality and efficient care is being provided, while Medicaid payments are used appropriately and with minimal waste. Program integrity efforts encompass a variety of administrative, review, and law enforcement strategies.

State stakeholders—Medicaid managed care offices, state Medicaid program integrity units, Medicaid Fraud Control Units (MFCUs), and in many cases state auditors—and MCO stakeholders—MCOs that contract with states to deliver Medicaid services—play important roles in the oversight of managed care payment risks and have a variety of program integrity responsibilities. A stakeholder's program integrity responsibilities can be specialized—such as for MFCUs, which focus on fraudulent behavior—or varied—such as for state Medicaid managed care offices and MCOs, which are responsible for monitoring fraud and other issues, such as compliance with quality standards or ensuring MCOs meet contract requirements. (See table 1.)

Two of the stakeholders—state Medicaid managed care offices and MCOs—have responsibilities for program operation in addition to program integrity oversight responsibilities. For example, state Medicaid managed care offices' program operations responsibilities include enrolling beneficiaries, negotiating contracts with MCOs, developing capitation rates, and making monthly capitation payments to MCOs. MCOs' program operation responsibilities include establishing contracts with providers, creating provider networks, ensuring that enrollees have an ongoing source of primary care and timely access to needed services, and processing and paying provider claims.

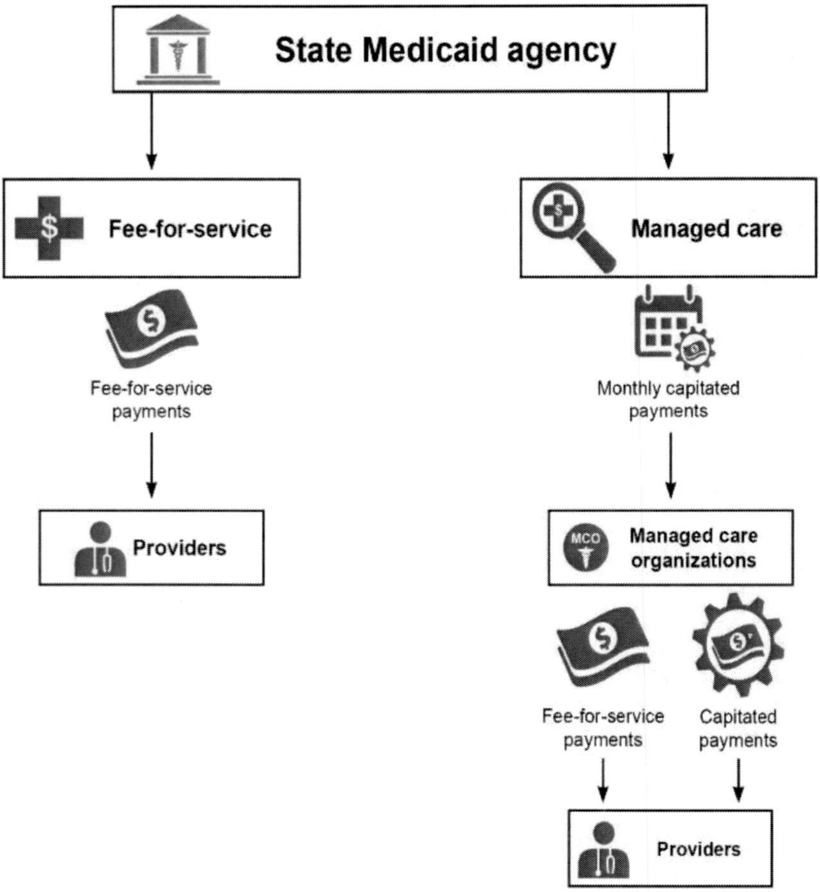


Source: GAO. | GAO-18-528.

Notes:

States may have different types of managed care arrangements in their Medicaid programs, some of which have a limited benefit package or do not assume financial risk for services provided. In this chapter, we are referring to comprehensive, risk-based managed care provided through MCOs, which is the most common managed care arrangement.

Managed care organizations may also pay providers through other payment approaches in which the provider assumes some risk for covered services.

Figure 1. Medicaid Fee-for-Service and Managed Care Delivery Models.

**Table 1. Examples of Program Integrity Oversight Responsibilities of State-Level Stakeholders in Medicaid Managed Care**

| State-level stakeholder | Examples of program integrity oversight responsibilities |
|---|---|
| State Medicaid managed care offices | State Medicaid managed care offices are responsible for reviewing MCO quality standard reports, and monitoring MCO compliance with contract requirements, such as those related to network adequacy, reporting overpayments to, or fraud by, providers, and reporting ineligible or deceased individuals. |
| State program integrity units | State program integrity units may have responsibility for program integrity for services delivered under both managed care and fee-for-service. These units are responsible for developing policies to prevent Medicaid improper payments, identify improper payments the Medicaid agency has made, and recover improper payments. They also may be responsible for ensuring that providers that engage in fraudulent or abuse activities do not enroll in the program and are reported as terminated providers. |
| Medicaid Fraud Control Units (MFCU) | MFCUs are responsible for investigating and prosecuting Medicaid fraud. MFCUs are generally located in state Attorney General offices. State program integrity units refer potential fraud cases to MFCUs for further investigation and legal action. |
| State auditors | State auditors are responsible for assessing financial management and accountability in state government agencies and programs. The extent to which state audit offices conduct audits of a state Medicaid program—and audits particularly of Medicaid managed care—can vary by state. |
| Managed care organizations (MCO) | MCOs are responsible for developing policies and implementing procedures to prevent incorrect payments to providers, monitoring providers to ensure they are complying with program requirements, reporting overpayments made to providers, reporting ineligible or deceased individuals, and reporting providers engaged in fraudulent activity. |

Source: GAO analysis of information from state auditors, the Medicaid and CHIP Payment and Access Commission, and the National Association of State Medicaid Fraud Control Units. I GAO-18-528.

Note: States vary in the organizational structure of their Medicaid program. For example, in some states the program integrity unit may be within the managed care office, while in other states it may be separate.

In a previous report, we found that state Medicaid program integrity efforts focus primarily on payments and services delivered under fee-for-service, and do not closely examine program integrity in managed care.[194] For example, officials from five of seven states that we spoke to for that report said that they primarily focused their program integrity efforts on fee-for-service claims. They also noted that program integrity in Medicaid managed care was more complex than for fee-for-service.

## CMS's Program Integrity Responsibilities

CMS's program integrity responsibilities take a variety of forms. CMS issues program requirements for states through regulations and guidance; for example, regulations requiring states to establish actuarially sound capitation rates and to ensure that MCOs have an adequate network of providers, as well as to ensure that all covered services are available and accessible to beneficiaries in a timely manner.[195] CMS also requires states to submit MCO contracts and capitation rates to CMS for review and approval, and report key information such as encounter data collected from MCOs. The agency provides technical assistance and educational support to states, including having staff available to help states with specific issues or questions, and providing courses on program integrity issues. The agency also conducts periodic reviews to assess state program integrity policies, processes, and capabilities. In addition, CMS has engaged audit contractors to help states audit providers receiving Medicaid payments, including payments made by MCOs to providers.

---

[194] See GAO, *Medicaid Program Integrity: Increased Oversight Needed to Ensure Integrity of Growing Managed Care Expenditures*, GAO-14-341 (Washington, D.C.: May 19, 2014). In this report we recommended that CMS require states to conduct audits of managed care payments, update its guidance on program integrity in managed care, and provide additional support to states. CMS implemented these recommendations.

[195] In May 2016, CMS issued a final rule on Medicaid managed care to enhance regulatory provisions in a range of program integrity areas. In general, actuarially sound capitation rates are certified by an actuary as being appropriate for the populations and services covered. Rates are to be adequate for MCOs to meet requirements for ensuring availability and timely access to services, adequate networks, and coordination and continuity of care. See 42 C.F.R. §§ 438.4, 438.206, 438.207, 438.208 (2017).

# SIX TYPES OF PAYMENT RISKS EXIST FOR MANAGED CARE, WITH STAKEHOLDERS VIEWING SOME RISKS AS GREATER THAN OTHERS

We identified six types of payment risks through our review of Medicaid audit reports and other sources. Most of the stakeholders we spoke to agreed that these payment risks exist in Medicaid managed care. Four of these risks relate to the payments state Medicaid agencies make to MCOs, and two relate to payments that MCOs make to providers. (See figures 2 and 3.)

| PAYMENT RISK | GENERAL DESCRIPTION |
|---|---|
| **Improper state capitation payments** | State makes monthly capitation payments to an MCO for beneficiaries who are ineligible for Medicaid, not enrolled in Medicaid or who have died. |
| **Inaccurate state capitation rates** | State establishes capitation rates that are inaccurate, primarily due to issues with the data used to set the rates.[a] |
| **State payments to noncompliant MCO** | State makes monthly capitation payments to an MCO for beneficiaries even though the MCO has not fulfilled state contract requirements.[b] |
| **Duplicate state payments** | State makes duplicate payments—for example, when a health care provider submits a fee-for-service claim to the state Medicaid program for services that were covered by the MCO contract. |

Source: GAO analysis of audit and other reports. | GAO-18-528.

[a] Examples of data issues include inaccurate encounter data, MCO reported costs that are not allowable, overpayments that are not adjusted, or data that do not reflect changes in care delivery practices that have affected MCO costs.

[b] Examples of unfulfilled contract requirements may include an MCO not establishing an adequate provider network, reporting inaccurate encounter data for services, or not reporting the amount of overpayments the MCO made to providers.

Figure 2. Payment Risks Related to State Medicaid Program Payments to Managed Care Organizations (MCO).

| | PAYMENT RISK | GENERAL DESCRIPTION |
|---|---|---|
|  | **Incorrect MCO fee-for-service payments** | MCO pays providers for improper or false claims, such as claims for services (a) not provided, or provided by ineligible providers, or (b) that represent inappropriate billing, such as billing individually for bundled services or for a higher intensity of services than needed. |
|  | **Incorrect MCO capitation payments** | MCO pays providers without assurance they have provided needed services.[a] |

Source: GAO analysis of audit and other reports. | GAO-18-528.

[a] Incorrect MCO capitation payments may result from false claims submitted by providers, data that do not reflect changes in care delivery practices and related costs, or lack of assurance that providers are delivering all medically necessary services to beneficiaries.

Figure 3. Payment Risks Related to Medicaid Managed Care Organization (MCO) Payments to Providers.

In terms of the relative importance of these payment risks, two payment risks were more frequently cited by stakeholders as having a higher level of risk than other types—incorrect MCO fee-for-service payments to providers and inaccurate state capitation rates. The remaining four payment risks were more frequently cited as having lower or unknown levels of risk: improper state capitation payments, state payments to noncompliant MCOs, incorrect MCO capitation payments, and duplicate state payments. (See figure 4.) When we asked stakeholders to designate a level of risk, stakeholders whose primary responsibility is program integrity—state auditors, MFCU officials, and state Medicaid program integrity staff—were more likely to assign a higher level of risk for certain types of payment risks than state Medicaid managed care officials and MCO officials. (See app. I for additional information on risk level designation by stakeholder group.)

Stakeholders provided the following examples of payment risks that they rated as having "some" or "high" risk in the state. (See table 2.) See appendix II for further examples of payment risks identified as part of our review of audits and other reports.

# Multiple Challenges Exist for Effective Program Integrity Oversight and Stakeholders Identified Strategies to Address Them

We identified six challenges to effective program integrity oversight in Medicaid managed care based on our review of Medicaid audit reports and other sources.

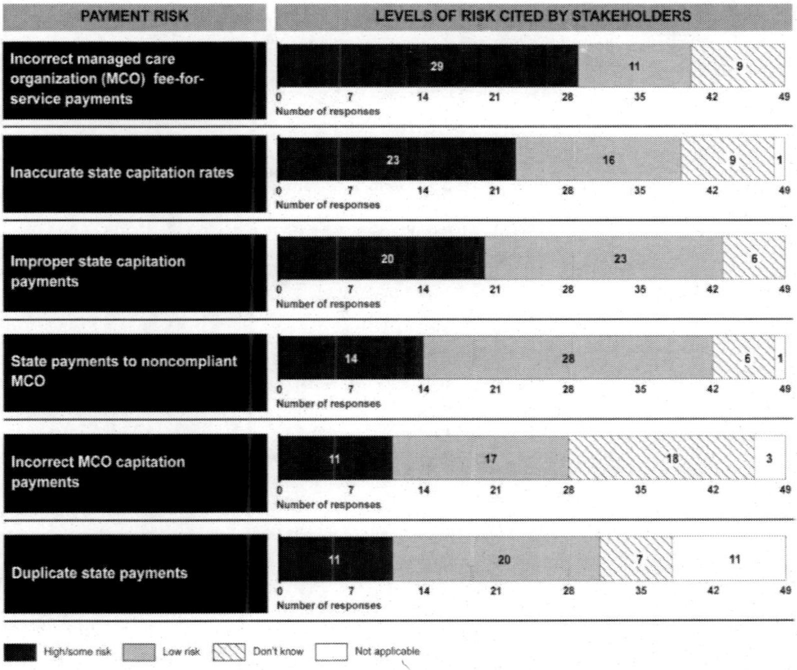


Source: GAO analysis of information from interviews with program integrity stakeholders. | GAO-18-528.

Note: We interviewed 49 stakeholders in 10 states, including the state Medicaid managed care office, the state Medicaid program integrity unit, the state auditor, the state Medicaid Fraud Control Unit, and a managed care organization. Some stakeholders occasionally said they did not have enough information to assign a level of risk ("Don't know") or that one of the payment risks did not apply in the state ("Not applicable").

Figure 4. Stakeholders' Views of the Level of Risk Associated with Each Type of Medicaid Managed Care Payment Risk.

## Table 2. Examples of Types of Payment Risks in Medicaid Managed Care

| Payment risk | Examples cited by stakeholders |
|---|---|
| Incorrect managed care organization (MCO) fee-for-service payments | • A Medicaid program integrity official said his state had experienced a range of cases relating to this payment risk, including in-home care and psychiatric providers who billed MCOs for services they did not provide; providers giving excessive prescriptions and drug tests; billing for multiple services when only one was provided; providing services that were not medically necessary.<br>• A Medicaid Fraud Control Unit (MFCU) official in one state noted that MCOs paid providers for certain ineligible services for several years before it became known, and a MFCU official in another state cited MCOs paying people who are not enrolled as Medicaid providers.<br>• A state auditor described a case of a provider who was submitting upcoded bills—billing for more severe illnesses than what existed or for more expensive services than what was provided. |
| Inaccurate state capitation rates | • A Medicaid program integrity official said there was no verification that adjustments were made to the capitation rate for potentially fraudulent claims.<br>• A Medicaid managed care official in another state said there were problems with encounter data accuracy that could affect rate-setting.<br>• A MFCU official said there could be an appreciable amount of overpayments "baked into" the state's capitation rates.<br>• A Medicaid program integrity official in another state noted that it was unclear whether MCOs were reporting overpayments. |
| Improper state capitation Payments | • A Medicaid program integrity official said that the state had been unable to access information on deceased individuals from the federal government for close to 2 months.<br>• A state auditor said that the state had lost access to a key database, and that one tenth of their beneficiaries may be ineligible.<br>• Another state auditor said that beneficiaries' eligibility status changed frequently in their Medicaid population, and validating eligibility changes over time was challenging. |

| Payment risk | Examples cited by stakeholders |
|---|---|
| State payments to noncompliant MCO | • A state auditor explained that while there are lots of reporting requirements for MCOs, the state does not always do a good job of reviewing the MCOs' reports and taking any necessary action.<br>• A MFCU official expressed concern that MCOs were not meeting contract requirements to report fraud, because there were a relatively low number of referrals of possible fraud in managed care compared with referrals in fee-for-service. |
| Incorrect MCO capitation payments | • A state Medicaid managed care official said there was not much the state could do to mitigate this risk, because it is dependent on the MCO to monitor providers.<br>• One of the MCO officials said there is some risk of this, because it is very resource intensive for a health plan to audit medical records to confirm that providers are providing needed services. |
| Duplicate state payments | • A MFCU official said that providers know this is a payment area they can easily abuse.<br>• A state auditor explained that providers are "creatures of habit" and will continue to bill the state as long as they get paid. In those cases, it is the responsibility of the state agency to check the providers' claims |

Source: GAO analysis of information from interviews with program integrity stakeholders. | GAO-18-528.

Note: We interviewed 49 stakeholders in 10 states, including the state Medicaid managed care office, the state Medicaid program integrity unit, the state auditor, the state MFCU, and a managed care organization.

Among these six challenges, stakeholders most frequently cited allocation of resources, quality of data and technology, and adequacy of state policies and practices as key challenges. Some stakeholders also described strategies to address these challenges.

## Key Challenges to Oversight Included Resource Allocation, the Quality of Data and Technology, and the Adequacy of State Policies and Practices

Through our research on examples of payment risks in Medicaid managed care, we identified six areas that can present challenges to program integrity oversight, including (1) availability and allocation of resources; (2) access to and quality of data and technology; (3) state policies and practices; (4) provider compliance with program requirements; (5) MCO management of program integrity; and (6) federal regulations, guidance, and review. Allocation of resources, quality of data and technology, and state policies and practices were the three most commonly cited challenges to program integrity oversight by stakeholders. (See figure 5.)

Stakeholders described the following examples of challenges to program integrity oversight they had observed. See appendix III for more information on the particular challenges for each of the payment risks.

### *Availability and Allocation of Resources*

Stakeholders who cited resource allocation as an oversight challenge to managed care cited several key issues, such as the number of staff allocated to an activity, the expertise needed, and the ability to retain and replace staff. (See table 3.) Some stakeholders identified resource issues within their own organizations, while some identified resource issues they said existed in other organizations.

### *Access to and Quality of Data and Technology*

Stakeholders who cited the quality of data and technology as oversight challenges to managed care provided examples related to timely access to data, inaccurate and unreliable data, and problems with information systems and interfaces. (See table 4.)

### *State Policies and Practices*

Stakeholders who cited state policies and practices as an oversight challenge to managed care described insufficient contract requirements, lack of state monitoring, and problems with state oversight. (See table 5.) Stakeholders from the state program integrity office, the MFCU, and the state auditor's office more frequently identified state policies and practices as a challenge than stakeholders from the state Medicaid managed care agency.

# Table 3. Stakeholder Examples of Oversight Challenges Related to Resource Allocation for Medicaid Managed Care

| Type of resource challenge | Examples of challenges cited |
|---|---|
| Funds and staff | • A state auditor said the state's Medicaid applications have grown dramatically in recent years, but resources to determine eligibility have not.<br>• Several stakeholders—including a managed care organization (MCO) official, two state program integrity officials, and two Medicaid Fraud Control Unit (MFCU) officials—noted that some MCOs lack sufficient staff resources to detect incorrect MCO payments to their providers.<br>• A Medicaid managed care official said the state does not have enough staff to review data on deceased and ineligible individuals and therefore they rely on MCOs to do it. |
| Expertise | • One state auditor cited the lack of in-house expertise as a challenge. They explained that all expertise with information technology systems has become the purview of contractors, and that very few state employees are able to access the information resulting in extensive delays in identifying deceased and ineligible individuals. Additionally, even though the state relies on MCO encounter data in setting capitation rates, there are no staff at the state level with sufficient knowledge to look at the data without the use of consultants.<br>• A Medicaid managed care official noted that they have been unable to fill several budgeted vacancies in the actuarial division, because the state has not found people with the right expertise. |
| Retaining and replacing staff | • A state auditor said that the state was not timely in identifying risks of paying for ineligible or deceased beneficiaries, because of personnel turnover and difficulty in filling vacancies in the eligibility determination and oversight and monitoring units.<br>• A Medicaid managed care official said that, given the state pay scale, it has been hard to recruit staff with clinical training. |

Source: GAO analysis of information from interviews with program integrity stakeholders. I GAO-18-528.

Note: We interviewed 49 stakeholders in 10 states, including the state Medicaid managed care office, the state Medicaid program integrity unit, the state auditor, the state MFCU, and a managed care organization.

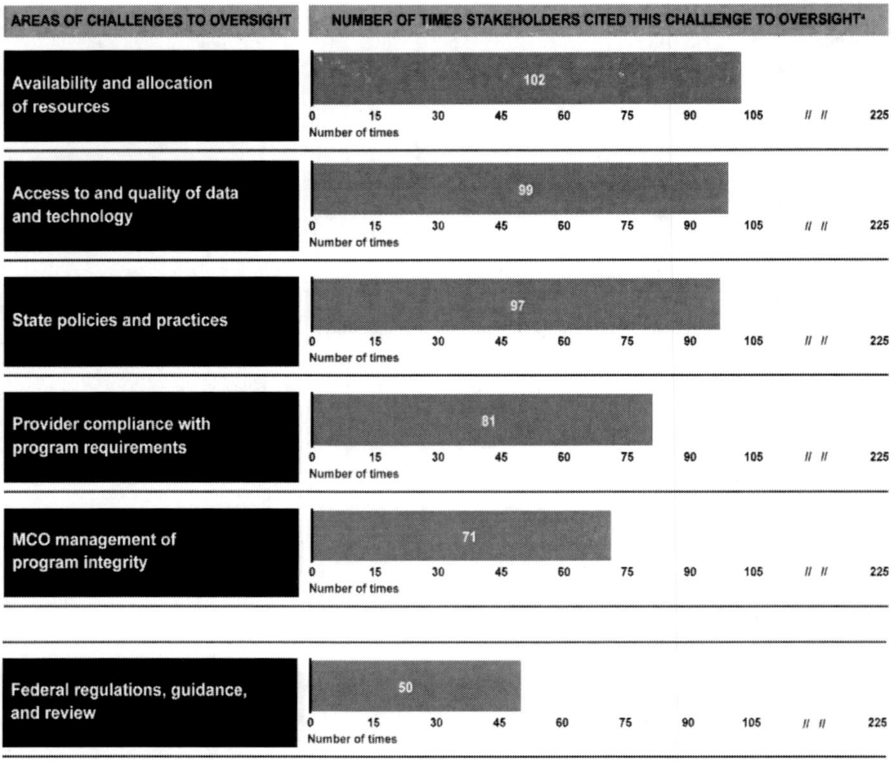


Source: GAO analysis of information from interviews with program integrity stakeholders. | GAO-18-528.

[a] These data are out of 228 total responses. We interviewed 49 stakeholders in 10 states, including the state Medicaid managed care office, the state Medicaid program integrity unit, the state auditor, the state Medicaid Fraud Control Unit, and a managed care organization (MCO). Stakeholders were asked to state whether each challenge was present for each of the six payment risks. Stakeholder responses were not included in the total if the respondent either did not know enough to discuss a particular payment risk (answered "don't know" for risk level and did not answer questions regarding challenges), or stated that the questions were not applicable for a payment type (answered "N/A" for risk level).

Figure 5. Frequency of Stakeholder Citing of Six Challenges to Medicaid Managed Care Oversight.

# Table 4. Stakeholder Examples of Oversight Challenges Related to Data and Technology for Medicaid Managed Care

| Type of data and technology challenge | Examples of challenges cited |
|---|---|
| Access to data | • Stakeholders in three states reported challenges in getting access to federal data on deceased individuals.<br>• A Medicaid program integrity official said they could not access the state's death records due to lack of agreement within the state over departmental responsibilities. |
| Encounter data accuracy and reliability | • Two Medicaid program integrity officials said they have had problems getting accurate and complete encounter data from managed care organizations (MCO).<br>• A Medicaid managed care official said there were problems with the quality of data received from MCOs for providers of non-traditional services, such as transportation to medical appointments.<br>• One Medicaid Fraud Control Unit (MFCU) official explained that MCOs report data in different formats, and another MFCU said that the data MCOs report to the state agency are not consistent with the data the MCOs provided to the MFCU.<br>• An MCO official said that the state's algorithm for calculating capitation rates did not incorporate all of the encounter data they submitted to the state, potentially affecting the accuracy of the rates in covering medical costs. |
| Information systems | • A Medicaid program integrity official said the state did not have a way to determine whether an individual is enrolled in more than one plan.<br>• A state auditor reported problems with the interface between the state's eligibility and claims processing systems, which affected their ability to ensure they were not paying for deceased individuals.<br>• A MFCU official said that the risk of the state making duplicate payments is related to the lack of interface between eligibility and claims payment systems. |

Source: GAO analysis of information from interviews with program integrity stakeholders. I GAO-18-528.

Note: We interviewed 49 stakeholders in 10 states, including the state Medicaid managed care office, the state Medicaid program integrity unit, the state auditor, the state MFCU, and a managed care organization.

## Table 5. Stakeholder Examples of Oversight Challenges Related to State Policies and Practices for Medicaid Managed Care

| Type of state policy and practice challenge | Examples of challenges cited |
|---|---|
| State MCO contracts and guidance | • A Medicaid Fraud Control Unit (MFCU) official noted a lack of fraud referrals from managed care organizations (MCO) and said this could be related to a lack of effective contract provisions related to MCO identification of overpayments. |
| State MCO contracts and guidance | • A state managed care official said that MCOs reported minimal information to the state, because the state did not provide guidelines or a template of reporting requirements.<br>• A state auditor said there is nothing in the contract about recovering capitation payments from MCOs for ineligible individuals.<br>• MCO officials from two states said that with respect to inaccurate payments to providers, there has been a lack of consistent guidance from the state about what services are covered and what are not covered. |
| Monitoring | • Multiple stakeholders noted the lack of state efforts to monitor important information related to payment risks. For example, a state auditor said no one was validating the accuracy of MCO beneficiary eligibility. A Medicaid program integrity official said that no one in the state was monitoring whether overpayments were being reported by MCOs or if adjustments for overpayments are made in setting capitation rates. A state auditor conducted multiple audits that showed that the state was not checking claims and was making fee-for-service payments to providers for services that should be covered by the MCOs.<br>• An MCO official said that because of state delays in reviewing beneficiary eligibility, the utilization data used by the state to set capitation rates reflected a different beneficiary population than was ultimately enrolled in the program. |
| Oversight | • A state auditor said that sanctions were used very infrequently, and even if the contract allowed for a penalty, the state did not exercise the right to enforce it.<br>• An MCO official said that because the state does not get back to the MCO about reported cases of potential fraud in a timely manner, it becomes difficult not to pay the provider. |

Source: GAO analysis of information from interviews with program integrity stakeholders. I GAO-18-528.

Note: We interviewed 49 stakeholders in 10 states, including the state Medicaid managed care office, the state Medicaid program integrity unit, the state auditor, the state MFCU, and a managed care organization.

### *MCO Management of Program Integrity*

Stakeholders who cited MCO management as an oversight challenge to managed care described how inadequate MCO oversight and monitoring—as well as incomplete MCO reporting to the state agency—can increase the risk of different types of payment risks. (See table 6.) Stakeholders from the state Medicaid managed care agency, the state program integrity office, and the MFCU were more likely than MCO stakeholders to cite these issues as challenges. In particular, a few state officials noted that there was variation in size and resources among the MCOs in their respective states.

### *Provider Compliance with Program Requirements*

Stakeholders who cited provider compliance as a challenge to oversight indicated that providers are the primary source of inaccurate payments, because of improper billing, which may include fraudulent billing. These stakeholders also stated that some types of providers presented a higher risk than others in their state. Several stakeholders pointed out that certain providers intentionally commit fraud, while others may be unaware of changes in policies or procedures and therefore unintentionally submit inaccurate claims.

Several stakeholders noted that it is the responsibility of providers to bill correctly, while a few others pointed out that because the payment process is complicated, MCOs and state agencies may not identify inaccurate payments. Stakeholders also selected from a list of 19 types of providers the 3 or 4 that in their view represented the highest payment risks in the state. The two most frequently mentioned health care providers or services were (1) durable medical equipment, and (2) psychiatric and behavioral health care providers. (See table 7.)

## Table 6. Stakeholder Examples of Oversight Challenges Related to Managed Care Organization (MCO) Management

| Type of MCO Management challenge | Examples of challenges |
|---|---|
| Oversight and monitoring | • An MCO official said smaller MCOs in the state do not do as good a job in oversight of certain subcontracted partners—such as dental care organizations—as other MCOs, and this may negatively affect other MCOs ability to oversee these organizations.<br>• A Medicaid Fraud Control Unit (MFCU) official said MCOs in the state needed to do a better job of communicating state regulations to providers, and of monitoring provider claims. |
| Reporting to the state agency | • A Medicaid program integrity official said that MCOs do not investigate the accuracy of provider claims or report updated claims to the state, and therefore needed adjustments are not made to the capitation rate.<br>• Two MFCU officials and a Medicaid managed care official said that MCOs do not report overpayments, because they want to maintain good relationships with providers. One explained that MCOs are under pressure to maintain an adequate network, so they will address problems internally rather than report and lose a provider who fills a key clinical need. Another official said that MCOs seek to avoid creating "provider abrasion." The third said that MCOs may be likely to determine that a provider should be educated rather than referred for prosecution.[a]<br>• Four officials said that MCOs lack financial incentives to identify and report inaccurate payments. A state auditor said that MCOs do not have an incentive to report inaccurate payments, because they get higher payments. A MFCU official said that MCOs in the state did not have the incentive to refer providers for prosecution, because they may not recover the money that is overpaid. |

Source: GAO analysis of information from interviews with program integrity stakeholders. I GAO-18-528.

Note: We interviewed 49 stakeholders in 10 states, including the state Medicaid managed care office, the state Medicaid program integrity unit, the state auditor, the state MFCU, and a managed care organization.

[a]"Provider abrasion" is a term used in the health care industry to refer to cases where providers express frustration due to delayed or rejected claims payments, or what they view as excessive oversight.

### Table 7. Health Care Providers and Services Most Frequently Identified by Stakeholders as Having the Highest Risk for Payment Error in Medicaid Managed Care

| Type of provider or service | Number of times identified as among the top four providers or services at risk for payment error[a] |
|---|---|
| Durable medical equipment | 19 |
| Psychiatric and behavioral health care (including both mental illness and substance abuse | 19 |
| Prescription drugs | 13 |
| Laboratory, x-ray, and imaging | 12 |
| Personal care or support | 11 |
| Pharmacy | 10 |
| Home health | 9 |
| Long term care services and supports in the home and community generally | 8 |
| Primary care physicians and related licensed practitioners | 8 |

Source: GAO analysis of information from interviews with program integrity stakeholders. I GAO-18-528.

Note: We interviewed 49 stakeholders in 10 states, including the state Medicaid managed care office, the state Medicaid program integrity unit, the state auditor, the state Medicaid Fraud Control Unit, and a managed care organization.

[a] Forty-three of 49 stakeholders answered this question, while the remaining 6 stakeholders said that they did not have enough information to make this determination. Other providers and services that four, five, or six stakeholders identified as presenting high risks included dental and other oral surgery services, inpatient hospitals, transportation and other accommodations, and long term care institutions, such as nursing homes and intermediate care facilities.

### *Federal Regulations, Guidance, and Review*

Over half of the stakeholders who identified federal regulations, guidance, and review as oversight challenges to managed care cited the complexity of federal regulations and the lack of federal guidance as key issues. For example, one stakeholder said that there needed to be more clarity about the new regulations for setting capitation rates for MCOs, while another said that there was a lack of clarity about the respective roles of states and MCOs in program integrity oversight. One stakeholder noted that most of the responsibility for operating the Medicaid program lies with the state, not with the federal government.

## Strategies Identified by Stakeholders to Address Managed Care Oversight Challenges Included Ensuring High Quality Data and Collaboration among State Agencies and MCOs

Some stakeholders we interviewed identified strategies, controls, or best practices to address the challenges to oversight of Medicaid managed care payment risks. As shown in table 8, they identified a variety of strategies such as ensuring high quality data, collaboration among state agencies and MCOs, imposing sanctions on noncompliant MCOs, enhancing contract requirements, and conducting regular monitoring.

**Table 8. Strategies Identified by Stakeholders to Address Selected Medicaid Managed Care Payment Risks**

| Strategy | Examples | Payment risks addressed |
|---|---|---|
| Ensure high quality and useful data through automated edit checks | Conduct editing of encounter data sent by managed care organizations (MCO) to determine if it can be accepted. In one state, if too many encounters are rejected, all of the data are sent back to the MCO. | Inaccurate state capitation rates |
| | Implement a system edit that automatically recoups payments after an individual has unenrolled. | Improper state capitation payments |
| | Implement edits in claims processing systems to prevent claims that should be covered by MCOs from being paid by the state through feefor-service. | Duplicate state payments |
| Facilitate collaboration between state agencies and MCOs | Collaboration among stakeholders to more easily identify common fraud schemes. Because each stakeholder may have limited data and a narrowly defined role in the process, collaboration allows the stakeholders to share their data to more efficiently catch and prosecute fraudulent behavior. | State payments to noncompliant MCOs Incorrect MCO fee-for-service payments |

| Strategy | Examples | Payment risks addressed |
|---|---|---|
| | Meet with MCOs on a monthly or quarterly basis to facilitate in the reporting of information required by the contract. In one state, these meetings lead to clarification of contract language. | State payments to noncompliant MCOs |
| Regularly audit plans and providers | Conduct annual audits of plans' quality performance, and review utilization against state and national averages in order to identify potential underutilization patterns. An MCO official reported that the MCO audited its capitated provider networks. | Incorrect MCO capitation payments |
| Enhance contract requirements | Require MCOs to provide a daily electronic eligibility file to the state, and to inform the state if the MCO is aware that an enrollee's eligibility should be terminated due to death or ineligibility. | Improper state capitation payments |
| Regularly assess and prioritize resource allocation | Employ a risk assessment process to continually set priorities on where to use staff and other resources. The official described this as an effort to manage resource limitations. | Improper state capitation payments |
| Regularly monitor health care providers | Regularly monitor capitated networks for under- and over-utilization, including review of utilization for common services and comparing them to state and national averages. | Incorrect MCO capitation payments |
| Target reporting needs | Require MCOs to submit on a quarterly basis the number of complaints, referrals, or inquiries that they've received, as well as overpayments identified, and providers that the MCO has unenrolled. | Incorrect MCO fee-for-service payments |
| Provide focused education | Educate MCOs and providers about what fraud, waste, and abuse are, as well as benefit policies and coverage. | Incorrect MCO fee-for-service payment risks addressed |
| Actively employ sanctions | In one state, 95 percent of encounters must be submitted within a certain time frame to avoid sanction by the state, which allows the state time to review the data. | Inaccurate state capitation rates |

Source: GAO analysis of information from interviews with program integrity stakeholders. I GAO-18-528.

Note: We interviewed 49 stakeholders in 10 states, including the state Medicaid managed care office, the state Medicaid program integrity unit, the state auditor, the state Medicaid Fraud Control Unit, and a managed care organization.

# CMS Has Assisted States in Addressing Payment Risks, but Some Efforts Have Been Delayed and There Are Gaps in Oversight

CMS has taken important steps to address payment risks in Medicaid managed care, issuing a final rule, increasing guidance, and conducting oversight activities. However, some efforts are incomplete, and there are gaps in key oversight activities.

## CMS Issued a Final Rule, Provided Additional Guidance, and Updated Certain Oversight Activities Related to Managed Care Program Integrity

In May 2016, CMS issued a final rule on Medicaid managed care. According to CMS, the rule is intended to enhance regulatory provisions related to program integrity and payment risks, among other things.[196] These regulatory provisions varied in terms of when the requirements were applicable. For example, for contracts beginning on or after July 1, 2017, the rule requires

- state contracts with MCOs to require MCOs to promptly report all overpayments made to providers, and to specify the overpayments due to potential fraud; [197]
- states to account for overpayments when setting capitation payment amounts;[198] and

---

[196] The rule was issued to strengthen actuarial soundness payment provisions to promote accountability of Medicaid managed care program rates, promote the quality of care and strengthen efforts to reform delivery systems, and ensure beneficiary protections, in addition to enhancing policies related to program integrity. A number of the provisions of the rule were applicable for state contracts with MCOs for rating periods starting on or after July 1, 2017, while some were scheduled to take effect for later rating periods.

[197] See 42 C.F.R. § 438.608(a)(2) (2017).

[198] See 42 C.F.R. § 438.608(d)(4) (2017).

- states to establish procedures and quality assurance protocols to ensure that MCOs submit encounter data that is complete and accurate.[199]

These requirements have the potential to enhance MCO and state oversight of managed care, and address payment risks involving incorrect MCO payments to providers and inaccurate state capitation rates for MCOs. CMS is currently reviewing the rule for possible revision of its requirements and an announcement on the results of the review is expected in 2018.[200]

Most stakeholders we spoke to identified ways in which the managed care rule could have a positive impact on managed care program integrity oversight. Of the 49 stakeholders we spoke to, 28 made positive statements about the rule's potential impact on program integrity oversight of payment risks in managed care, 9 stakeholders said they were not familiar enough with the managed care rule to comment on it, and the remaining 12 stakeholders provided a range of comments about the rule. The 28 stakeholders with positive comments identified a variety of ways in which they said the managed care rule would help, including

- reducing improper payments;
- establishing transparency in setting state capitation rates;
- providing clear guidelines for MCO reporting, and clear authority for states to require reporting;
- obtaining information on overpayments identified and collected by MCOs;
- holding MCO leadership accountable for meeting program requirements; and
- reducing medical costs, despite additional short-term administrative costs.

---

[199] See 42 C.F.R. §§ 438.242(d), 438.818(a)(2).

[200] CMS indicated it will issue a Notice of Proposed Rulemaking in 2018 to streamline Medicaid managed care regulations and reduce burden. See Department of Health and Human Services, Medicaid and CHIP Managed Care, *Spring 2018 Unified Agenda of Federal Regulatory and Deregulatory Actions*, (CMS-2480-P), RIN 0938-AT40, accessed May 14, 2018, http://www.reginfo.gov.

- Comments by the other 12 stakeholders who were familiar with the rule included statements that the rule
- should have been more aggressive in requiring MCOs to implement efforts related to program integrity;
- would have limited impact for them, because many of its requirements were already in place in their state; and set time frames for implementation that were hard to meet.

In addition to issuing the rule, CMS has sought to increase guidance available to states through training, technical assistance, and other educational resources. (See table 9.)

**Table 9. CMS Steps to Increase Guidance on Oversight of Payment Risks in Medicaid Managed Care**

| Type of guidance | CMS steps |
|---|---|
| Training | In 2017, the Centers for Medicare & Medicaid Services (CMS) expanded the course offerings of the Medicaid Integrity Institute—a national training program for state program integrity officials—to include courses on vulnerabilities in Medicaid managed care, state enrollment of managed care contracted providers, and how to handle denials and terminations of ineligible providers. CMS officials told us that these courses, as well as other ongoing courses at the institute, cover multiple payment risks in Medicaid managed care through case studies and participant discussion.<br>The Medicaid Fraud and Abuse Technical Advisory Group convened a Managed Care Audits & Overpayments subgroup from July to October 2017 to facilitate exchanges between CMS, the institute, and states on issues states are facing.[a] |
| Technical assistance | CMS officials told us that they have increased the availability of staff to provide technical assistance to states.<br>Key topics that state officials raise with CMS include questions related to (1) overpayments that managed care organizations (MCO) make to providers; and (2) actuarial soundness issues associated with setting capitation rates for MCOs, including how to address overpayments in rate development, among other topics. |
| Other educational resources | In January 2017, the agency issued an information bulletin to facilitate state oversight of certain services for children and youth in Medicaid managed care.[b]<br>In April 2017, CMS issued a toolkit for states to assess whether MCOs have an adequate number of providers to serve beneficiaries.[c] |

| Type of guidance | CMS steps |
|---|---|
| | In June 2017, CMS issued an update to its Medicaid Provider Enrollment Compendium, which helps states ensure that their provider screening and enrollment will exclude ineligible providers and avoid making improper payments, among other things. The update includes guidance on the provider screening requirements for Medicaid managed care network providers.[d] |
| | In September 2017, CMS awarded a contract for the purpose of updating educational materials related to program integrity. CMS officials stated that they expected a shift in focus of educational tools toward managed care. |
| | In May 2018, CMS issued guidance about best practices that were identified through the agency's program integrity reviews. The guidance was issued to states and to the agency's Regional Information Sharing System. |

Source: CMS. I GAO-18-528.

[a] The Medicaid Fraud and Abuse Technical Advisory Group has been working with CMS since 1997, and includes state program integrity directors representing every CMS region. The group is divided into workgroups charged with identifying and developing suggestions that can be shared during monthly calls with states, CMS, and the Medicaid Integrity Institute.

[b] Department of Health and Human Services, Centers for Medicare & Medicaid Services, The Early and Periodic Screening, Diagnostic and Treatment (EPSDT) Benefit for Children and Youth in Managed Care, Informational Bulletin, Jan. 5, 2017.

[c] Centers for Medicare & Medicaid Services, Promoting Access in Medicaid and CHIP Managed Care: A Toolkit for Ensuring Provider Network Adequacy and Service Availability, April 2017.

[d] Centers for Medicare & Medicaid Services, Medicaid Provider Enrollment Compendium, updated June 2017.

Lastly, CMS efforts have included updating the requirements used in capitation rate setting reviews, contract oversight, and other types of audits and reviews, as described below.

- *Review of state capitation rates for Medicaid MCOs.* CMS reviews states' capitation rates at least once every year, and in 2017 made revisions to its rate review guidance to states, incorporating new requirements from the managed care rule. According to CMS officials, the agency typically conducts between 250 and 300 rate reviews annually to determine whether states' rate development methodologies meet generally accepted actuarial principles, as well as federal laws and requirements.

- *Review of state Medicaid MCO contracts*. CMS regularly reviews state contracts with MCOs to ensure that contract provisions meet federal requirements. In 2017, CMS updated its criteria for Medicaid managed care contract review and approval, and revised the guide that it provides to states to help them develop effective MCO contracts.[201]
- CMS contracted audits. In 2016, CMS began to transition and consolidate audits of providers to a type of contractor called Unified Program Integrity Contractors (UPIC). This transition is intended to integrate contracted audit activities across CMS health care programs, such as Medicaid and Medicare, according to CMS. Additionally, UPIC audits can include health care providers who participate in multiple federal programs. Within the Medicaid program, UPICs may conduct audits with states interested in pursuing what are called "collaborative audits." CMS's contract with UPICs allows for audits of providers in MCO networks.[202]
- Focused program integrity reviews. CMS officials said that in 2016, the agency updated the review guide used to conduct focused program integrity reviews of state Medicaid managed care programs.[203] CMS program integrity reviews have identified some common issues, such as a low number of investigations of overpayments conducted by managed care plans and a low amount

---

[201] See Centers for Medicare & Medicaid Services, State Guide to CMS Criteria for Medicaid Managed Care Contract Review and Approval, Jan. 20, 2017.

[202] The UPIC statement of work indicates that they shall investigate suspected instances of fraud, waste, and abuse involving providers performing under Medicaid managed care; and maintain an ongoing dialogue with the appropriate personnel of units in managed care organizations, including Medicaid MCOs in their region, as well as coordinate with the state Medicaid agency to develop contacts at the Medicaid MCOs. The managed care rule requires that all state contracts with MCOs provide the state, CMS, and the HHS-OIG with access to any records or documents of the MCO or its subcontractors, and such access supports the ability to conduct such audits.

[203] CMS officials said that program integrity reviews are conducted to assess the effectiveness of state program integrity efforts, including compliance with federal statutory and regulatory requirements. As we previously reported, in 2014, CMS shifted the emphasis of its reviews from a comprehensive approach to an approach that provided a more "focused review" on high risk areas of concern in each state, including managed care. See GAO-18-291.

of recoveries by plans.[204] However, CMS officials stated these reviews are not focused primarily on assessing specific payment risks. For example, these reviews do not involve an actual review or audit of MCO payments to providers to assess the extent that inaccurate payments were made. Instead, they review program integrity policies and processes, such as whether and how the state monitors overpayments, and whether MCOs comply with state requirements.

## CMS Efforts to Address Payment Risks Have Been Delayed and Gaps Exist in Key Oversight Activities

Despite CMS's efforts to improve oversight of program integrity in Medicaid managed care, there have been delays in issuing guidance, and gaps in key auditing and monitoring activities. These delays and gaps are inconsistent with the agency's current program integrity plan, which established goals for improving state oversight of program integrity in Medicaid managed care, as well as the financial accountability of Medicaid MCOs.[205]

### *Delays in the Development and Issuance of Guidance*

Publication of CMS guidance that would assist states in oversight of payment risks has been delayed. CMS officials told us in April 2017 that they planned to issue a compendium of guidance related to the managed care rule's program integrity regulations. The compendium is intended to provide guidance on (1) MCO program integrity requirements, (2) state audits of MCO encounter data that must be conducted at least every 3 years, and (3) MCO overpayments to providers. However, in September 2017, CMS

---

[204] See GAO, Medicaid Program Integrity: CMS Should Build on Current Oversight Efforts by Further Enhancing Collaboration with States, GAO-17-277 (Washington, D.C.: March 15, 2017).

[205] See Department of Health and Human Services, Centers for Medicare & Medicaid Services, *Comprehensive Medicaid Integrity Plan, Fiscal Years 2014-2018.*

officials told us that although they had a draft of the compendium, they did not have a timeline for issuing it, because the managed care rule was under review. As of May 2018, no issuance date has been set for the guidance. Over half of the stakeholders we interviewed who identified federal responsibilities as an oversight challenge to managed care cited the complexity of federal regulations and the lack of federal guidance as key issues. The lack of available federal guidance resulting from delays in issuing such guidance is inconsistent with federal internal control standards that call for federal agencies to communicate quality information to those responsible for program implementation for the purposes of achieving program objectives and addressing program risks.[206] Until such guidance is issued, stakeholders' ability to effectively address challenges to payment risks in Medicaid managed care will continue to be hindered.

### *Gaps in Auditing*

Although audits of providers that bill and are paid by MCOs can provide important information about payment risks and are included in the UPIC statement of work, only 14 of the 762 audits initiated by CMS contractors during the period of fiscal year 2014 through 2017 were managed care audits. Our review of three CMS contracted managed care audits indicated that the amount of inaccurate MCO payments to providers—as well as MCO and provider noncompliance with contracts—can be significant. For example, one audit of an MCO's payments to selected providers found that 8.94 percent of payments were in error, representing over $4 million in overpayments for a 6-month period. This audit also identified a lack of provider compliance with requirements to provide preventive care services and care coordination to members, and a lack of MCO compliance with requirements to monitor member enrollment, resulting in the MCO paying providers for individuals who were not enrolled.[207]

---

[206] See GAO-14-704G, Section 15.03.

[207] Among 27 audits and investigations of Medicaid managed care programs we recently reviewed, 10 identified about $68 million in MCO overpayments to providers and other unallowable MCO costs, and 1 investigation resulted in a $137.5 million settlement to resolve allegations of false claims. See GAO-18-291.

CMS officials shared plans to increase collaborative audits in managed care in the future. CMS officials said the agency is in the early planning stages to pilot an audit of MCO providers in one state, with the goal of addressing challenges encountered in prior managed care audits. CMS is also in discussions with states and audit contractors to conduct potential audits and investigations in fiscal years 2018 and 2019.

However, CMS and audit contractor officials identified several circumstances related to states' contracts with MCOs that they said have created gaps in their auditing activity.

- According to CMS officials, states have reported a reluctance to conduct provider audits when states' contracts with MCOs (1) allow the MCO to retain identified overpayments, or (2) do not explicitly discuss how identified overpayments are addressed.
- Officials with the two operating UPICs told us that CMS's general guidance to them was to restrict their audits to states with MCO contracts where the states can recoup overpayments from the MCOs.[208]
- According to one contractor, because few states have such contracts, the vast majority of the contractors' audits are of providers paid on a fee-for-service basis. However, overpayments to providers can affect state and federal expenditures regardless of a state's particular recoupment policy, because if they are not accounted for, they may increase future capitation rates paid to MCOs.[209]
- Audit contractor officials also said the lack of access to MCO coverage and policy materials, and the inability to directly access encounter or claims data, prevent them from doing analyses to identify potential provider fraud, abuse, and waste for investigation.

---

[208] We spoke with the two UPICs that were operational at the time of our study, as well as one of the Medicaid Program Integrity Contractors that conducted audits prior to CMS contracts with UPICs.

[209] See GAO-18-291.

While CMS officials said they encourage states to participate in additional collaborative audits of managed care, they did not identify steps the agency is taking to address the circumstances that limit collaborative audits conducted. The lack of sufficient auditing in managed care is inconsistent with federal internal control standards that require federal agencies to identify risks through such activities as auditing.[210]

### *Gaps in Monitoring*

CMS has incomplete information on the scope and extent of MCO overpayments to providers, which results in a gap in monitoring MCO payments. Gaps in monitoring also exist because CMS lacks a process for consistently collecting information about overpayments and documenting that states account for overpayments when setting capitation rates. A few examples of these issues include the following:

- While CMS regularly reviews states' proposed capitation rates, it lacks a process to consistently ensure any overpayments are accounted for by the states. According to an official with CMS's Office of the Actuary, their review of state capitation rates does not require documentation of the amount of overpayments that occurred the prior year, how they were determined, or how they were incorporated into setting capitation rates. According to this official, issues between states and MCOs—such as contractual issues related to how overpayments are handled—are beyond the scope of their review and responsibilities. However, such information could be important to program integrity oversight; for example, 11 stakeholders we interviewed said that state capitation rates did not account for overpayments, because they had observed that overpayments were not reported by MCOs, were not monitored by the state, or both.
- Although some of CMS's focused program integrity reviews have suggested that there is under-reporting of MCO overpayments to

[210] See GAO-14-704G, Sections 7.02 and 7.04.

providers, CMS officials explained that these reviews are intended to assess state compliance with regulations, and not to determine the extent of under-reporting or why overpayments are under-reported.[211]

- States' and CMS's contracted auditors have conducted only a few collaborative audits in managed care, even though such audits can identify overpayments made by MCOs to providers.

These gaps in monitoring of overpayments are inconsistent with federal internal control standards that require federal agencies to monitor operating effectiveness through audits and reviews.[212] Without more complete information on the extent of overpayments and a process to ensure they are accounted for in state capitation rates, CMS is unable to ensure that MCOs are effectively identifying overpayments and documenting that they are accounted for when reviewing and approving state capitation rates. As a result, CMS cannot be sure that states are holding MCOs financially accountable for making proper payments, that states are paying accurate capitation payments to MCOs, or that the federal government's share of Medicaid expenditures is accurate.

## CONCLUSION

Managed care has the potential to help states reduce Medicaid program costs and better manage utilization of health care services. However, oversight of managed care is critical to achieving these goals. Payment risks are not eliminated under managed care; in fact, they are more complex and difficult to oversee. While CMS has taken important steps to improve program integrity in managed care—including strengthening regulations,

---

[211] In focused integrity reviews that CMS conducted in 27 states from 2014 to 2017, the agency found that MCOs in 17 states reported fewer overpayments to their state Medicaid agencies than CMS would expect.

[212] See GAO-14-704G, Sections 16.06–16.08.

developing guidance for states on provider enrollment in Medicaid managed care, and beginning to include managed care in the monitoring and auditing process—the efforts remain incomplete, because of delays and limited implementation. To date, CMS has not issued its planned compendium with guidance on program integrity in Medicaid managed care, taken steps to address known factors limiting collaborative audits, or developed a process to help ensure that overpayments to providers are identified by the states. Without taking actions to address these issues, CMS is missing an opportunity to develop more robust program integrity safeguards that will best mitigate payment risks in managed care.

## RECOMMENDATIONS FOR EXECUTIVE ACTION

We are making the following three recommendations to CMS:

- The Administrator of CMS should expedite the planned efforts to communicate guidance, such as its compendium on Medicaid managed care program integrity, to state stakeholders related to Medicaid managed care program integrity. (Recommendation 1)
- The Administrator of CMS should eliminate impediments to collaborative audits in managed care conducted by audit contractors and states, by ensuring that managed care audits are conducted regardless of which entity—the state or the managed care organization—recoups any identified overpayments. (Recommendation 2)
- The Administrator of CMS should require states to report and document the amount of MCO overpayments to providers and how they are accounted for in capitation rate-setting. (Recommendation 3)

## Agency Comments

We provided a draft of this product to the Department of Health and Human Services for comment. HHS concurred with these recommendations, stating that it is committed to Medicaid program integrity. HHS also cited examples of activities underway to improve oversight of the Medicaid program, such as training offered through the Medicaid Integrity Institute, and guidance provided in the Medicaid Provider Enrollment Compendium. The full text of HHS's comments is reproduced in appendix IV. HHS also provided technical comments, which we incorporated as appropriate.

We are sending copies of this chapter to the Secretary of Health and Human Services and the Administrator of CMS.

GAO staff that made key contributions to this chapter are listed in appendix V.

Carolyn L. Yocom
Director, Health Care

## Appendix I: Risk Level Designations by Stakeholder Group

We asked stakeholders involved in program integrity oversight to assign a level of risk—either low, some, or high—to six types of payment risks in Medicaid managed care.[1] We interviewed officials in the following five organizations in each of 10 states: state Medicaid managed care office, state program integrity unit, Medicaid Fraud Control Unit (MFCU), state

[1] The six payment risks are (1) improper state capitation payments to MCOs for ineligible or deceased individuals; (2) inaccurate state capitation rate; (3) state payments to MCOs that have not fulfilled contract requirements; (4) state duplicate payment to MCOs and providers; (5) incorrect MCO fee-for-service payments to providers for improper claims, which may include fraudulent claims; and (6) incorrect MCO capitation payments to providers that have not complied with program requirements.

auditor's office, and a managed care organization (MCO).[2] (See table 1 for a description of each of these entities.) Figures 6 through 9 below illustrate the risk level stakeholders assigned to the four types of payment risk that are associated with states' periodic capitation payments to MCOs. Figures 10 and 11 illustrate the risk level stakeholders assigned the two types of payment risks associated with MCO payments to providers. In some cases, stakeholders said they did not have enough information to assign a level of risk ("Don't know") or that one of the payment risks did not apply in their state ("Not applicable").

For some payment risks, the stakeholders whose primary responsibility is program integrity—state auditors, MFCU officials, and state Medicaid program integrity staff—were more likely to assign a higher level of risk than state Medicaid managed care officials and MCO officials who have responsibilities both for program operation and program integrity. For example, some of the risk levels cited in our interviews by state auditors, MFCU officials, and state Medicaid program integrity staff included the following:

- State auditors most frequently cited improper state capitation payments as high risk in the state.
- Three state auditors identified duplicate state payments as high risk.
- Just over half of all state auditors, MFCU officials, and state Medicaid program integrity staff identified inaccurate state capitation rates as some or high risk.

In contrast, state Medicaid managed care officials and MCO officials were less likely to assign high risk to payment types. Some examples include the following:

[2] We interviewed a total of 49 stakeholders. One state auditor declined to participate. Selected states included California, Florida, Georgia, Hawaii, Massachusetts, Michigan, Nevada, Oregon, Tennessee, and Wisconsin. We selected states that had a significant share of their Medicaid populations enrolled in MCOs and to provide a mix of population sizes and geographic locations.

- No state Medicaid managed care officials cited a high level of risk for any of the six payment types.
- Two MCO officials cited a high level of risk for incorrect MCO fee-for-service payments. No other MCO officials cited a high level of risk for any of the other payment types.

Stakeholder views on the risk level of different payment risks are outlined in the figures that follow.

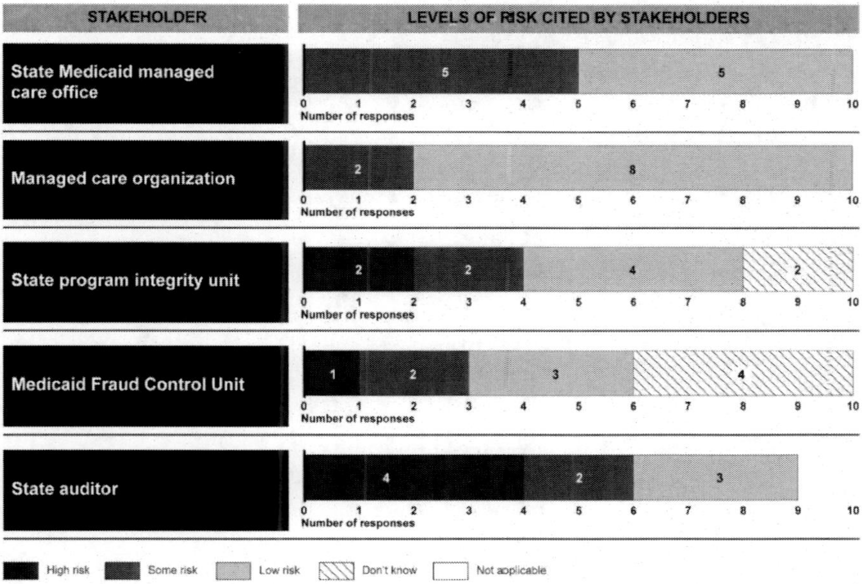


Source: GAO analysis of information from interviews with program integrity stakeholders. | GAO-18-528.

Notes: Improper state capitation payments may occur when the state makes monthly capitation payments to a managed care organization for beneficiaries who are ineligible for or not enrolled in Medicaid, or who have died.

We interviewed 49 stakeholders in 10 states, including the state Medicaid managed care office, the state Medicaid program integrity unit, the state auditor, the state Medicaid Fraud Control Unit, and a managed care organization.

Figure 6. Stakeholders' Views on the Level of Risk for Improper State Capitation Payments for Medicaid Managed Care.

Improper state capitation payments may occur when the state makes monthly capitation payments to an MCO for beneficiaries who are ineligible for or not enrolled in Medicaid, or who have died. (See figure 6.)

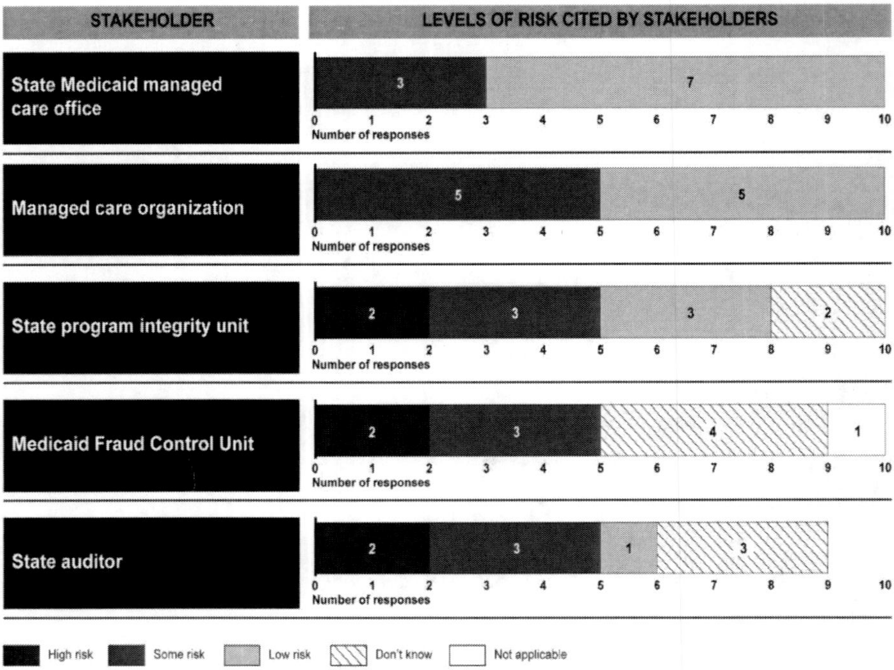


Source: GAO analysis of information from interviews with program integrity stakeholders. | GAO-18-528.

Notes: Inaccurate state capitation rates occur when a state sets a capitation rate that is inaccurate, primarily due to issues with the data used to set the rates.

We interviewed 49 stakeholders in 10 states, including the state Medicaid managed care office, the state Medicaid program integrity unit, the state auditor, the state Medicaid Fraud Control Unit, and a managed care organization.

Figure 7. Stakeholders' Views on the Level of Risk for Inaccurate State Capitation Rates for Medicaid Managed Care.

Inaccurate state capitation rates occur when a state established a capitation rate that is inaccurate primarily due to issues with the data used to set the rates. Data issues could include inaccurate encounter data, unallowable costs, overpayments that are not adjusted for in the rate, or older data that do not reflect changes in care delivery practices that affect MCO costs. (See figure 7.)

State payments to noncompliant MCOs occur when a state pays MCOs a periodic capitation per beneficiary even though the MCO has not fulfilled state contract requirements. Examples of unfulfilled contract requirements include an MCO failing to establish an adequate provider network, reporting inaccurate encounter data for services, or failing to report the amount of overpayments the MCO has made to providers. (See figure 8.)

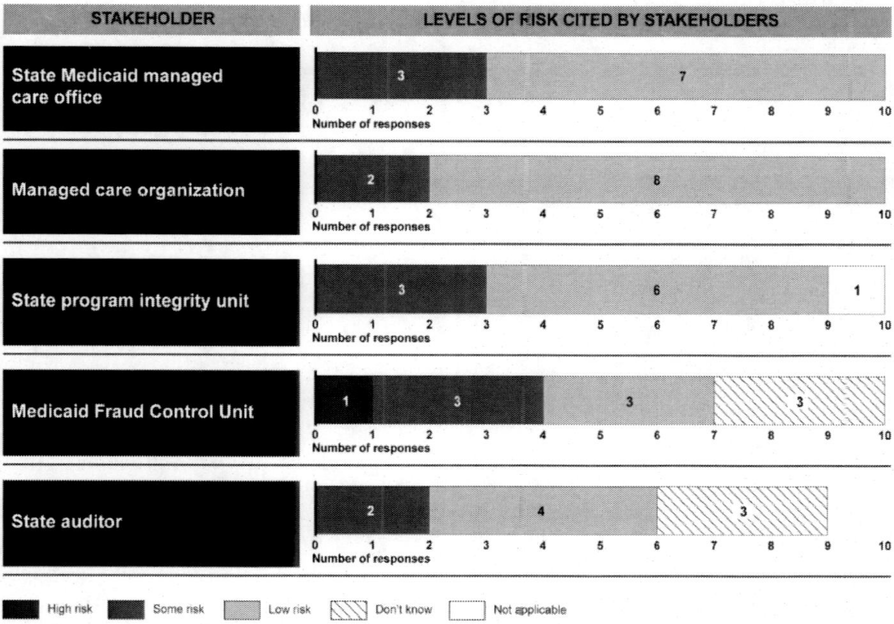


Source: GAO analysis of information from interviews with program integrity stakeholders. | GAO-18-528.

Notes: State payments to noncompliant MCOs occur when a state pays MCOs a monthly capitation per beneficiary even though the MCO has not fulfilled state contract requirements.

We interviewed 49 stakeholders in 10 states, including the state Medicaid managed care office, the state Medicaid program integrity unit, the state auditor, the state Medicaid Fraud Control Unit, and a managed care organization.

Figure 8. Stakeholders' Views on the Level of Risk for State Payments to Noncompliant Medicaid Managed Care Organizations (MCO).

Duplicate state payments to an MCO occur when a health care provider submits a fee-for-service claim to the state Medicaid program for services that were covered under the MCO contract. (See figure 9.)

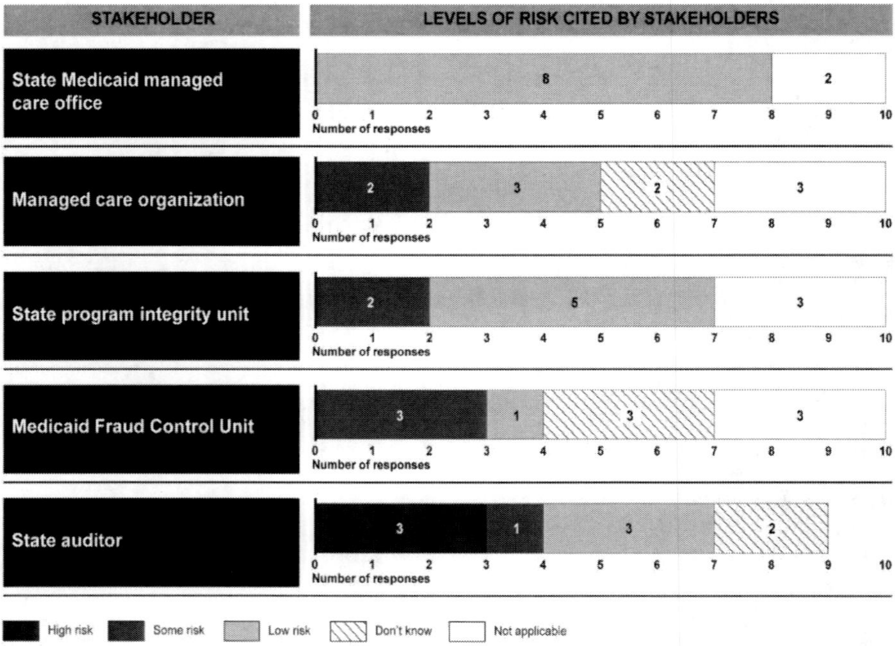


Source: GAO analysis of information from interviews with program integrity stakeholders. | GAO-18-528.

Notes: Duplicate state payments to a managed care organization (MCO) occur when a health care provider submits a fee-for-service claim to the state Medicaid program for services that were covered under the MCO contract.

We interviewed 49 stakeholders in 10 states, including the state Medicaid managed care office, the state Medicaid program integrity unit, the state auditor, the state Medicaid Fraud Control Unit, and an MCO.

Figure 9. Stakeholders' Views of the Level of Risk for Duplicate State Payments for Medicaid Managed Care.

Incorrect MCO fee-for-service payments occur when the MCO pays providers for improper claims, such as claims for services (1) not provided, or provided by ineligible providers; or (2) that represent inappropriate billing, such as billing individually for bundled services or for a higher intensity of services than needed. (See figure 10.)

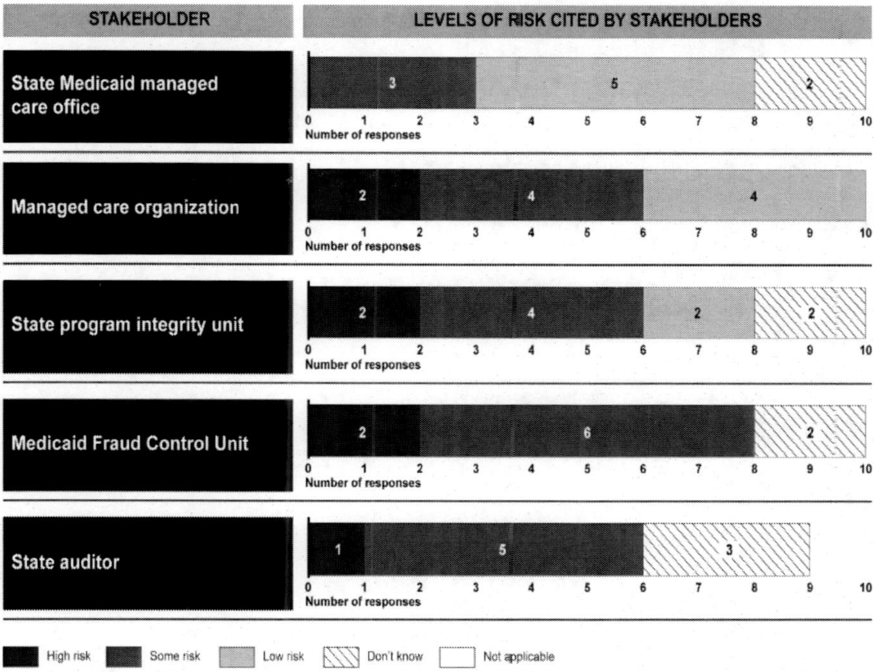


Source: GAO analysis of information from interviews with program integrity stakeholders. | GAO-18-528.

Notes: Incorrect MCO fee-for-service payments occur when the MCO pays providers for improper claims, such as claims for services not provided appropriately or that represent inappropriate billing.

We interviewed 49 stakeholders in 10 states, including the state Medicaid managed care office, the state Medicaid program integrity unit, the state auditor, the state Medicaid Fraud Control Unit, and a managed care organization.

Figure 10. Stakeholders' Views of the Level of Risk for Incorrect Medicaid Managed Care Organization (MCO) Fee-for-Service Payments.

Incorrect MCO capitation payments occur when MCOs pay providers a periodic fixed payment without assurances they have provided needed services. (See figure 11.)

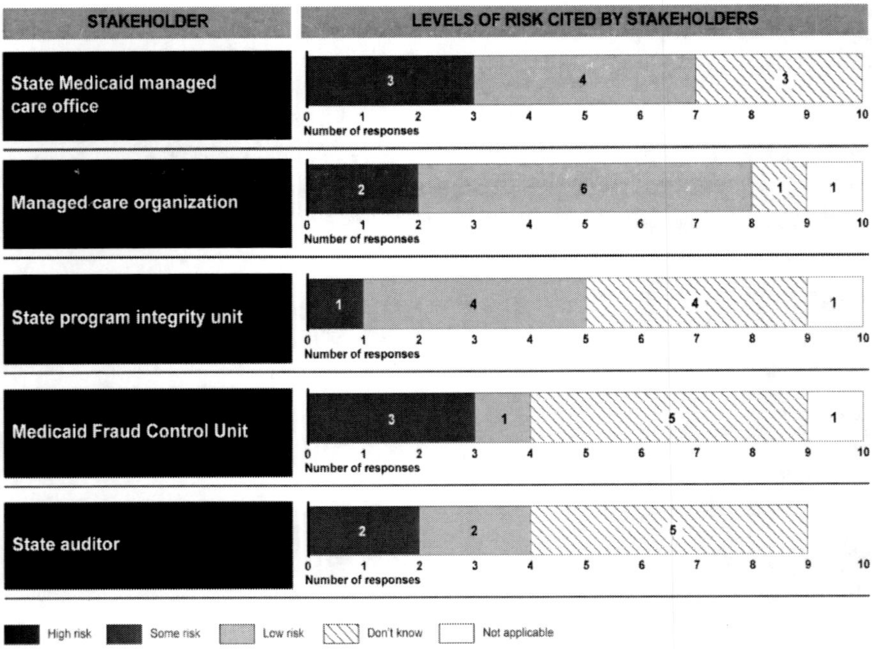


Source: GAO analysis of information from interviews with program integrity stakeholders. | GAO-18-528.

Notes: Incorrect MCO capitation payments occur when MCOs pay providers a periodic fixed payment without assurances they have provided needed services.

We interviewed 49 stakeholders in 10 states, including the state Medicaid managed care office, the state Medicaid program integrity unit, the state auditor, the state Medicaid Fraud Control Unit, and a managed care organization.

Figure 11. Stakeholders' Views of the Level of Risk for Incorrect Medicaid Managed Care Organizations (MCO) Capitation Payments.

# Appendix II: Examples of Different Types of Payment Risks in Medicaid Managed Care

To identify examples of payment risks in Medicaid managed care, we reviewed Department of Health and Human Services' (HHS) Office of Inspector General (HHS-OIG) publications and our prior work; obtained

## Table 10. Examples of Improper State Capitation Payments for Medicaid Managed Care

| State | Finding | Report or source (descending order by date) |
|---|---|---|
| Louisiana | The Louisiana Legislative Auditor found that the state Department of Health paid $637,745 in improper capitation payments to managed care organizations (MCO) for 203 deceased Medicaid recipients over a 4-year period. | Louisiana Legislative Auditor. Medicaid Audit Unit: Improper Payments for Deceased Medicaid Recipients. Louisiana Department of Health. November 29, 2017. |
| Texas | The Department of Health and Human Services, Office of the Inspector General (HHS-OIG) found that Texas Medicaid paid $6.4 million for 8,496 capitation payments from 2013 through 2015 for beneficiaries with death dates reported as prior to this period. | HHS-OIG. Texas Managed Care Organizations Received Medicaid Capitation Payments After Beneficiary's Death. Report A-06-16-05004. November 2017. |
| New York | The New York State Comptroller found that the state Medicaid agency made $72.6 million in capitated payments for disenrolled and deceased individuals. | New York State Office of the State Comptroller. Inappropriate Premium Payments for Recipients No Longer Enrolled in Mainstream Managed Care and Family Health Plus. Report 2015-S-47. Albany, N.Y. July 2017. |
| Florida | HHS-OIG found that the Florida Medicaid agency paid an estimated $26 million over 5 years, from 2009 through 2014, to Medicaid MCOs for coverage of people who had already died. | HHS-OIG. Florida Managed Care Organizations Received Medicaid Capitation Payments After Beneficiary's Death. Report A-04-15-06182. November 2016. |
| Arizona | The State of Arizona Auditor General estimated that its Medicaid program was paying between approximately $3.5 and $4.8 million in monthly capitation payments for enrolled, but ineligible members. | State of Arizona Office of the Auditor General. Medicaid Applicants Must Be Approved Through Eligibility Determination Process. Report No. 12-02. June 2012. |

Source: GAO analysis of audit and other reports. I GAO-18-528.

Note: Improper state capitation payments occur when the state makes monthly capitation payments to an MCO for beneficiaries who are ineligible for Medicaid, not enrolled in Medicaid, or who have died.

input from the National State Auditor's Association; and conducted literature searches and key word searches of online databases, which identified additional state audits and investigations involving Medicaid managed care payment. We grouped these examples of payment risks into six broad categories or types based on similar key characteristics. Tables 10 through 15 provide examples of each of the six types of payment risks we identified: (1) improper state capitation payments, which are state capitation payments to MCOs for ineligible or deceased individuals; (2) inaccurate state capitation rates; (3) state payments to non-compliant managed care organizations (MCO); (4) duplicate state payments to MCOs and providers; (5) incorrect MCO fee-for-service payments to providers; and (6) incorrect MCO capitation payments to providers that have not complied with program requirements.

### Table 11. Examples of Inaccurate State Capitation Rates for Medicaid Managed Care

| State | Finding | Report or source (descending order by date) |
|---|---|---|
| Virginia | The Virginia Joint Legislative Audit and Review Commission found that the state has paid managed care organizations (MCO) for potentially avoidable health care services, and could have saved up to $36 million annually if it had reduced capitation rates for inefficient health care spending. | Commonwealth of Virginia Joint Legislative Audit and Review Commission. Managing Spending in Virginia's Medicaid Program. December 2016. |
| New York | The New York State Comptroller found that an MCO claimed over $260,000 in unallowable administrative expenses, which contributed to an increase in capitation rates across the state. In addition, the Department of Health overpaid more than $18.9 million in premiums to MCOs, because it improperly included certain unallowable costs in calculating premiums. | New York State Office of the State Comptroller. Mainstream Managed Care Organizations – Administrative Costs Used in Premium Rate Setting. Report 2014-S-55. Albany, N.Y. October 2016. |

| State | Finding | Report or source (descending order by date) |
|---|---|---|
| Rhode Island | The Rhode Island Office of the Auditor General found that Medicaid managed care organizations were overpaid more than $200 million due to overstated capitation rates for the Medicaid expansion population. | Office of the Auditor General, State of Rhode Island and Providence Plantations. Single Audit Report Fiscal Year Ended June 30, 2015. March 2016. |
| Washington | The Washington State Auditor's Office found that two MCOs made $17.5 million in overpayments to providers in 2010. The auditor estimated that for every $1 million in overpayments in 2010, the state Medicaid agency potentially paid an estimated additional $1.26 million in capitated payments to all MCOs statewide in 2013, because 2010 expenditures that included the overpayments were used to calculate premium rates for 2013. | Washington State Auditor. Performance Audit: Health Care Authority's Oversight of the Medicaid Managed Care Program. Audit No. 1011450. April 14, 2014. |
| Multiple states | The Department of Justice alleged that an MCO submitted inflated expenditure information to the state Medicaid agencies in nine states. The MCO agreed to pay over $137.5 million in a settlement with the nine states and the federal government to resolve these claims. | United States Department of Justice. Florida-Based Wellcare Health Plans Agrees to Pay $137.5 Million to Resolve False Claims Act Allegations. Washington, D.C. April 3, 2012. |

Source: GAO analysis of audit and other reports. I GAO-18-528.

Note: Inaccurate state capitation rates occur when a state established a capitation rate that is inaccurate, primarily due to issues with the data used to set the rates. Data issues could include inaccurate encounter data, unallowable costs, overpayments that are not adjusted for in the rate, or older data that do not reflect changes in care delivery practices that affect MCO costs.

## Table 12. Examples of State Payments to Noncompliant Medicaid Managed Care Organizations (MCO)

| State | Finding | Report or source (descending order by date) |
|---|---|---|
| Texas | The Texas State Auditor found that an MCO reported payments in its financial statistical report that were not allowed under its contract, and also that the… | Texas State Auditor. An Audit Report on The Health and Human Services Commission's Management of its Medicaid Managed Care… |

**Table 12. (Continued)**

| State | Finding | Report or source (descending order by date) |
|---|---|---|
| | Texas Health and Human Services Commission did not ensure that its own business practices and oversight of MCOs aligned with the managed care contract. | Contract with Superior HealthPlan, Inc. and Superior HealthPlan Network, and Superior's Compliance with Reporting Requirements. Report No. 18-015. Austin, Tex. January 2018. |
| Oregon | The State of Oregon Audits Division found that while MCOs were required to develop policies and procedures for detecting fraud, waste, and abuse, some MCO policies lacked sufficient detail and some MCOs appeared to perform only limited activities to detect improper payments. | State of Oregon Audits Division. Oregon Health Authority Should Improve Efforts to Detect and Prevent Improper Medicaid Payments. Report 2017 – 25. Salem, Ore. November 2017. |
| Texas | The Texas State Auditor found that an MCO reported $3.8 million in unallowable expenses for advertising, company events, gifts, and stock options; and an additional $34 million in other questionable costs in 2015. Further, the MCO did not prepare required certifications and personnel activity reports, or adequately document financial reports, as required by the state's Uniform Managed Care Manual. | Texas State Auditor. An Audit Report on HealthSpring Life and Health Insurance Company, Inc., a Medicaid STAR+PLUS Managed Care Organization. Report No. 17-025. Austin, Tex. February 2017. |
| California | The California State Auditor found that the California Department of Health Care Services did not verify that the provider network data it received from the MCOs were accurate. The Medi-Cal managed care contract requires MCOs to maintain a network of primary care providers that meets certain location requirements. However, the auditor's review of the provider directories of three MCOs found inaccuracies, including providers no longer participating in the network. | California State Auditor. California Department of Health Care Services: Improved Monitoring of Medi-Cal Managed Care Health Plans is Necessary to Better Ensure Access to Care. Report 2014-134. June 2015. |

Source: GAO analysis of audit and other reports. I GAO-18-528.

Note: State payments to noncompliant MCOs occur when a state pays MCOs a periodic capitation per beneficiary even though the MCO has not fulfilled state contract requirements. Examples of unfulfilled contract requirements include an MCO failing to establish an adequate provider network, reporting inaccurate encounter data for services, or failing to report the amount of overpayments the MCO has made to providers.

## Table 13. Examples of Duplicate State Payments for Medicaid Managed Care

| State | Finding | Report or source (descending order by date) |
|---|---|---|
| Oregon | The State of Oregon Audits Division found that the state Medicaid agency could not provide an inventory of carve out services not covered by managed care organizations (MCO). Without such an inventory, the division found that it is difficult to detect or prevent potential duplicate payments to MCOs and to fee-for-service providers. The Audits Division analyzed both fee-for-service payments and capitated payments to MCOs and found 31,300 potential duplicate payments for a 15 month period. | State of Oregon Audits Division. Oregon Health Authority Should Improve Efforts to Detect and Prevent Improper Medicaid Payments. Report 2017 – 25. Salem, Ore. November 2017. |
| Massachusetts | The Massachusetts state auditor identified $193 million in improper payments, mostly duplicate payments, for behavioral health services that resulted from problems with MassHealth's system for identifying which claims it should cover in its fee-for-service program and which claims should be covered through its capitated contract with a behavioral health services MCO. | Commonwealth of Massachusetts Office of the State Auditor. Office of Medicaid (MassHealth) – Review of Fee-for-Service Payments for Services Covered by the Massachusetts Behavioral Health Partnership for the Period July 1, 2010 through June 30, 2015. Official Auditor Report. April 3, 2017. |

Source: GAO analysis of audit and other reports. I GAO-18-528.

Note: Duplicate state payments to an MCO occur when a health care provider submits a fee-for-service claim to the state Medicaid program for services that were covered under the MCO contract.

## Table 14. Examples of Incorrect Medicaid Managed Care Organization Fee-for-Service Payments

| State | Finding | Report or source (descending order by date) |
|---|---|---|
| Louisiana | The Louisiana Legislative Auditor found that managed care organizations (MCO) paid $2.4 million for 157,232 laboratory claims where the provider did not have the appropriate certification to provide the level of service provided. | Louisiana Legislative Auditor. Medicaid Audit Unit. Improper Payments in the Medicaid Laboratory Program. Louisiana Department of Health. Baton Rouge, La. September 6, 2017. |

**Table 14. (Continued)**

| State | Finding | Report or source (descending order by date) |
|---|---|---|
| New Jersey | The New Jersey Attorney General reported that a medical supply provider pleaded guilty to submitting $100,000 in fraudulent claims to a MCO for durable medical equipment that was never distributed. | State of New Jersey Office of the Attorney General. Owner of Hudson County Medical Equipment Supply Store Pleads Guilty To $100,000 from Medicaid Fraud Scam. Trenton, N.J. August 21, 2017. |
| West Virginia | The Department of Justice found that a West Virginia MCO and state Medicaid program made over $700,000 in payments to a dentist who submitted exaggerated claims, claims for services not provided, and duplicate claims for a single procedure. | Department of Justice. Enforcement Actions. U.S. Attorney; Southern District of West Virginia: Charleston. Charleston Dentist Pleads Guilty to Health Care Fraud. Charleston, W.Va.: August 21, 2017. |
| New York | The New York State Comptroller found that two MCOs made more than $6.6 million in payments to excluded and deceased providers, including almost $60,000 in payments to pharmacies for medications prescribed by deceased providers. | New York State Office of the State Comptroller. Medicaid Managed Care Organization Fraud and Abuse Detection. Report 2014-S-51. Albany, N.Y. July 15, 2016. |
| Texas | The Department of Justice found that the Texas Medicaid agency and MCOs made payments to two individuals who were not licensed to provide psychotherapy services and who submitted $7.1 million in false claims. | Department of Justice. U.S. Attorney, Northern District of Texas. Ellis County Woman Sentenced to 105 Months in Federal Prison for Defrauding Medicaid. Dallas, Tex. April 8, 2016. |
| Multiple states | The Department of Health and Human Services' Office of Inspector General (HHS-OIG) found, in interviewing state officials in 13 states, that these officials expressed concerns about provider and beneficiary fraud and abuse including rendering services that are not medically necessary and upcoding by providers. | HHS-OIG. Medicaid Managed Care: Fraud and Abuse Concerns Remain Despite Safeguards. OEI-01-09-00550. December 2011. |

Source: GAO analysis of audit and other reports. I GAO-18-528.

Note: Incorrect MCO fee-for-service payments occur when the MCO pays providers for improper claims, such as claims for services (1) not provided, or provided by ineligible providers; or (2) that represent inappropriate billing, such as billing individually for bundled services or for a higher intensity of services than needed.

**Table 15. Example of Incorrect Medicaid Managed Care Organization Capitation Payments**

| State | Finding | Report or Source (descending order by date) |
|---|---|---|
| California | The California Department of Health Care Services, in response to a whistleblower complaint within a utilization management company that subcontracted to managed care organizations (MCO), found that Medicaid beneficiaries were in imminent danger of not receiving medically necessary health care services, because the company was not processing requests for health care services on a timely basis. | State of California Health and Human Services Agency. Department of Health Care Services. Syner Med Corrective Action Plan. November 17, 2017. |

Source: GAO analysis of audit and other reports. I GAO-18-528.

Note: Incorrect MCO capitation payments occur when MCOs pay providers without assurances they have provided needed services.

# APPENDIX III: CHALLENGES TO EFFECTIVE PROGRAM INTEGRITY OVERSIGHT IN MEDICAID MANAGED CARE

We asked 49 stakeholders involved in program integrity oversight to consider the following six challenges to effective program integrity oversight: (1) availability and allocation of resources; (2) access to and quality of data and technology; (3) state policies and practices; (4) provider compliance with program requirements; (5) managed care organization (MCO) management of program integrity; and (6) federal regulations, guidance, and review.[1] Stakeholders were asked whether any of these presented a challenge to each of six types of payment risks in Medicaid managed care in their state, including (1) improper state capitation payments to MCOs for ineligible or deceased individuals; (2) inaccurate state

[1] We interviewed 49 officials, including officials in the following five organizations in 10 states: state Medicaid managed care office, state program integrity unit, Medicaid Fraud control Unit, state auditor's office, and a managed care organization. Selected states included California, Florida, Georgia, Hawaii, Massachusetts, Michigan, Nevada, Oregon, Tennessee, and Wisconsin.

capitation rates; (3) state payments to MCOs that have not fulfilled contract requirements; (4) state duplicate payments to MCOs and providers; (5) incorrect MCO fee-for-service payments to providers for improper claims; and (6) incorrect MCO capitation payments to providers that have not complied with program requirements.

Figure 12 illustrates the number of times stakeholders cited a particular challenge for each of the payment risks. The frequency with which each of the challenges was identified differed to some extent for different payment risks. Some examples include the following:

- Quality of data and technology was the most cited challenge for duplicate state payments.
- State policies and practices was the most cited challenge for inaccurate state capitation rates.
- Provider compliance with program requirements was the most cited challenge for two payment types: (1) incorrect MCO fee-for-service payments to providers, and (2) incorrect MCO capitation payments to providers.
- Resource allocation was the second most cited challenge for five of the six payment risk types, although it was not the most cited challenge for any one payment risk type.

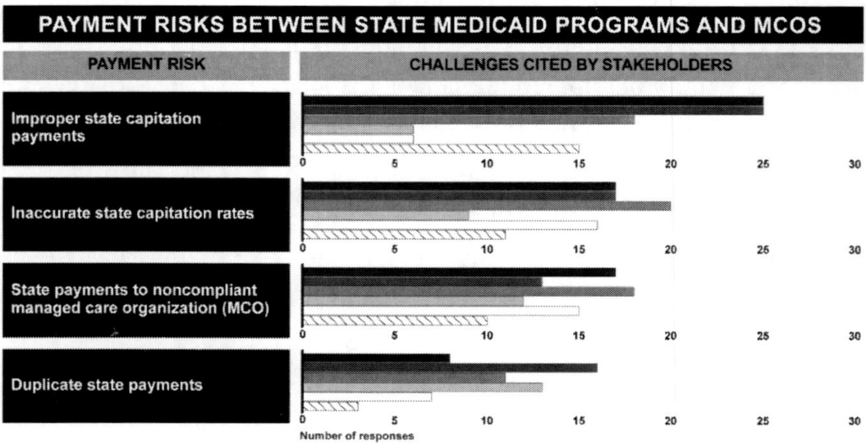


Figure 12. (Continued).

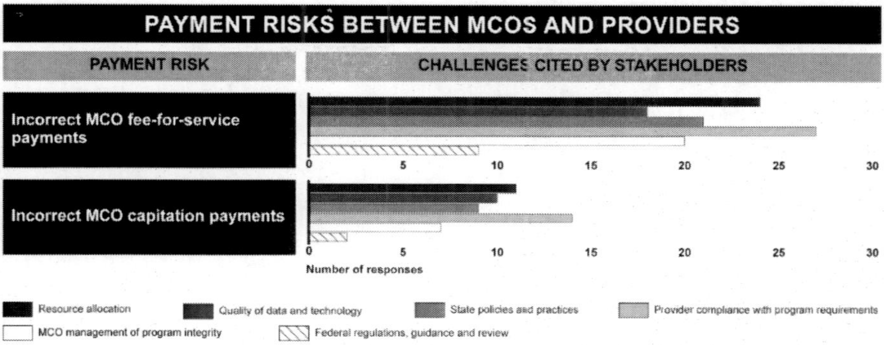


Source: GAO analysis of information from interviews with program integrity stakeholders. | GAO-18-528.

Notes: Payment risks are described here.

*Improper state capitation payments* occur when the state makes periodic capitation payments to an MCO for beneficiaries who are ineligible for or not enrolled in Medicaid, or who have died.

*Inaccurate state capitation rates* occur when a state sets a capitation rate that is inaccurate, primarily due to issues with the data used to set the rates.

*State payments to noncompliant MCOs* occur when a state pays MCOs a periodic capitation per beneficiary even though the MCO has not fulfilled state contract requirements.

*Duplicate state payments to an MCO* occur when a health care provider submits a fee-for-service claim to the state Medicaid program for services that were covered under the MCO contract.

*Incorrect MCO fee-for-service payments* occur when the MCO pays providers for improper claims, such as claims for services not provided appropriately or that represent inappropriate billing.

*Incorrect MCO capitation payments* occur when MCOs pay providers without assurances they have provided needed services.

We interviewed 49 stakeholders in 10 states, including the state Medicaid managed care office, the state Medicaid program integrity unit, the state auditor, the state Medicaid Fraud Control Unit, and a managed care organization.

Figure 12. Number of Times Stakeholders Cited Each Challenge to Medicaid Managed Care Program Integrity Oversight, by Payment Risk.

# Appendix IV: Comments from the Department of Health and Human Services

DEPARTMENT OF HEALTH & HUMAN SERVICES OFFICE OF THE SECRETARY

Assistant Secretary for Legislation
Washington, DC 20201

JUN 28 2018

Carolyn Yocom
Director, Health Care
U.S. Government Accountability Office
441 G Street NW
Washington, DC 20548

Dear Ms. Yocom:

Attached are comments on the U.S. Government Accountability Office's (GAO) report entitled, "*Medicaid Managed Care: Improvements Needed to Better Oversee Payment Risks*" (GAO-18-528).

The Department appreciates the opportunity to review this report prior to publication.

Sincerely,

Matthew D. Bassett
Assistant Secretary for Legislation

**GENERAL COMMENTS OF THE DEPARTMENT OF HEALTH AND HUMAN SERVICES (HHS) ON THE GOVERNMENT ACCOUNTABILITY OFFICE'S DRAFT REPORT ENTITLED: MEDICAID MANAGED CARE: IMPROVEMENTS NEEDED TO BETTER OVERSEE PROGRAM RISK (GAO-18-528)**

The U.S. Department of Health and Human Services (HHS) appreciates the opportunity to review and comment on the draft report from the Government Accountability Office (GAO). HHS is strongly committed to program integrity efforts in Medicaid.

While states have primary responsibility for direct oversight of their managed care contractors and their compliance with program integrity standards, HHS undertakes a wide array of activities to oversee and support states' Medicaid program integrity efforts. These efforts include ongoing program monitoring, state program integrity focused reviews, desk reviews, collaborative audits, and the provision of state training and technical assistance.

Through state program integrity focused reviews, HHS assesses the effectiveness of the state's program integrity efforts, including determining if states' policies and practices comply with federal regulations, identifying program vulnerabilities that may not rise to the level of regulatory non-compliance, identifying states' best practices in managed care program integrity, and monitoring state corrective action plans. Onsite reviews during 2014-2018 focused on specific areas of program integrity concern, including oversight of managed care organizations.

To supplement the onsite focused reviews, program integrity desk reviews allow HHS to increase the number of states that receive customized program integrity oversight by conducting offsite reviews of documentation submitted by states on specified topics. Desk review topics target specific issues, such as states' progress on corrective action plans from previous state program integrity reviews.

Collaborative audits conducted by Unified Program Integrity Contractors contribute to HHS's oversight of state Medicaid programs, including managed care organizations. These audits allow HHS and the states to discuss and agree upon potential audit targets while utilizing state data. Collaborative audits have proven to be an effective way to augment states' own audit capacities by leveraging HHS resources, resulting in more timely and accurate audits. HHS has completed 14 collaborative audits of managed care organization network providers. In addition, CMS is in the early planning stages of piloting targeted audits of managed care organizations to provide states with feedback about potential vulnerabilities in their managed care programs.

HHS also offers substantive training, technical assistance, and support to states in a structured learning environment via the Medicaid Integrity Institute. The Medicaid Integrity Institute regularly refreshes course offerings to focus on emerging program integrity issues in areas such as Medicaid managed care, provider screening and enrollment, and data analysis. From its inception in 2008, the Medicaid Integrity Institute has trained state employees from all 50 states, the District of Columbia, and Puerto Rico through more than 8,000 enrollments in 170 courses and 14 workgroups.

**GENERAL COMMENTS OF THE DEPARTMENT OF HEALTH AND HUMAN SERVICES (HHS) ON THE GOVERNMENT ACCOUNTABILITY OFFICE'S DRAFT REPORT ENTITLED: MEDICAID MANAGED CARE: IMPROVEMENTS NEEDED TO BETTER OVERSEE PROGRAM RISK (GAO-18-528)**

The Medicaid managed care final rule published in 2016 takes important steps to strengthen program integrity in managed care while maintaining state flexibility, including requiring more transparency in the rate setting process, requiring the enrollment of managed care organization network providers in Medicaid, mandatory reporting of potential fraud, waste, or abuse to the state, mandatory reporting of any changes in a provider's circumstances that may impact that provider's participation in the managed care plan's network, and the suspension of payments to a network provider when the state determines a credible allegation of fraud exists. The rule provides flexibility as to how the state addresses treatment of recoveries by plans through the contract. However, states need to specify how managed care plan recoveries due to fraud, waste, and abuse are addressed in the contract and take recoveries into account in the rate setting process.

In addition, HHS has published, and updates as needed, the Medicaid Provider Enrollment Compendium to help states in implementing various provider enrollment requirements, including the requirement to enroll managed care organization network providers in Medicaid. The Medicaid Provider Enrollment Compendium serves as a consolidated resource for certain Medicaid provider enrollment regulations and guidance so states have the information in a central document. Lastly, HHS is providing substantial technical support and conducting on-site reviews of states to refine their provider enrollment and screening activities in concert with federal rules.

GAO's recommendations and HHS's responses are below.

**GAO Recommendation 1**
The Administrator of CMS should expedite the planned efforts to communicate guidance, such as its compendium on Medicaid managed care program integrity to state stakeholders related to Medicaid managed care program integrity.

**HHS Response**
HHS concurs with this recommendation. HHS will work to communicate planned guidance to stakeholders.

**GAO Recommendation 2**
The Administrator of CMS should eliminate impediments to collaborative audits in managed care conducted by audit contractors and states, such as using its periodic review of state managed care contracts to recommend modification of contracts that do not explicitly support provider auditing.

**HHS Response**

**GENERAL COMMENTS OF THE DEPARTMENT OF HEALTH AND HUMAN SERVICES (HHS) ON THE GOVERNMENT ACCOUNTABILITY OFFICE'S DRAFT REPORT ENTITLED: MEDICAID MANAGED CARE: IMPROVEMENTS NEEDED TO BETTER OVERSEE PROGRAM RISK (GAO-18-528)**

HHS concurs with this recommendation and will use the pilot audits to address challenges encountered in prior managed care audits including developing audits in states where contract language does not specifically allow for recovery of overpayments by the state.

**GAO Recommendation 3**
The Administrator of CMS should require states to report and document the amount of MCO overpayments to providers and how they are accounted for in capitation rate setting.

**HHS Response**
HHS concurs with this recommendation and will work with states to require them to report MCO overpayments to providers and document how overpayments are accounted for in capitation rate setting.

# APPENDIX V: GAO STAFF ACKNOWLEDGMENTS

In addition to Carolyn L. Yocom, Tim Bushfield (Assistant Director), Mary Giffin (Analyst-in-Charge), Arushi Kumar, Julie Flowers, Drew Long, Vikki Porter, Katie Thomson made key contributions to this chapter. Other staff who made contributions to the report were Jessica Broadus, Barbie Hansen and Erika Huber.

# APPENDIX VI: ACCESSIBLE DATA

## Data Tables

### Data Table for Figure 2: Payment Risks Related to State Medicaid Program Payments to Managed Care Organizations (MCO)

| Payment Risk | General Description |
|---|---|
| Improper state capitation payments | State makes monthly capitation payments to an MCO for beneficiaries who are ineligible for Medicaid, not enrolled in Medicaid or who have died. |
| Inaccurate state capitation rates | State establishes capitation rates that are inaccurate, primarily due to issues with the data used to set the rates. |
| State payments to noncompliant MCO | State makes monthly capitation payments to an MCO for beneficiaries even though the MCO has not fulfilled state contract requirements. |
| Duplicate state payments | State makes duplicate payments- for example, when a health care provider submits a fee-for-service claim to the state Medicaid program for services that were covered by the MCO contract. |

### Data Table for Figure 3: Payment Risks Related to Medicaid Managed Care Organization (MCO) Payments to Providers

| Payment Risk | General Description |
|---|---|
| Incorrect MCO fee-for-service payments | MCO pays providers for improper or false claims, such as claims for services (a) not provided, or provided by ineligible providers, or (b) that represent inappropriate billing, such as billing individually for bundled services or for a higher intensity of services than needed. |
| Incorrect MCO capitation payments | MCO pays providers without assurance they have provided needed services. |

## Data Table for Figure 4: Stakeholders' Views of the Level of Risk Associated with Each Type of Medicaid Managed Care Payment Risk Levels of Risk Cited by Stakeholders (Number of Responses)

| Payment Risk | High/ some risk | Low risk | Don't know | Not applicable |
|---|---|---|---|---|
| Incorrect managed care organization (MCO) fee-for-service payments | 29 | 11 | 9 | 0 |
| Inaccurate state capitation rates | 23 | 16 | 9 | 1 |
| Improper state capitation payments | 20 | 23 | 6 | 0 |
| State payments to noncompliant MCO | 14 | 28 | 6 | 1 |
| Incorrect MCO capitation payments | 11 | 20 | 7 | 3 |
| Duplicate state payments | 11 | 20 | 7 | 11 |

## Data Table for Figure 5: Frequency of Stakeholder Citing of Six Challenges to Medicaid Managed Care Oversight

| Areas of Challenges to Oversight | Number of Times Stakeholders Cited this Challenge to Oversight |
|---|---|
| Availability and allocation of resources | 102 |
| Access to and quality of data and technology | 99 |
| State policies and practices | 97 |
| Provider compliance with program requirements | 81 |
| MCO management of program integrity | 71 |
| Federal regulations, guidance, and review | 50 |

**Data Table for Figure 6: Stakeholders' Views on the Level of Risk for Improper State Capitation Payments for Medicaid Managed Care Levels of Risk Cited by Stakeholders (Number of Responses).**

| Stakeholder | High risk | Some risk | Low risk | Don't know | Not applicable |
|---|---|---|---|---|---|
| State Medicaid managed care office | 0 | 5 | 5 | 0 | 0 |
| Managed care organization | 0 | 2 | 8 | 0 | 0 |
| State program integrity unit | 2 | 2 | 4 | 2 | 0 |
| Medicaid Fraud Control Unit | 1 | 2 | 3 | 4 | 0 |
| State auditor | 4 | 2 | 3 | 0 | 0 |

**Data Table for Figure 7: Stakeholders' Views on the Level of Risk for Inaccurate State Capitation Rates for Medicaid Managed Care Levels of Risk Cited by Stakeholders (Number of Responses)**

| Stakeholder | High risk | Some risk | Low risk | Don't know | Not applicable |
|---|---|---|---|---|---|
| State Medicaid managed care office | 0 | 3 | 7 | 0 | 0 |
| Managed care organization | 0 | 5 | 5 | 0 | 0 |
| State program integrity unit | 2 | 3 | 3 | 2 | 0 |
| Medicaid Fraud Control Unit | 2 | 3 | 0 | 4 | 1 |
| State auditor | 2 | 3 | 1 | 3 | 0 |

### Data Table for Figure 8: Stakeholders' Views on the Level of Risk for State Payments to Noncompliant Medicaid Managed Care Organizations (MCO) Levels of Risk Cited by Stakeholders (Number of Responses)

| Stakeholder | High risk | Some risk | Low risk | Don't know | Not applicable |
|---|---|---|---|---|---|
| State Medicaid managed care office | 0 | 3 | 7 | 0 | 0 |
| Managed care organization | 0 | 2 | 8 | 0 | 0 |
| State program integrity unit | 0 | 3 | 6 | 0 | 1 |
| Medicaid Fraud Control Unit | 1 | 3 | 3 | 3 | 0 |
| State auditor | 0 | 2 | 4 | 3 | 0 |

### Data Table for Figure 9: Stakeholders' Views of the Level of Risk for Duplicate State Payments for Medicaid Managed Care Levels of Risk Cited by Stakeholders (Number of Responses)

| Stakeholder | High risk | Some risk | Low risk | Don't know | Not applicable |
|---|---|---|---|---|---|
| State Medicaid managed care office | 0 | 0 | 8 | 0 | 2 |
| Managed care organization | 0 | 2 | 3 | 2 | 3 |
| State program integrity unit | 0 | 2 | 5 | 0 | 3 |
| Medicaid Fraud Control Unit | 0 | 3 | 1 | 3 | 3 |
| State auditor | 3 | 1 | 3 | 2 | 0 |

**Data Table for Figure 10: Stakeholders' Views of the Level of Risk for Incorrect Medicaid Managed Care Organization (MCO) Fee-for-Service Payments Levels of Risk Cited by Stakeholders (Number of Responses)**

| Stakeholder | High risk | Some risk | Low risk | Don't know | Not applicable |
|---|---|---|---|---|---|
| State Medicaid managed care office | 0 | 3 | 5 | 2 | 0 |
| Managed care organization | 2 | 4 | 4 | 0 | 0 |
| State program integrity unit | 2 | 4 | 2 | 2 | 0 |
| Medicaid Fraud Control Unit | 2 | 6 | 0 | 2 | 0 |
| State auditor | 1 | 5 | 0 | 3 | 0 |

**Data Table for Figure 11: Stakeholders' Views of the Level of Risk for Incorrect Medicaid Managed Care Organizations (MCO) Capitation Payments Levels of Risk Cited by Stakeholders (Number of Responses)**

| Stakeholder | High risk | Some risk | Low risk | Don't know | Not applicable |
|---|---|---|---|---|---|
| State Medicaid managed care office | 0 | 3 | 5 | 2 | 0 |
| Managed care organization | 2 | 4 | 4 | 0 | 0 |
| State program integrity unit | 2 | 4 | 2 | 2 | 0 |
| Medicaid Fraud Control Unit | 2 | 6 | 0 | 2 | 0 |
| State auditor | 1 | 5 | 0 | 3 | 0 |

## Data Table for Figure 12: Number of Times Stakeholders Cited Each Challenge to Medicaid Managed Care Program Integrity Oversight, by Payment Risk Payment risks between state Medicaid programs and MCOs. Challenges cited by stakeholders

| Payment Risk | Resource allocation | Quality of data and technology | State policies and practices | Provider compliance with program require-ments | MCO manage ment of program integrity | Federal regula-tions, guidance and review |
|---|---|---|---|---|---|---|
| Improper state capitation payments | 25 | 25 | 18 | 6 | 6 | 15 |
| Inaccurate state capitation rates | 17 | 17 | 20 | 9 | 16 | 11 |
| State payments to noncompliant managed care organization (MCO) | 17 | 13 | 18 | 12 | 15 | 10 |
| Duplicate state payments | 3 | 3 | 3 | 3 | 3 | 3 |

## Payment risks between MCOs and providers. Challenges cited by stakeholders

| Payment Risk | Resource allocation | Quality of data and techno-logy | State policies and practices | Provider compliance with program requirements | MCO manage-ment of program | Federal regula-tions, guidance |
|---|---|---|---|---|---|---|
| Incorrect MCO fee-for-service | 24 | 18 | 21 | 27 | 20 | 9 |
| Incorrect MCO capitation | 11 | 10 | 9 | 14 | 7 | 2 |

# AGENCY COMMENT LETTER

## Text of Appendix IV: Comments from the Department of Health and Human Services

Dear Ms. Yocom:

Attached are comments on the U.S. Government Accountability Office's (GAO) report entitled, "Medicaid Managed Care: Improvements Needed to Better Oversee Payment Risks" (GAO-18- 528).

The Department appreciates the opportunity to review this chapter prior to publication.

Sincerely,

Matthew D. Bassett
Assistant Secretary for Legislation
Attachment

## GENERAL COMMENTS OF THE DEPARTMENT OF HEALTH AND HUMAN SERVICES (HHS) ON THE GOVERNMENT ACCOUNTABILITY OFFICE'S DRAFT REPORT ENTITLED: MEDICAID MANAGED CARE: IMPROVEMENTS NEEDED TO BETTER OVERSEE PROGRAM RISK (GAO-18-528)

The U.S. Department of Health and Human Services (HHS) appreciates the opportunity to review and comment on the draft repo11 from the Government Accountability Office (GAO). HHS is strongly committed to program integrity efforts in Medicaid.

While states have primary responsibility for direct oversight of their managed care contractors and their compliance with program integrity standards, HHS undertakes a wide array of activities to oversee and support states' Medicaid program integrity efforts. These efforts include ongoing program monitoring, state program integrity focused reviews, desk reviews, collaborative audits, and the provision of state training and technical assistance.

Through state program integrity focused reviews, HHS assesses the effectiveness of the state's program integrity efforts, including determining if states' policies and practices comply with federal regulations, identifying program vulnerabilities that may not rise to the level of regulatory non-compliance, identifying states' best practices in managed care program integrity, and monitoring state corrective action plans. Onsite reviews during 2014-2018 focused on specific areas of program integrity concern, including oversight of managed care organizations.

To supplement the onsite focused reviews, program integrity desk reviews allow HHS to increase the number of states that receive customized program integrity oversight by conducting offsite reviews of documentation submitted by states on specified topics. Desk review topics target specific issues, such as states' progress on corrective action plans from previous state program integrity reviews.

Collaborative audits conducted by Unified Program Integrity Contractors contribute to HHS's oversight of state Medicaid programs, including managed care organizations. These audits allow HHS and the states to discuss and agree upon potential audit targets while utilizing state data.

Collaborative audits have proven to be an effective way to augment states' own audit capacities by leveraging HHS resources, resulting in more timely and accurate audits. HHS has completed 14 collaborative audits of managed care organization network providers. In addition, CMS is in the early planning stages of piloting targeted audits of managed care organizations to provide states with feedback about potential vulnerabilities in their managed care programs.

HHS also offers substantive training, technical assistance, and support to states in a structured learning environment via the Medicaid Integrity Institute. The Medicaid Integrity Institute regularly refreshes course offerings to focus on emerging program integrity issues in areas such as Medicaid managed care, provider screening and enrollment, and data analysis. From its inception in 2008, the Medicaid Integrity Institute has trained state employees from all 50 states, the District of Columbia, and Puerto Rico through more than 8,000 enrollments in 170 courses and 14 workgroups.

The Medicaid managed care final rule published in 2016 takes important steps to strengthen program integrity in managed care while maintaining state flexibility, including requiring more transparency in the rate setting process, requiring the enrollment of managed care organization network providers in Medicaid, mandatory reporting of potential fraud, waste, or abuse to the state, mandatory reporting of any changes in a provider's circumstances that may impact that provider's participation in the managed care plan's network, and the suspension of payments to a network provider when the state determines a credible allegation of fraud exists. The rule provides flexibility as to how the state addresses treatment of recoveries by plans through the contract. However, states need to specify how managed care plan recoveries due to fraud, waste, and abuse are addressed in the contract and take recoveries into account in the rate setting process.

In addition, HHS has published, and updates as needed, the Medicaid Provider Enrollment Compendium to help states in implementing various provider enrollment requirements, including the requirement to enroll managed care organization network providers in Medicaid. The Medicaid Provider Enrollment Compendium serves as a consolidated resource for certain Medicaid provider enrollment regulations and guidance so states have the information in a central document. Lastly, HHS is providing substantial technical support and conducting on-site reviews of states to refine their provider enrollment and screening activities in concert with federal rules. GAO's recommendations and HHS's responses are below.

## GAO Recommendation 1

The Administrator of CMS should expedite the planned efforts to communicate guidance, such as its compendium on Medicaid managed care program integrity to state stakeholders related to Medicaid managed care program integrity.

## HHS Response

HHS concurs with this recommendation. HHS will work to communicate planned guidance to stakeholders.

## GAO Recommendation 2

The Administrator of CMS should eliminate impediments to collaborative audits in managed care conducted by audit contractors and states, such as using its periodic review of state managed care contracts to recommend modification of contracts that do not explicitly support provider auditing.

## HHS Response

HHS concurs with this recommendation and will use the pilot audits to address challenges encountered in prior managed care audits including developing audits in states where contract language does not specifically allow for recovery of overpayments by the state.

## GAO Recommendation 3

The Administrator of CMS should require states to report and document the amount of MCO overpayments to providers and how they are accounted for in capitation rate setting.

## HHS Response

HHS concurs with this recommendation and will work with states to require them to report MCO overpayments to providers and document how overpayments are accounted for in capitation rate setting.

# INDEX

## A



## B



## C

## D



## E



## F

## H



## I

## L



## M

## R



## S



## T

## U



## W

## Progress in Medical Research: Government Programs and Key Issues

**Editor:** Nima Gustavsson

**Series:** Medical Procedures, Testing and Technology

**Book Description:** The first chapter in this book examines legislation as it relates to expanding telehealth services, including the five conditions that a telehealth service must meet to be covered and paid for under Medicare Part B. The second chapter focuses on the background and key issues surrounding biologics and biosimilars.

**Softcover ISBN:** 978-1-53614-105-4
**Retail Price:** $82

## Improving Outcomes of Extremely Premature Infants through Infant-Driven Care

**Author:** Jenn Gonya, Ph.D., Nicole Cistone, Amy Baughcum, Ph.D., Jennifer Hofherr, Leslie Thomas, Rebecca Romero, Amee Szyperski (Nationwide Children's Hospital Neonatal Intensive Care Small Baby Program, Columbus, Ohio, US)

**Series:** Neonatology Research Developments

**Book Description:** This book describes a set of guidelines that have been established for the specific care of extremely premature infants and discusses the ways in which the implementation of these guidelines in the neonatal intensive care unit setting ensures an approach that addresses both the medical and developmental needs of this highly vulnerable population.

**Softcover ISBN:** 978-1-53613-954-9
**Retail Price:** $82